"IN SOLITUDE AND AGAINST TERRIFYING ODDS, (FLORINDA DONNER) HAS REMAINED FAITHFUL TO THE WARRIOR'S PATH."
—*Carlos Castaneda*

"COMPLEX, SPELLBINDING STORIES . . . Doña Mercedes is a non-invasive healer/teacher, gentler than Castaneda's Juan Matus, but as wise, charming, and unpredictable."
—*Library Journal*

"Florinda Donner shows us first hand the ancient lore of curing disease . . . through prayers, incantations, massage and the 'casting off of negative energy.' . . . *THE WITCH'S DREAM* offers much new material for understanding faith and the power to heal."
—*Richmond Times-Dispatch*

"COMPELLING . . . Donner's three-page epilogue might be expanded into a psychosocial study on how healing 'works,' whether from cultural bias, the placebo effect, etc. A STIMULATING, THOUGHT-PROVOKING TEXT."
—*ALA Booklist*

"Donner is uncommonly good at getting a skeptical reader to suspend disbelief. . . . WONDERFULLY RICH MATERIAL . . . REMARKABLE."
—*Kirkus Reviews*

THE WITCH'S DREAM

FLORINDA DONNER

Foreword by
CARLOS CASTANEDA

PUBLISHED BY POCKET BOOKS NEW YORK

POCKET BOOKS, a division of Simon & Schuster, Inc.
1230 Avenue of the Americas, New York, N.Y. 10020

*To All Those
Whom I Cannot
Mention By Name*

Foreword

The work of Florinda Donner has a most special significance for me. It is, in fact, in agreement with my own work, and at the same time it deviates from it. Florinda Donner is my co-worker. We are both involved in the same pursuit; both of us belong to the world of don Juan Matus. The difference stems from her being female. In don Juan's world, males and females go in the same direction, on the same warrior's path, but on opposite sides of the road. Therefore, the views of the same phenomena obtained from those two positions have to be different in detail but not in flavor.

This proximity to Florinda Donner under any other circumstance would unavoidably engender a sense of loyalty rather than one of ruthless examination. But under the premises of the warrior's path, which we both follow, loyalty is expressed only in terms of demanding the best of ourselves. That best, for us, entails total examination of whatever we do.

Following don Juan's teachings, I have applied the warrior's premise of ruthless examination to Florinda Donner's work. I find that for me there are three different levels, three distinct spheres, of appreciation in it.

The first is the rich detail of her descriptions and narrative. To me, that detail is ethnography. The minutiae of daily life, which is commonplace in the cultural setting of the characters she describes, is something thoroughly unknown to us.

The second has to do with art. I would dare say that an ethnographer should also be a writer. In order to place us vicariously in the ethnographic horizon he or she describes, an ethnographer would have to be more than a social scientist; an ethnographer would have to be an artist.

The third is the honesty, simplicity, and directness of the work. It is here, without doubt, where I am most exigent. Florinda Donner and I have been molded by the same forces; therefore, her work must conform to a general pattern of striving for excellence. Don Juan has taught us that our work has to be a complete reflection of our lives.

I can't help having a warrior's sense of admiration and respect for Florinda Donner, who in solitude and against terrifying odds has maintained her equanimity, has remained faithful to the warrior's path, and has followed don Juan's teachings to the letter.

—CARLOS CASTANEDA

Author's Note

The state of Miranda, in northeastern Venezuela, was populated by Carib and Ciparicoto Indians during prehispanic times. During colonial times, two other racial and cultural groups became prominent there: the Spanish colonizers and the African slaves that the Spaniards brought to work their plantations and mines.

The descendants of those Indians, Spaniards, and Africans make up the mixed population that presently inhabits the small hamlets, villages, and towns scattered over the inland and coastal areas.

Some of the towns in the state of Miranda are famous for their healers, many of whom are also spiritualists, mediums, and sorcerers.

In the midseventies, I made a trip to Miranda. Being at that time an anthropology student interested in healing practices, I worked with a woman healer. To honor her request for anonymity, I have given her the name Mercedes Peralta, and I have called her town Curmina.

As faithfully and accurately as I could, and with the healer's permission, I recorded in a field diary everything about my relation with her, from the moment I came to her house. I also recorded separately what some of her patients told me about themselves. The present work consists of portions of my field diary and the stories of those patients who were selected by Mercedes Peralta herself. The parts taken from my field diary are written in the first person. I have, however, rendered the patient's stories into the third person. This is the only liberty I have taken with the material, other than changing the names and the personal data of the characters of the stories.

PART ONE

1

It began for me with a transcendental event; an event that shaped the course of my life. I met a *nagual*. He was an Indian from northern Mexico.

The dictionary of the Spanish Royal Academy defines *nagual* as the Spanish adaptation of a word that means sorcerer or wizard in the Nahuatl language of southern Mexico.

Traditional stories of naguals, men of ancient times who possessed extraordinary powers and performed acts that defied the imagination, do exist in modern Mexico. But in an urban or even rural setting today, actual naguals are purely legendary. They seem to live only in folktales, through hearsay, or in the world of fantasy.

The nagual I met, however, was real. There was nothing illusory about him. When I asked him out of well-meant curiosity what made him a nagual, he presented a seemingly simple, and yet utterly complex idea as an explanation for what he did and what he was. He told me that nagualism begins with two certainties: the certainty that human beings are extraordinary beings living in an extraordinary world; and the certainty that neither men nor the world should ever be taken for granted under any circumstances.

From those sweet, simple premises, he said, grows a simple conclusion: Nagualism is at once taking off one mask and wearing another. Naguals take off the mask that makes us see ourselves and the world we live in as ordinary, lusterless, predictable, and repetitious and put on the second mask, the one that helps us see ourselves—and our surroundings—for what we really are—breathtaking events that bloom into transitory existence once and are never to be repeated again.

After meeting that unforgettable nagual, I had a moment's hesitation due solely to the fear I felt on examining such an imposing paradigm. I wanted to run away from that nagual and his quest, but I could not do it. Some time later, I took a drastic step and joined him and his party.

But this is not a story about that nagual, although his ideas and his influence bear heavily in everything I do. It is not my task to write about him or even to name him. There are others in his group who do that.

When I joined him, he took me to Mexico to meet a strange, striking woman—without telling me that she was perhaps the most knowledgeable and influential woman of his group. Her name was Florinda Matus. In spite of her worn, drab clothes, she had the innate elegance of most tall, thin women. Her pale complexioned face, gaunt and severe, was crowned by braided white hair and highlighted by large, luminous eyes. Her husky voice and her joyful, youthful laughter eased my irrational fear of her.

The nagual left me in her charge. The first thing I asked Florinda was whether she was a nagual herself. Smiling rather enigmatically, she further refined the definition of the word. She said, "To be a sorcerer or a wizard or a witch doesn't mean to be a nagual. But any of them can be one if he or she is responsible for and leads a group of men and women involved in a specific quest of knowledge."

When I asked her what that quest was, she responded that for those men and women it was to find the second mask, the one that helps us see ourselves and the world for what we really are—breathtaking events.

But this is not the story of Florinda either, despite the fact that she is the woman who guides me in every act I perform. This is, rather, the story of one of the many things she made me do.

"For women the quest of knowledge is indeed a very curious affair," Florinda told me once. "We have to go through strange maneuvers."

"Why is that so, Florinda?"

"Because women really don't care."

"I care."

"You say you care. You really don't."

"I'm here with you. Doesn't that speak for my caring?"

"No. What happened is that you like the nagual. His personality overwhelms you. I am the same myself. I was overwhelmed by the preceding nagual. The most irresistible sorcerer there was."

"I admit you are right but only partially. I do care about the nagual's quest."

"I don't doubt it. But that's not enough. Women need some specific maneuvers, in order to get at the core of themselves."

"What maneuvers? What core of ourselves are you talking about, Florinda?"

"If there is something inside us that we don't know about, such as hidden resources, unsuspected guts and cunning, or nobility of the spirit in the face of sorrow and pain, it will come out if we are confronted by the unknown while we are alone, without friends, without familiar boundaries, without support. If nothing comes out of us under those circumstances, it's because we have nothing. And before you say you really care for the nagual's quest, you must first find out for yourself whether there is something inside you. I demand that you do that."

"I don't think I am any good at being tested, Florinda."

"My question is: Can you live without knowing whether or not you have something hidden inside you?"

"But what if I am one of those who have nothing?"

"If that's the case, then I will have to ask you my second question: Can you go on being in the world you have chosen if you have nothing inside you?"

"Why, of course I can continue to be here. I've already joined you."

"No. You only think you have chosen my world. To choose the nagual's world is not just a matter of saying you have. You must prove it."

"How do you think I should go about doing that?"

"I'll give you a suggestion. You don't have to follow it, but if you do, you should go alone to the place where you were born. Nothing could be easier than that. Go there and take your chances, whatever they may be."

"But your suggestion is impractical. I don't have good feelings about that place. I didn't leave in good standing."

"So much the better; the odds will be stacked against

6

you. That's why I picked your country. Women don't like to be bothered too much; if they have to bother with things, they go to pieces. Prove to me that you are not that way."

"What would you suggest I do in that place?"

"Be yourself. Do your work. You said that you want to be an anthropologist. Be one. What could be simpler?"

2

Years later, following Florinda's suggestions, I finally went to Venezuela, the country of my birth. On the surface, I went to gather anthropological data on healing practices. Actually, I was there to carry out, under Florinda's guidance, the maneuvers necessary to discover whether I possessed hidden resources, without which I could not remain in the nagual's world.

The agreement that my journey must be a solitary one was nearly drawn out of me by force. With strong words and decisive gestures, Florinda served notice that under no circumstances should I seek counsel from anyone around me during the trip. Knowing that I was in college, she strongly advised me not to use the trappings of academic life while in the field. I should not ask for a grant, have academic supervisors, or even ask my family and friends for help. I should let circumstances dictate the path to follow; once I had taken it, I must plunge into it with the fierceness of women on the warrior's path.

I arranged to go to Venezuela on an informal visit. I would see my relatives, I thought, and gather information on any possibility for a future study in cultural anthropology. Florinda praised me for my speed and thoroughness. I thought she was humoring me. There was nothing to praise me for. I mentioned to her that what worried me was her lack of instructions. Again and again I asked her for more details about my role in Venezuela. As the date of my departure approached, I became increasingly anxious about the outcome of it all. I insisted, in no uncertain terms, that I needed more specific instructions.

We were sitting in wicker chairs, comfortably padded by soft cushions, under the shade of one of the many fruit trees growing in her huge court patio. In her long unbleached muslin dress, her wide-brimmed hat, fanning herself with a lace fan, she looked like someone from another time.

"Forget about specific information," she said impatiently. "It won't do you any good."

"It certainly will do me a lot of good," I insisted. "I really don't understand why you're doing this to me, Florinda."

"Blame it on the fact that I am in the nagual's world; on the fact that I am a woman and that I belong to a different mood."

"Mood? What do you mean by a different mood?"

She gazed at me with remote, disinterested eyes. "I wish you could hear yourself talking. What mood?" she mocked me. Her face expressed tolerant contempt. "I don't go for seemingly orderly arrangements of thought and deed. For me, order is different from arranging things neatly. I don't give a damn about stupidity and I have no patience. That's the mood."

"That sounds dreadful, Florinda. I was led to believe that in the nagual's world, people are above pettiness and don't behave impatiently."

"Being in the nagual's world has nothing to do with

9

my impatience," she said, making a humorous, hopeless gesture. "You see, I'm impeccably impatient."

"I really would like to know what it means to be impeccably impatient."

"It means that I am, for instance, perfectly conscious that you are boring me now with your stupid insistence on having detailed instructions. My impatience tells me that I should stop you. But it is my impeccability that will make you shut up at once.

"All this boils down to the following: If you persist in asking for details guided only by your bad habit of having everything spelled out, in spite of my telling you to stop, I'll hit you. But I'll never be angry at you or hold it against you."

In spite of her serious tone I had to laugh. "Would you really hit me, Florinda? Well, hit me if you have to," I added, seeing her determined face. "But I've got to know what I am going to do in Venezuela. I'm going crazy with worry."

"All right! If you insist on knowing the details I consider important, I'll tell you. I hope you understand we're separated by an abyss and that abyss can't be bridged by talk. Males can build bridges with their words; women can't. You're imitating males now. Women have to make the bridge with their acts. We give birth, you know. We make people. I want you to go away so that in aloneness you'll find out what your strengths or weaknesses are."

"I understand what you say, Florinda, but consider my position."

Florinda relented, dismissing the retort that arose to her lips.

"All right, all right," she said wearily, motioning me to move my chair next to hers. "I'm going to give you the details I consider important for your trip. Fortunately for you, they are not the detailed instructions you are after. What you want is for me to tell you exactly what to do in a future situation, and when to do it. That's something quite stupid to ask. How can I give you instructions about something that doesn't yet exist? I'll give you, instead, instructions on how to arrange your thoughts, feelings, and reactions. With that in hand, you'll take care of any eventuality that might arise."

"Are you really serious, Florinda?" I asked in disbelief.

"I'm deadly serious," she assured me. Leaning forward in her chair, she went on speaking with a half smile about to break into a laugh. "The first detailed item to consider is taking stock of yourself. You see, in the nagual's world, we must be responsible for our actions."

She reminded me that I knew the warrior's path. In the time I had been with her, she said, I had received extensive training in the laborious practical philosophy of the nagual's world. Therefore, any detailed instructions she might give me now would have to be, actually, a detailed reminder of the warrior's path.

"In the warrior's path, women don't feel important," she went on, in the tone of someone reciting from memory, "because importance waters down fierceness. In the warrior's path women are fierce. They remain fiercely impassive under any conditions. They don't demand anything, yet they are willing to give anything of themselves. They fiercely seek a signal from the spirit of things in the form of a kind word, an appropriate gesture; and when they get it, they express their thanks by redoubling their fierceness.

"In the warrior's path, women don't judge. They fiercely reduce themselves to nothing in order to listen, to watch, so that they can conquer and be humbled by their conquest or be defeated and be enhanced by their defeat.

"In the warrior's path, women don't surrender. They may be defeated a thousand times, but they never surrender. And above all, in the warrior's path, women are free."

Unable to interrupt her, I had kept gazing at Florinda, fascinated though not quite grasping what she was saying. I felt acute despair when she stopped as though she had nothing more to tell me. Without quite wanting to, I began crying uncontrollably. I knew that what she had just told me could not help me to resolve my problems.

She let me cry for a long time and then she laughed. "You really are weeping!" she said in disbelief.

"You are the most heartless, unfeeling person I've ever met," I said between sobs. "You're ready to send me God knows where, and you don't even tell me what I should do."

"But I just did," she said still laughing.

"What you just said has no value in a real-life situation," I retorted angrily. "You sounded like a dictator spouting slogans."

Florinda regarded me cheerfully. "You'll be surprised how much use you can get out of those stupid slogans," she said. "But now, let us come to an understanding. I'm not sending you any place. You're a woman in the warrior's path, you're free to do what you wish, you know that. You haven't yet grasped what the nagual's world is all about. I'm not your teacher; I'm not your mentor; I'm not responsible for you. No one but yourself is. The hardest thing to grasp about the nagual's world is that it offers total freedom. But freedom is not free.

"I took you under my wing because you have a natural ability to see things as they are, to remove yourself from a situation and see the wonder of it all. That's a gift; you were born like that. It takes years for average persons in the nagual's world to remove themselves from their involvement with themselves and be capable of seeing the wonder of it all."

Regardless of her praise, I was nearly beyond myself with anxiety. She finally calmed me down by promising that just before my plane left she would give me the specific detailed information I wanted.

I waited in the departure lobby of the airline, but Florinda didn't show up at all. Despondent and filled with self-pity, I gave free rein to my despair and disappointment. With no concern for the curious glances around me, I sat down and wept. I felt lonelier than I had ever felt before. All I could think of was that no one had come to see me off; no one had come to help me with my suitcase. I was used to having relatives and friends see me off.

Florinda had warned me that anyone who chose the nagual's world had to be prepared for fierce aloneness. She had made it clear that to her, aloneness did not mean loneliness but a physical state of solitude.

3

Never had I realized how sheltered my life had been.
In a hotel room in Caracas, alone and without any
idea of what to do next, I came to experience first
hand the solitariness Florinda had talked about. All I
felt like doing was sitting on the hotel bed and watching TV. I didn't want to touch my suitcase. I even
thought of taking the plane back to Los Angeles. My
parents were not in Venezuela at the time, and I had
been unable to contact my brothers by telephone.

Only after tremendous effort did I begin to unpack.
Neatly tucked inside a pair of folded slacks I found a
piece of paper with Florinda's handwriting. I read it
avidly.

Don't worry about details. Details tend to adjust
themselves to serve the circumstances if one has
conviction. Your plans should be as follows. Pick
anything and call that the beginning. Then go and
face the beginning. Once you are face to face
with the beginning, let it take you wherever it
may. I trust that your convictions won't let you
pick a capricious beginning. Be realistic and fru-
gal, so as to select wisely. Do it now!!
P.S. Anything would do for a start.

Possessed by Florinda's decisiveness, I picked up the phone and dialed the number of an old friend of mine. I was not sure she would still be in Caracas. The polite lady who answered the phone gave me other possible numbers to call because my friend was no longer at that address. I called all of them, for I could no longer stop. The beginning was taking hold of me. Finally I located a married couple I knew from childhood, my parents' friends. They wanted to see me immediately, but they were going to a wedding in an hour so they insisted on taking me along. They assured me it was all right.

At the wedding I met an ex-Jesuit priest, who was an amateur anthropologist. We talked for hours on end. I told him of my interest in anthropological studies. As if he had been waiting for me to say a magical word, he began to expound on the controversial value of folk healers and the social role they play in their societies.

I had not mentioned healers or healing in general as a possible topic for my study, although it was foremost in my mind. Instead of feeling happy that he seemed to be addressing himself to my inner thoughts, I was filled with an apprehension that verged on fear. When he told me that I should not go to the town of Sortes, even though it was purported to be the center of spiritualism in western Venezuela, I felt genuinely annoyed with him. He seemed to be anticipating me at every turn. It was precisely to that small town that I had planned to go if nothing else happened.

I was just about to excuse myself and leave the party, when he said in quite a loud tone that I should seriously consider going to the town of Curmina, in northern Venezuela, where I could have phenomenal success because the town was a new, true center of spiritualism and healing.

"I don't know how I know it, but I know you're dying to be with the witches of Curmina," he said in a dry, matter-of-fact tone.

He took a piece of paper and drew a map of the region. He gave me exact distances in kilometers from Caracas to the various points in the area where he said spiritualists, sorcerers, witches, and healers lived. He placed special emphasis on one name: Mercedes Peralta. He underlined it and, totally unaware of it, first encircled it, then drew a heavy square around it and boxed it in.

"She's a spiritualist, a witch, and a healer," he said smiling at me. "Be sure you go and see her, will you?"

I knew what he was talking about. Under Florinda's guidance, I had met and worked with spiritualists, sorcerers, witches, and healers in northern Mexico and among the Latino population of southern California. From the very beginning Florinda classified them. Spiritualists are practitioners who entreat the spirits of saints or devils to intercede for them, with a higher order, on behalf of their patients. Their function is to get in touch with spirits and interpret their advice. The advice is obtained in meetings during which spirits are called. Sorcerers and witches are practitioners who affect their patients directly. Through their knowledge of occult arts, they bring unknown and unpredictable elements to bear on the two kinds of people who come to see them: patients in search of help and clients in search of their witchcraft services. Healers are practitioners who strive exclusively to restore health and well-being.

Florinda made sure she added to her classification the possible combinations of all three.

In a joking way but in all seriousness, she claimed that in matters of restoring health, I was predisposed to believe that non-Western healing practices were more holistic than Western medicine. She made it clear that I was wrong, because healing, she said, depended on the practitioner and not on a body of knowledge. She maintained that there was no such thing as non-Western healing practices, since healing, unlike medicine, was not a formalized discipline. She used to tease that in my own way, I was as prejudiced as those who believe that if a patient is cured by means of medicinal plants, massages, or incantations, either the disease was psychosomatic or the cure was the result of a lucky accident that the practitioner did not understand.

Florinda was convinced that a person who successfully restored health, whether a doctor or a folk healer, was someone who could alter the body's fundamental feelings about itself and its link with the world—that is, someone who offered the body, as well as the mind, new possibilities so that the habitual mold to which body and mind had learned to conform could be systematically broken down. Other dimensions of awareness would then become accessible, and the commonsense expectations of disease and health could become transformed as new bodily meanings became crystalized.

Florinda had laughed when I expressed genuine surprise upon hearing such thoughts, which were revolutionary to me at the time. She told me that everything she said stemmed from the knowledge she shared with her companions in the nagual's world.

* * *

Having followed the instructions in Florinda's note, I let the situation guide me; I let it develop with minimal interference on my part. I felt I had to go to Curmina and look up the woman that the ex-Jesuit priest had talked about.

When I first arrived at Mercedes Peralta's house, I did not have to wait long in the shadowy corridor before a voice called me from behind the curtain directly in front of me that served as a door. I climbed the two steps leading to a large, dimly lit room that smelled of cigar smoke and ammonia. Several candles, burning on a massive altar that stood against the far wall, illuminated the figurines and pictures of saints arranged around the blue-robed Virgin of Coromoto. It was a finely carved statue with red smiling lips, rouged cheeks, and eyes that seemed to fix me with a benign, forgiving gaze.

I stepped closer. In the corner, almost hidden between the altar and a high rectangular table, sat Mercedes Peralta. She appeared to be asleep, with her head resting against the back of her chair, her eyes closed. She looked extremely old. I had never seen such a face. Even in its restful immobility, it revealed a frightening strength. The glow of the candles, rather than softening her sharply chiseled features, only accentuated the determination etched in the network of wrinkles.

Slowly, she opened her eyes; they were large and almond shaped. The whites of her eyes were slightly discolored. At first her eyes were almost blank, but then they became alive and stared at me with the unnerving directness of a child. Seconds passed and gradually under her unwavering gaze, which was neither friendly nor unfriendly, I began to feel uncomfortable.

"Good afternoon, doña Mercedes," I greeted her before I started to lose all my courage and run out of the house. "My name is Florinda Donner, and I am going to be very direct so as not to waste your valuable time."

She blinked repeatedly, adjusting her eyes to look at me.

"I've come to Venezuela to study healing methods," I went on, gaining confidence. "I study at a university in the United States, but I truly would like to be a healer. I can pay you if you take me as your student. But even if you don't take me as your student, I can pay you for any information you would give me."

The old woman did not say a word. She motioned me to sit down on a stool, then rose and gazed at a metal instrument on the table. There was a comical expression on her face as she turned to look at me.

"What is that apparatus?" I asked daringly.

"It's a nautical compass," she said casually. "It tells me all kinds of things." She picked it up and placed it on the topmost shelf of a glass cabinet that stood against the opposite wall. Apparently struck by a funny thought, she began to laugh. "I'm going to make something clear to you right now," she said. "Yes, I'll give you all kinds of information about healing, not because you ask me, but because you're lucky. I already know that for sure. What I don't know is if you're strong as well."

The old woman was silent, then she spoke again in a forced whisper without looking at me, her attention on something inside the glass cabinet.

"Luck and strength are all that count in everything,"

she said. "I knew the night I saw you by the plaza that you are lucky and that you were looking for me."

"I don't understand what you're talking about," I said.

Mercedes Peralta turned to face me, then laughed in such a discordant manner that I felt certain she was mad. She opened her mouth so wide I could see the few molars she still had left. She stopped abruptly, sat on her chair, and insisted that she had seen me exactly two weeks ago late at night in the plaza. She had been with a friend, she explained, who was driving her home from a séance that had taken place in one of the coastal towns. Although her friend had been baffled to see me alone so late at night, she herself had not been in the least surprised. "You reminded me instantly of someone I once knew," she said. "It was past midnight. You smiled at me."

I did not remember seeing her or being alone in the plaza at that hour. But it could have been that she had seen me the night I had arrived from Caracas. After waiting in vain for the week-long rain to stop, I had finally risked the drive from Caracas to Curmina. I knew full well that there would be landslides; it turned out that instead of the usual two hours, the drive took me four. By the time I had arrived, the whole town was asleep, and I had trouble finding the hostel near the plaza, which had also been recommended to me by the former priest.

Mystified by her insistence that she knew I was coming to see her, I told her about him and what he had said to me at the wedding in Caracas. "He was quite insistent that I look you up," I said. "He mentioned that your ancestors were sorcerers and healers, famous during colonial times, and that they were persecuted by the Holy Inquisition."

A flicker of surprise widened her eyes slightly. "Did you know that in those days accused witches were sent to Cartagena in Colombia to be tried?" she asked and immediately went on to say, "Venezuela wasn't important enough to have an Inquisitorial tribunal." She paused and, looking straight into my eyes, asked, "Where had you originally planned to study healing methods?"

"In the state of Yaracuy," I said vaguely.

"Sortes?" she inquired. "Maria Lionza?"

I nodded. Sortes is the town where the cult of Maria Lionza is centered. Said to have been born of an Indian princess and a Spanish conquistador, Maria Lionza is purported to have had supernatural powers. Today, she is revered by thousands in Venezuela as a saintly miraculous woman.

"But I took the ex-priest's advice and came to Curmina instead," I said. "I've already talked with two women healers. Both agreed that you're the most knowledgeable, the only one who could explain healing matters to me."

I talked about the methods I wanted to follow, making it all up on the spur of the moment: direct observation and participation in some of the healing sessions while tape recording them and, most important of all, systematic interviewing of the patients I observed.

The old woman nodded, giggling from time to time. To my great surprise, she was totally amenable to my proposed methods. She proudly informed me that years ago she had been interviewed by a psychologist from a university in Caracas, who had stayed for a week right there in her house.

"To make it easier for you," she suggested, "you can come and live with us. We have plenty of rooms in the house."

I accepted her invitation but told her that I had planned to stay for at least six months in the area. She seemed unperturbed. As far as she was concerned, I could stay for years. "I'm glad you're here, Musiúa," she added softly.

I smiled. Although born and raised in Venezuela, I have been called a *musiúa* (moo-see-yua) all my life. It is usually a derogatory term, but depending on the tone in which it is said, it can be turned into a rather affectionate expression referring to anyone who is blond and blue-eyed.

4

Startled by the faint rustle of a skirt swishing past me, I opened my eyes and gazed at the candle burning on the altar in the semidarkness of the room. The flame flickered and sent up a single black thread of smoke. On the wall appeared a woman's shadow with a stick in its hand. The shadow seemed to impale the heads of the men and women who, with closed eyes, were sitting beside me on old wooden chairs arranged in a circle. I could barely stifle a nervous giggle upon realizing that it was Mercedes Peralta, placing big, hand-rolled cigars in everyone's mouth. She then took the candle from the altar, lit each cigar with it, and returned to her chair in the middle of the circle. In a deep monotonous voice she began to chant an unintelligible, repetitious incantation.

Suppressing a fit of coughing, I tried to synchronize my smoking with the rapid puffing of the people around me. Through teary eyes I watched their solemn, mask-like faces becoming momentarily animated with every puff until they seemed to dissolve in the thickening smoke. Like a disembodied object, Mercedes Peralta's hand materialized out of that vaporous haze. Snapping her fingers, she repeatedly traced the air with the imaginary lines connecting the four cardinal points.

Imitating the others, I began to sway my head to and fro, to the rhythmic sound of her snapping fingers and her low-voiced incantations. Ignoring my growing nausea, I forced myself to keep my eyes open so as not to miss a single detail of what was occurring around me. This was the first time I had been allowed to attend a meeting of spiritualists. Doña Mercedes was going to serve as the medium and contact the spirits.

Her own definition of spiritualists, witches, and healers was the same as Florinda's, with the exception that she recognized another independent class: Mediums. She defined mediums as the interpreting intermediaries who serve as conduits for the spirits to express themselves. She understood that mediums were so independent that they did not have to belong to any of the three other categories. But they could also be all four categories in one.

"There is a disturbing force in the room." A man's voice interrupted doña Mercedes' incantations.

Smoldering cigars perforated the smoky darkness like accusing eyes as the rest of the group mumbled their agreement.

"I'll see to it," she said, rising from her chair. She went from person to person, pausing for an instant behind each one.

I yelled out in pain as I felt something sharp piercing my shoulder.

"Come with me," she whispered into my ear. "You aren't in a trance." Afraid I would resist, she took me firmly by the arm and led me to the red curtain that served as a door.

"But you yourself asked me to come," I insisted before I was pushed out of the room. "I won't bother anyone if I sit quietly in a corner."

"You'll bother the spirits," she murmured and noise-lessly drew the curtain shut.

I walked to the kitchen at the back of the house, where I usually worked at night transcribing tapes and organizing my gradually growing field notes. Swarms of insects clustered around the single bulb dangling from the kitchen ceiling. Its weak light illuminated the wooden table standing in the middle of the room but left the corners in shadows, where the flea-ridden, mangy dogs slept. One side of the rectangular kitchen was open to the yard. Against the other three walls, blackened by soot, stood a raised adobe cooking pit, a kerosene stove, and a round metal tub filled with water.

I walked into the moonlit yard. The cement slab where doña Mercedes' companion Candelaria spread out well-soaped clothes to whiten in the sun each day shone like a silvery puddle of water. The wash hanging on the lines looked like white stains against the darkness of the stucco wall encircling the yard. Outlined by the moon, fruit trees, medicinal plants, and vegetable patches formed a uniform dark mass humming with insects and the strident call of crickets.

I returned to the kitchen and checked the pot simmering on the stove. No matter what time of day or night, there was always something to eat. Usually it was a hearty soup made of meat, chicken, or fish, depending on what was available, and an assortment of vegetables and roots.

I searched for a soup plate among the dishes piled on the wide adobe shelves built into the wall. There were dozens of unmatched china, metal, and plastic plates. I served myself a large bowl of chicken soup, but before sitting down, I remembered to scoop out some water from the nearby tub and replenish the pot on the stove. It had not taken me long to familiarize myself with the habits of that eccentric household.

I started to write down what had transpired in the meeting. Trying to recollect every detail of an event or every word of a conversation was always the best exercise to fight off the sense of loneliness that invariably came upon me.

The cold nose of a dog rubbed against my leg. I searched for leftover pieces of bread, fed them to the dog, and then returned to my notes.

I worked until I felt sleepy and my eyes burned, strained by the weak light. I collected my tape recorder and papers, then headed toward my room, situated at the other end of the house. I paused for an instant in the inside patio. It was patched with moonlight. A faint breeze stirred the leaves of the gnarled grape vine; its jagged shadows painted lacy patterns on the brick courtyard.

Before actually seeing the woman, I felt her presence. She was squatting on the ground, almost hidden by the large terra-cotta pots scattered throughout the patio. A wooly mop of hair crowned her head like a white halo, but her dark face remained indistinct, blending in with the shadows around her.

I had never seen her in the house before. I recovered from my initial fright by reasoning that she must be one of doña Mercedes' friends, or perhaps one of her patients, or even one of Candelaria's relatives, who was waiting for her to come out of the séance.

"Pardon me," I said. "I'm new here. I work with doña Mercedes."

The woman nodded as I spoke. She gave me the impression she knew what I was talking about. But she did not break her silence. Possessed by an inexplicable uneasiness, I tried not to succumb to hysterical fright. I kept repeating to myself that I had no reason to panic because an old woman was squatting in the patio.

"Were you at the séance?" I asked in an uncertain voice.

The woman shook her head affirmatively.

"I was there, too," I said, "but doña Mercedes kicked me out." I felt relieved all of a sudden and wanted to make fun of the situation.

"Are you afraid of me?" the old woman asked abruptly. Her voice had a cutting, raspy, yet youthful sound.

I laughed. I was about to say no with a flippant air, when something held me back. I heard myself saying that I was terrified of her.

"Come with me," the woman ordered me matter-of-factly.

Again my first reaction was to follow her boldly, but instead I heard myself saying something I had not intended. "I have to finish my work. If you care to talk to me, you can do it here and now."

"I command you to come!" the woman's voice boomed.

All the energy of my body seemed to drain out of me at once. Yet I stated, "Why don't you command yourself to stay." I could not believe I had said that. I was ready to apologize, when a strange reserve of energy flowed into my body and made me feel almost under control.

"Have it your way," the woman said and stood up from her squatting position. Her height was inconceivable. She grew and grew until her knees were at my eye level.

At that point I felt my energy leaving me and I let out a series of wild, piercing screams.

Candelaria came rushing to my side. She covered the distance between the room where the meeting of spiritualists was taking place and the patio before I had time to gasp for air and scream once more.

"Everything is all right now," she repeated in a soothing voice that seemed to come from far away.

Gently, she rubbed my neck and back, but I could not stop from shaking. And then without wanting to, I began to cry.

"I shouldn't have left you by yourself," she said apologetically. "But who would've thought a musiúa would see her?"

Before any of the other participants in the meeting came out to see what was going on, Candelaria took me to the kitchen. She helped me into a chair and gave me a glass of rum. I drank it and told her what had happened in the patio. The instant I had finished both the rum and my account, I felt drowsy, distracted, but far from drunk.

"Leave us alone, Candelaria," doña Mercedes said, stepping into my room. Not only had Candelaria put me to bed, she had also placed a cot alongside so that she could be there when I awoke.

"I don't know how to say this," doña Mercedes began after a long silence, "but you're a medium. I knew this all along." Her feverish eyes seemed to be suspended in a crystalline substance as she studied my face intently. "The only reason they did let you sit in the séance was because you're lucky. Mediums are lucky."

In spite of my apprehension I had to laugh.

"Don't laugh about this," she admonished. "It's serious. You called a spirit last night all by yourself. And the most important spirit of them all, the spirit of one of my ancestors, came to you. She doesn't come often, but when she does, it's for important reasons."

"Was she a ghost?" I asked stupidly.

"Of course she was a ghost," she said firmly. "We understand things the way we've been taught. There are no deviations from that. Our beliefs are that you saw a most frightening spirit and that a live medium can communicate with the spirit of a dead medium."

"Why would that spirit come to me?" I asked.

"I don't know. She came to me once to warn me," she replied, "but I didn't follow her advice." Her eyes became gentle, and her voice grew softer as she added, "The first thing I told you when you arrived was that you're lucky. I was lucky, too, until someone broke my luck. You remind me of that person. He was as blond as you are. His name was Federico and he also had luck, but he had no strength whatsoever. The spirit told me to leave him alone. I didn't, and I am still paying for it."

At a loss as to how to take the sudden turn of events or the sadness that had come upon her, I placed my hand over hers.

"He had no strength whatsoever," she repeated. "The spirit knew it."

Although Mercedes Peralta was always willing to discuss anything pertaining to her practices, she had quite emphatically discouraged my curiosity regarding her past. Once, and I don't know whether I caught her unaware or whether it was a deliberate move on her part, she revealed that she had suffered a great loss many years ago.

Before I had a chance to decide whether she was actually encouraging me to ask personal questions, she lifted my hand to her face and held it against her cheek. "Feel these scars," she whispered.

"What happened to you?" I asked, running my fingers over the rough scar tissue on her cheeks and neck. Until I touched them, the scars had been indistinguishable from the wrinkles. Her dark skin felt so brittle I was afraid it would disintegrate in my hand. A mysterious vibration emanated from her entire body. I could not shift my gaze from her eyes.

"We won't talk about what you saw in the patio," she said emphatically. "Things like that pertain only to the world of mediums, and you should never discuss that world with anyone. I would certainly advise you not to be afraid of that spirit but do not beckon her foolishly."

She helped me get out of my bed and led me outside to the same spot in the patio where I had seen the woman. As I stood there inspecting the darkness around us, I realized that I had no idea whether I had slept a few hours or an entire night and day.

Doña Mercedes seemed to be aware of my confusion. "It's four in the morning," she said. "You've slept almost five hours."

She crouched where the woman had been. I squatted beside her, between the shrubs of jasmine hanging down from wooden lattices like perfumed curtains.

"It never occurred to me that you didn't know how to smoke," she said and laughed her dry raspy laughter.

She reached inside her skirt pocket, pulled out a cigar, and lit it. "At a meeting of spiritualists, we smoke hand-rolled cigars. Spiritualists know that the smell of tobacco pleases the spirits." After a short pause, she put the lit cigar in my mouth. "Try to smoke," she ordered.

I drew on it, inhaling deeply. The heavy smoke made me cough.

"Don't inhale," she said impatiently. "Let me show you how." She reached for the cigar and puffed at it repeatedly, breathing in and out in short even spurts. "You don't want the smoke to go to your lungs but to your head," she explained. "That's the way a medium calls the spirits. From now on, you're going to call the spirits from this spot. And don't talk about it until you can conduct a spiritualist's meeting all by yourself."

"But I don't want to call the spirits," I laughingly protested. "All I want is to sit in one of the meetings and watch."

She regarded me with a threatening determination. "You are a medium, and no medium goes to a meeting to watch."

"What is the reason for a meeting?" I asked, changing the subject.

"To ask questions of the spirits," she promptly responded. "Some spirits give great advice. Others are malevolent." She chuckled with a touch of malice. "Which spirit shows up depends on the medium's state of being."

"Are mediums, then, at the mercy of the spirits?" I asked.

She was silent for a long time, looking at me without betraying any feelings in her face. Then, in a defiant tone she said, "They are not if they are strong." She continued staring at me fiercely, then she closed her eyes. When she opened them again, they were devoid of all expression. "Help me to my room," she murmured. Holding on to my head, she straightened up. Her hand slid down my shoulder, then to my arm, the stiff fingers curling around my wrist like carbonized roots.

Silently, we shuffled down the dark corridor, where wooden benches and chairs covered with goat hide stood rigidly against the wall. She stepped inside her bedroom. Before closing the door she reminded me again that mediums do not talk about their world. "I knew the instant I saw you in the plaza that you were a medium and that you would be coming to see me," she affirmed. A smile, the meaning of which I did not understand, crossed her face. "You have come to bring me something from my past."

"What?"

"I don't quite know myself. Memories, perhaps," she said vaguely. "Or perhaps you are bringing my old luck back." She brushed my cheek with the back of her hand and softly closed the door.

5

Lulled by the soft breeze and the laughter of children playing in the street, I dozed all afternoon in the hammock that hung between two soursop trees in the yard. I was even oblivious to the scent of powder detergent mingled with the pungent odor of creosol with which Candelaria washed the floors twice each day, regardless of whether they were dirty.

I waited until it was nearly six o'clock. Then, as Mercedes Peralta had requested, I went and knocked on her bedroom door. There was no answer. Quietly, I stepped inside. Usually at that time, she was through with the people who came to her to be treated for one malady or another. She never saw more than two a day. On her bad days, which were quite frequent, she saw no one. On those occasions, I took her for rides in my jeep and for long walks in the surrounding hills.

"Is that you, Musiúa?" doña Mercedes asked, stretching in her low-hanging hammock, fastened to metal rings built into the wall.

I greeted her and sat on the double bed by the window. She never slept in it. She maintained that from a bed, regardless of its size, one could have a fatal fall. Waiting for her to get up, I looked around the oddly furnished room that never failed to enchant me.

Things had been arranged there with a look of purposeful incongruity. The two night tables at the head and foot of the bed, cluttered with candles and figurines of saints, served as altars. A low wooden wardrobe painted blue and pink blocked the door that opened to the street. I wondered what was inside, for doña Mercedes' clothes—she never wore anything but black—hung everywhere, from hooks on the walls and behind the door, at the head and foot of the iron bedstead, and even from the ropes holding the hammock. A crystal chandelier, which did not work, dangled precariously from the cane ceiling. It was gray with dust, and spiders had spun their webs around its prisms. An almanac, the kind one tears a page from each day, hung behind the door.

Combing her fingers through her white mop of hair, Mercedes Peralta heaved a deep sigh, then swung her legs out of the hammock and hunted about with her feet for her cloth sandals. She sat still for a moment, then moved to the high narrow window facing the street and opened its wooden panels. She blinked repeatedly until her eyes adjusted to the late-afternoon light beaming into the room. Intently, she gazed at the sky, as if she were expecting some message from the sunset.

"Are we going for a walk?" I asked.

Slowly, she turned around. "A walk?" she repeated, arching her brows in surprise. "How can we go for a walk when I have a person waiting for me."

I opened my mouth ready to inform her there was no one outside, but the mocking expression in her tired eyes compelled me to silence. She took my hand, and we walked out of her room.

With his chin buried in his chest, a frail-looking old

man dozed on the wooden bench outside the room where Mercedes Peralta treated people who came for help. Sensing our presence, he straightened up. "I don't feel too well," he said in a toneless voice, reaching for his straw hat and the walking stick lying beside him.

"Octavio Cantú," Mercedes Peralta said, addressing herself to me, but shaking his hand. She led him up the two steps into the room. I followed close behind. He turned around with an inquiring expression in his eyes as he gazed at me.

"She's been helping me," she said. "But if you don't want her with us, she'll go outside."

He stood there for a moment nervously shifting his feet. His mouth twisted into a lopsided smile. "If she has been helping you," he murmured with a touch of helplessness, "I suppose it's all right."

With a swift movement of her head, Mercedes Peralta motioned me to my stool by the altar, then helped the old man into the chair directly in front of the high rectangular table. She seated herself to his right, facing him. "Where could it be?" she mumbled repeatedly, searching among the assortment of jars, candles and cigars, dried roots, and scraps of material scattered on the table. She sighed with relief upon finding her nautical compass, which she placed in front of Octavio Cantú. Attentively, she studied the round-shaped metal box. "Look at this!" she cried out, beckoning me to move closer.

It was the same compass I had seen her examine so intently the first day I walked into that room. The needle, barely visible through the opaque, badly scratched glass, moved vigorously to and fro, as if animated by some invisible force emanating from Octavio Cantú.

Mercedes Peralta used the compass as a diagnostic device only if she believed the person to be suffering from a spiritual ailment rather than a natural disease. So far, I had been unable to determine what criteria she used to differentiate between the two kinds of maladies. For her, a spiritual ailment could manifest itself in the form of a bout of bad luck as well as a common cold, which, depending on the circumstances, might also be diagnosed as a natural ailment.

Expecting to find some mechanical contraption that activated the needle, I examined the compass at every opportunity. Since there was none, I accepted her explanation as a bonafide truth: Whenever a person is centered, that is, when body, spirit, and soul are in harmony, the needle does not move at all. To prove her point, she placed the compass in front of herself, Candelaria, and me. To my great astonishment, the needle moved only when the compass was in front of me.

Octavio Cantú craned his neck to peer at the instrument. "Am I sick?" he asked softly, gazing up at doña Mercedes.

"It's your spirit," she murmured. "Your spirit is in great turmoil." She returned the compass to the glass cabinet, then positioned herself behind the old man and rested both hands on his head. She remained that way for a long time; then with quick, sure movements, she ran her fingers down his shoulders and arms. Swiftly, she stepped in front of him, her hands brushing lightly down his chest, his legs, all the way to his feet. Reciting a prayer that was part church litany, part incantation—she maintained that every good healer knew that Catholicism and spiritualism complemented each other—she alternately massaged his back and chest for nearly a half hour. To give momentary relief to her tired hands, she periodically shook them vigorously behind her back. She called it casting off the accumulation of negative energy.

To mark the end of the first part of her treatment, she stamped her right foot three times on the ground. Octavio Cantú shuddered uncontrollably. She held his head from behind, pressing her palms to his temples until he began to draw slow, difficult breaths. Mumbling a prayer, she moved to the altar, lit a candle and then a hand-rolled cigar, which she began to smoke with even, rapid puffs.

"I should be used to it by now," the old man said, breaking the smoky silence.

Startled by his voice, she began to cough until tears rolled down her cheeks. I wondered whether she had accidentally inhaled the smoke.

Octavio Cantú, oblivious to her coughing, continued to talk. "I've told you many, many times that whether I'm sober or drunk, I only dream one dream. I'm standing in my shack. It's empty. I feel the wind and see shadows moving everywhere. But there are no more dogs to bark at the emptiness and at the shadows. I awake with a terrible pressure; it feels like someone were sitting on my chest; and as I open my eyes, I see the yellow pupils of a dog. They open wider and wider, until they swallow me. . . ." His voice trailed off. Gasping for breath, he looked around the room. He no longer seemed to know where he was.

Mercedes Peralta dropped the cigar stub on the floor. Grabbing his chair from behind, she swiftly turned him around, so that he was now facing the altar. With slow, mesmerizing movements, she massaged him around his eyes.

I must have dozed off, for I found myself alone in the room. I quickly looked around. The candle on the altar was almost burned down. Right above me in the corner close to the ceiling sat a moth the size of a small bird. It had enormous black circles on its wings; they stared at me like curious eyes.

A sudden rustle made me turn around. Mercedes Peralta was sitting in her chair by the altar. I muffled a scream. I could have sworn she had not been there a moment before.

"I didn't know you were there," I said. "Look at that big moth above my head." I searched for the insect, but it was gone.

There was something about the way she looked at me that made me shudder. "I got too tired and fell asleep," I explained. "I didn't even find out what was wrong with Octavio Cantú."

"He comes to see me from time to time," she said. "He needs me as a spiritualist and a healer. I lighten the burden that weighs on his soul." She turned to the altar and lit three candles. In the flickering light her eyes were the color of the moth's wings. "You'd better go to sleep," she suggested. "Remember, we're going to go for a walk at dawn."

6

Certain that I had overslept again, I dressed quickly and headed down the dark corridor. Mindful of the creaking hinges, I carefully opened the door to Mercedes Peralta's room and tiptoed toward the hammock.

"Are you awake?" I whispered, pushing aside the gauzy material of the mosquito netting. "Do you still want to go for a walk?"

Her eyes opened instantly, but she was not really awake yet. She continued to stare quietly ahead. "I do," she finally said hoarsely, brushing the netting aside completely. She cleared her throat, spat in the bucket on the floor, and then moved over a little to make room for me in the hammock. "I'm glad you remembered our walk," she mumbled as she crossed herself. Closing her eyes, she folded her hands and prayed to the Virgin and to a number of saints in heaven. She thanked them individually for their guidance in helping her with the people she treated and then asked for their forgiveness.

"Why their forgiveness?" I inquired as soon as she finished her long prayer.

"Look at the lines on my palms," she said, placing her upturned hands in my lap.

With my index finger I traced the clearly delineated *V* and *M* lines that seemed to have been branded; the *V* on her left palm, and the *M* on her right.

"*V* stands for *vida,* life. *M* stands for *muerte,* death," she explained, enunciating the words with deliberate precision. "I was born with the power to heal and harm." She lifted her hands from my lap and brushed the air, as though she intended to erase the words she had spoken. She stared around the room, then deliberately maneuvered her thin, fleshless legs out of the hammock and slipped into a pair of cutout shoes through which her toes protruded. Her eyes twinkled with amusement as she straightened the black blouse and skirt, which she had slept in.

Holding on to my arm, she led me outside. "Let me show you something before we go for our walk," she said, heading toward the working room. She turned directly to the massive altar, which was made entirely out of melted wax. It had been started with a single candle, she said, by her great-great-grandmother, who had also been a healer.

Lovingly, she ran her hand over the glossy, almost transparent surface. "Search for the black wax amid the multicolored streaks," she urged me. "That's the evidence that witches light a black candle when they use their power to harm."

Countless strands of black wax ran into the colored bands.

"The ones closer to the top are mine," she said. Her eyes shone with an odd fierceness as she added, "A true healer is also a witch."

A glimmer of a smile lingered on her lips for a moment; then she went on to say that not only was she well known throughout the area but that people came for her treatments from as far as Caracas, Maracaibo, Mérida, and Cumaná. People knew about her abroad as well: Trinidad, Cuba, Colombia, Brazil, and Haiti. There were pictures somewhere in the house attesting that among those persons had been ministers of state, ambassadors, and even a bishop.

She regarded me enigmatically, then shrugged her shoulders. "My luck and my strength were peerless at one time," she said. "I ran out of both, and now I can only heal." Her grin widened, and her eyes took on a teasing gleam. "And how is your work progressing?" she asked with the innocent curiosity of a child. Before I had a chance to take in the sudden change of topic, she added, "Regardless of how many healers and patients you interview, you will never learn that way. A real healer must be first a medium and a spiritualist, and then a witch."

A dazzling smile lit up her face. "Don't be too upset when one of these days I burn your writing pads," she said casually. "You're wasting your time with all that nonsense."

I became utterly alarmed. I did not take kindly to the prospect of seeing my work go up in flames.

"Do you know what's of real interest?" she asked and then answered her own question. "The issues that go beyond the superficial aspects of healing. Things that can't be explained but may be experienced. There have been plenty of people who have studied healers. They believe that by watching and asking questions they may understand what mediums, witches, and healers do. Since there is no point in arguing with them, it's a lot easier to leave them alone to do whatever they want.

"It cannot be the same in your case," she went on.

"I cannot let you go to waste. So, instead of acting like you are studying healers, you're going to practice calling the spirit of my ancestor every night in the patio of this house. You can't take notes on that because the spirits count time in a different way. You'll see. To deal with the spirits is like entering inside the earth."

The memory of the woman I had seen in that patio perturbed me terribly. I wanted to abandon right then all my quest and forget Florinda's plans and run away.

Suddenly doña Mercedes laughed, a clear burst that dispelled my fears. "Musiúa, you should see your face," she said. "You're about to faint. Among other things, you're a coward." Despite her wry mocking tone, there was sympathy and affection in her smile. "I shouldn't push you. So I'm going to give you something you'll like—something that has more value than your study plans. A glimpse into the life of some personages of my choice. I will make them weave tales for you. Tales about fate. Tales about luck. Tales about love." She brought her face close to mine and in a soft whisper added, "Tales about strength and tales about weakness. That will be my gift to you to keep you appeased." She took my arm and led me outside. "Let's go for our walk."

Our steps rang lonely through the silent street bordered by high concrete sidewalks. In a faint murmur, obviously wary of waking the people sleeping inside the houses we passed, Mercedes Peralta remarked that during her days as a young healer, her house—the biggest one on the street—had stood isolated at what was then considered the outskirts of town. "But now," she said—the sweeping gesture of her arm encompassing everything around us—"it seems I live in the center of town."

We turned onto the main street and walked all the way to the plaza, where we rested on a bench facing the statue of Bolívar on a horse. The town hall stood at one side of the plaza, the church with its bell tower at the other. Many of the original buildings had been pulled down and replaced by boxlike structures. Yet, the old houses that still stood, with their wrought-iron grills, their red-tile roofs gray with age, and their wide eaves that permitted the rain water to splash clear of the brightly painted walls, gave the center of town its distinct colonial atmosphere.

"This town has not been the same since the day the clock in the tower of the city hall was fixed," she mused.

She explained that a long time ago, as if resenting the advent of progress, the clock had stopped at twelve o'clock. The local pharmacist had seen to it that it was fixed, and immediately afterward, as though conjured up by an act of magic, lampposts were put on the streets, and sprinklers were installed in the plaza so that the grass would stay green all year-round. And before anyone knew what was happening, industrial centers mushroomed everywhere.

She paused for an instant to catch her breath, then pointed to the shack-covered hills surrounding the city. "And so did the squatters' shanty towns," she added.

She rose and we walked to the end of the main street to where the hills began. Huts made of corrugated metal sheets, crates, and cardboard hung precariously on the steep slopes. The owners of the shacks close to the city streets had boldly tapped electricity from the lampposts. The insulated wires were crudely camouflaged with colored ribbons. We turned onto a side street, then into an alley, and finally we followed a narrow path winding up the only hill that had not yet been claimed by squatters.

The air, still damp from the night dew, smelled of wild rosemary. We climbed almost to the top of the hill, where a solitary saman tree grew. We sat down on the damp ground carpeted with tiny yellow daisies.

"Can you hear the sea?" Mercedes Peralta asked.

The faint breeze, rustling through the tree's intricately woven crown, scattered a shower of powdery golden blossoms. They alighted on her hair and shoulders like butterflies. Her face was suffused with an immeasurable calm. Her mouth opened slightly, revealing her few teeth, yellow with tobacco and age.

"Can you hear the sea?" she repeated, turning her dreamy, slightly misted eyes toward me.

I told her that the sea was too far away beyond the mountains.

"I know that the sea is far away," she said softly. "But at this early hour, when the town still sleeps, I always hear the sound of the waves carried by the wind." Closing her eyes, she leaned against the tree trunk, as if to sleep.

The morning stillness was shattered by the sound of a truck winding its way through a narrow street below. I wondered whether it was the Portuguese baker delivering his freshly baked rolls or the police picking up last night's drunks.

"See who it is," she urged me.

I walked a few steps down the path and watched an old man get out from a green truck parked at the bottom of the hill. His coat hung loosely on his stooped shoulders, and a straw hat covered his head. Aware of being watched, he looked up and waved his walking stick by way of greeting. I waved in return.

"It's the old man you treated last night," I told her.

"How fortunate!" she murmured. "Call him. Tell him to come up here. Tell him I want to see him. My gift to you begins now."

I walked down to where his truck was parked and asked the old man to walk back up the hill with me. He followed me without a word.

"No dogs today," he said to Mercedes Peralta by way of greeting and sat beside her.

"Let me tell you a secret, Musiúa," she said, beckoning me to sit across from her. "I am a medium, a witch, and a healer. Of the three, I like the second because witches have a particular way of understanding the mysteries of fate. Why is it that some people get rich, successful, and happy, while others find only hardship and pain? Whatever decides those things is not what you call fate; it's something more mysterious than that. And only witches know about it."

Her features strained for an instant with an expression I could not fathom as she turned to Octavio Cantú. "Some people say that we're born with our fate. Others claim that we make our fate with our actions. Witches say that it's neither and that something else catches us like the dog catcher catches a dog. The secret is to be there if we want to be caught or not to be there if we don't want to be caught."

Her glance strayed to the eastern sky, where the sun was rising over the distant mountains. After a few moments she faced the old man once more. Her eyes seemed to have absorbed the sun's radiance, for they shone as if smeared with fire.

"Octavio Cantú is coming to the house for his seasonal treatments," she said. "Perhaps little by little he'll weave a tale for you. A tale about how chance joins lives together and how that something that only witches know about fastens them into one bundle."

Octavio Cantú nodded his head in agreement. A tentative smile parted his lips. The scant beard on his chin was as white as the hair sticking out from under his straw hat.

Octavio Cantú came to doña Mercedes' house eight times. Apparently she had been treating him periodically since he was a young man. Besides being old and run down, he was an alcoholic. Doña Mercedes emphasized, however, that all his maladies were of the spirit. He needed incantations, not medicines.

At first, he hardly talked to me, but then he began to open up, feeling more confident perhaps. We spent long hours talking about his life. At the beginning of each of our sessions, he invariably seemed to succumb to despair, loneliness, suspicion. He demanded to know why I was interested in his life. But he always checked himself and regained his aplomb, and for the rest of the session—whether an hour or an entire afternoon— he would talk about himself as if he were some other person.

Octavio pushed the flat piece of cardboard aside and edged through the small doorlike opening of the shack. There was no light inside, and the pungent smoke of the dwindling fire in the stone hearth made his eyes tear. He shut them tight and groped his way in the darkness. He tripped over some tins and banged his shin on a wooden crate.

"Damn stinking place," he swore under his breath. He sat for a moment on the packed dirt floor and rubbed his leg. In the farthest corner of the wretched shack, he saw the old man asleep on a discarded, worn-out backseat of a car. Slowly, avoiding the crates, ropes, rags, and boxes scattered on the ground, he walked bent over to where the old man was lying.

Octavio lit a match. In the dim light the sleeping man looked dead. The rising and falling of his chest was so slight he hardly seemed to breathe. High cheekbones protruded from his black, emaciated face. His torn, dirty khaki pants were rolled up his calves. His long-sleeved khaki shirt was buttoned tightly around his wrinkled neck.

"Victor Julio!" Octavio shouted, shaking him vigorously. "Wake up, old man!"

Victor Julio's trembling, wrinkled eyelids opened for a moment. Only the discolored white of his eyes showed before he shut them again.

"Wake up!" Octavio cried out with exasperation. He reached for the narrow-brimmed straw hat on the ground and pushed it down hard on the old man's unkempt white hair.

"Who the hell are you?" Victor Julio grumbled. "What do you want?"

"I'm Octavio Cantú. I've been appointed by the mayor as your helper," he explained with an air of importance.

"Helper?" Unsteadily the old man sat up. "I need no helper." He slipped into his worn-out laceless shoes and staggered around the dark room until he found the gasoline lantern. He lit it. He rubbed the sleep out of his eyes and, blinking repeatedly, regarded the young man carefully.

Octavio Cantú was of medium height, with strong muscles, visible through his unbuttoned, faded blue jacket. His pants, which seemed too large for him, bagged over his new shiny boots. Victor Julio chuckled, wondering if Octavio Cantú had stolen them.

"So you're the new man," he said in a rasping voice, trying to determine the color of Octavio's eyes, shaded by a red baseball cap. They were shifty eyes, the color of moist earth. Victor Julio decided there was something decidedly suspicious about the young man. "I've never seen you around here," he said. "Where do you come from?"

"Paraguaná," Octavio answered curtly. "I've been here for a while. I've seen you several times at the plaza."

"Paraguaná," the old man repeated dreamily. "I've seen the sand dunes of Paraguaná." He shook his head and in a harsh voice demanded, "What are you doing in this godforsaken place? Don't you know that there is no future in this town? Haven't you noticed that the young people have migrated to the cities?"

"It's all going to change," Octavio declared, eager to steer the conversation away from himself. "This town is going to grow. Foreigners are buying up the cacao groves and the sugarcane fields. They are going to build factories. People are going to flock to this town. People are going to get rich."

Victor Julio doubled up with mocking laughter. "Factories aren't for those like us. If you stick around long enough, you'll end up like me." He put his hand on Octavio's arm. "I know why you're so far away from Paraguaná. You're running away from something, aren't you?" he asked, staring hard into the young man's restless eyes.

"What if I am?" Octavio shifted uncomfortably. He realized that he didn't have to tell him anything. No one knew about him in this town. Yet, something in the old man's eyes unnerved him. "I had some trouble back home," he muttered evasively.

Victor Julio shuffled over toward the opening of the shack, reached for his burlap sack hanging on a rusty nail, and took out a bottle of cheap rum. His hands, crisscrossed by protruding veins, shook uncontrollably as he unscrewed the lid of the bottle. He gulped repeatedly, heedless of the amber liquid trailing down his scraggly beard.

"There is a lot of work to be done," Octavio said. "We better get going."

"I was young like you when I was appointed by another mayor as a helper to an old man," Victor Julio reminisced. "I too was strong and eager to work. And look at me now. The rum doesn't even burn my throat any longer." Squatting on the ground, Victor Julio searched for his walking stick. "This cane belonged to the old man. He gave it to me before he died." He held up the dark, highly polished stick to Octavio. "It's made of hardwood from the Amazon jungle. It will never break."

Octavio glanced briefly at the cane and then asked impatiently, "Is the stuff we need here? Or do we still have to get it?"

The old man grinned. "The meat has been soaking since yesterday. It should be ready by now. It's outside behind the shack in a steel drum."

"Are you going to show me how to fix the meat?" Octavio asked.

Victor Julio laughed. All his front teeth were missing. The remaining yellow molars looked like two pillars in his cavernous mouth. "There is really nothing to show," he said in between giggles. "I just go to the pharmacist every time I want to prepare the meat. He's the one who mixes the beef tenderizer. Actually," he explained, "it's more like a marinade." His mouth spread into a wide grin. "I always get the meat from the slaughterhouse, compliments of the mayor." He took another gulp from the bottle. "Rum helps me to prepare myself." He rubbed his chin dry. "The dogs are going to catch up with me one of these days," he mumbled under his breath and handed the half-empty bottle to Octavio. "You better have some too."

"No thanks," Octavio refused politely. "I can't drink on an empty stomach."

Victor Julio opened his mouth ready to say something. Instead, he picked up his walking stick and his burlap sack and motioned Octavio to follow him outside. Absorbed, he stood for a moment and watched the sky. It was neither dark nor light but that strange oppressive gray that comes before dawn. In the distance he heard the barking of a dog. "There's the meat," he said, pointing with his chin to the steel drum standing on a tree stump. He handed Octavio a bundle of ropes. "It'll be easier to carry the drum if you tie it on your back."

Expertly, Octavio looped the ropes around the steel drum, lifted it on his back, then crossed the ropes over his chest and tied them securely below his navel. "Is this all we need?" he asked, avoiding the old man's gaze.

"I've some extra rope and a can of kerosene in my sack," Victor Julio explained and took another gulp of rum. Absentmindedly, he stuffed the bottle in his pocket.

In single file they followed the dry gully that cut across the cane break. All was silent except for the fading buzz of the crickets and the gentle breeze rustling through the bladelike leaves of the cane. Victor Julio had trouble breathing. His chest hurt. He felt so tired he wanted to lie down on the hard ground. He turned often to gaze at his shack in the distance. A foreboding feeling crossed his mind. The end was near. He had known for a long time that he was too old and feeble to do all the work he was supposed to do. It would be only a matter of time before they got a new man.

"Victor Julio, come on," Octavio called impatiently. "It's getting late."

The town was still asleep. Only a few old women on their way to church were about. With their heads covered by dark veils, they hurried past the two men without returning their greetings. On the narrow concrete sidewalks, seeking the protection of the silent houses, scrawny, sickly looking dogs lay curled up in front of closed doors.

At Victor Julio's command, Octavio lowered the steel drum on the ground and opened the tight lid. Using the long wooden pliers he had retrieved from his burlap sack, the old man picked chunks of meat from the drum. And as he and Octavio slowly made their way through town, he fed every stray dog they came across. Hungrily, wagging their tails, the animals devoured the fatal meal.

"The dogs will feed on you in hell," a fat woman shouted before disappearing through the large wooden door of the old colonial church at the other side of the plaza.

"No rabies this year," Victor Julio shouted back, wiping his nose on the sleeve of his shirt. "I think we got them all well fed for the hereafter."

"I counted seventeen," Octavio complained, stretching his sore back. "That's a lot of dead dogs to pull."

"The biggest one we won't have to carry," Victor Julio said, a sinister smile twisting his face. "There is one dog that won't die in the street."

"What do you mean?" Octavio asked, turning his red baseball cap around on his head, a puzzled look on his face.

Victor Julio's eyes narrowed, his pupils sparkled with an evil glint. His thin old body shivered with anticipation. "I'm all keyed up. Now, I'm going to kill the Lebanese storekeeper's black German shepherd."

"You can't do that," Octavio protested. "It's not a stray dog. It's not sick. It's well fed. The mayor said only stray sickly dogs."

Victor Julio swore loudly, then looked at his helper with a wicked expression. He was certain that this was the last time he would have access to the poison. If not Octavio, then someone else would be in charge of disposing of the dogs at the end of the next dry season. He could understand why the young man didn't want to cause any trouble in town, but that was not any of his concern. He had wanted to kill the Lebanese's dog ever since it had bitten him. This was his last chance.

"That dog is trained to attack," Victor Julio said. "Every time it gets loose it bites someone. It bit me some months ago." He pulled up his pant leg. "Look at the scar!" he muttered angrily, rubbing the purple, knotty spot on his calf. "The Lebanese didn't even bother to take me to a doctor. For all I knew that dog could have had rabies."

"But it didn't and you can't kill it," Octavio insisted. "The dog isn't in the street. It's got an owner." He looked imploringly at the old man. "You're only asking for trouble."

"Who cares," Victor Julio snapped belligerently. "I hate that animal and I won't have another chance to kill it." He flung his burlap sack over his shoulder. "Come on, let's go."

Unwillingly, Octavio followed the old man through a narrow side street toward the outskirts of town. They stopped in front of a large, green stucco house.

"The dog must be in the back," Victor Julio said. "Let's have a look." They walked along the brick wall encircling the backyard. There was no sign of the dog.

"We better leave," Octavio whispered. "I'm sure the dog sleeps inside the house."

"It'll come out," Victor Julio said, trailing his walking stick along the wall.

Loud barking splintered the morning stillness. Excitedly, the old man jumped up and down on his frail legs, brandishing his walking stick in the air above his head. "Give me the rest of the meat!" he demanded.

Octavio unfastened the ropes from his chest and reluctantly lowered the steel drum to the ground. The old man picked out the last pieces of meat with the wooden pliers and flung them over the wall.

"Just listen to that beast gulping down that poisoned meat," Victor Julio said gleefully. "That vicious brute is as hungry as the rest of them."

"Let's get out of here fast," Octavio hissed, lifting the steel drum on his back.

"There's no hurry." Victor Julio laughed. A sensation of elation invaded his body as he looked for something on which to stand.

"Let's go," Octavio insisted. "We're going to get caught."

"We won't," Victor Julio assured him calmly, climbing on the shaky wooden crate he had propped against the wall. He stood on his toes and looked at the raging dog. Barking furiously, the animal spat foam and blood in an effort to wrench loose whatever had stuck in its throat. Its legs grew rigid. It toppled over. Powerful spasms wheeled its body around.

Victor Julio shivered. "It's even hard to die," he murmured, stepping down from the crate. He didn't feel any satisfaction in having killed the Lebanese's German shepherd. In all the years of poisoning dogs, he had always avoided seeing them die. He had never enjoyed killing the town's stray mongrels, but it was the only job that had been available to him.

A vague fear filled Victor Julio's heart. He looked down the empty road. He curled his left thumb backward and placed the walking stick between it and his wrist. Holding his arm outstretched, he started to move the stick back and forth so rapidly the cane seemed to be suspended in midair.

"What kind of trick is that?" Octavio asked, watching him enthralled.

"It's no trick. It's an art. This is what I do best," Victor Julio explained sadly. "In the mornings and afternoons I entertain the small children in the plaza with my dancing stick. Some of the children are friendly to me." He handed the cane to Octavio. "Try it. See if you can do it."

Victor Julio laughed at Octavio's clumsy attempt to

hold the stick properly. "It takes years of practice," the old man said. "You've got to develop your thumb in order to stretch it backward until it touches the wrist. And you have got to move your arm much faster so the stick won't have time to fall on the ground."

Octavio handed him back the cane. "We better get those dogs!" he exclaimed, surprised by the suddenness of the morning glow and the flame-colored blotches appearing on the eastern sky.

"Victor Julio, wait for me," a child called after them.

Barefoot, her black tangled hair tied on top of her head, a six-year-old girl caught up with the two men. "Look what my aunt brought me to play with," she said, holding up a German shepherd puppy for the old man to see. "I named her Butterfly. She looks like one, doesn't she?"

Victor Julio sat on the curb. The little girl sat next to him and placed the cute, chubby puppy on his lap. Distractedly, he ran his fingers along the black and pale yellow fur.

"Show Butterfly how you make your walking stick dance," the child pleaded.

Victor Julio put the dog on the ground and retrieved the bottle of rum from his pocket. Without drawing a breath, he emptied its contents, then dropped the bottle into his burlap sack. There was a desolate expression in his eyes as he gazed into the child's smiling face. Soon she would grow up, he thought. She would no longer sit with him under the trees in the plaza and help him fill the trash cans with leaves and believe they would turn to gold during the night. He wondered if she, too, would shout at him, taunt him, like most of the older children did. He closed his eyes tightly.

"Let's see if the stick feels like dancing," he mumbled. Rubbing his creaking knees, he got up.

Mesmerized, both Octavio and the child watched the stick. It seemed to be dancing by itself, animated not only by the swift graceful movement of Victor Julio's arms but also by the rhythmic tapping of his foot and his hoarse, yet melodious, voice, as he sang a nursery rhyme.

Octavio put the drum down and sat on it to admire the old man's skill. Victor Julio stopped his song in midsentence. His stick fell on the ground. With a look of surprise and horror, he saw the puppy lapping up the juice of the poisoned meat, trickling from the drum.

The girl picked up the cane, caressed the finely carved head, and handed it to Victor Julio. "I've never seen you drop it," she remarked concerned. "Did the stick get tired?"

Victor Julio placed his trembling hand on her head, pulling her ponytail gently. "I'm going to take Butterfly for a walk," he said. "Go back to bed before your mother finds you out here. I'll see you later at the plaza. We'll pick leaves together." He lifted the chubby puppy in his arms and motioned Octavio to follow him up the street.

The stray dogs were no longer curled up in front of closed doors but lay rigid with their legs extended, scattered around the dusty streets, their glassy eyes staring blankly into space. One by one, Octavio tied them with the ropes Victor Julio had brought in his burlap sack.

Butterfly, her whole body shaking convulsively, sent a stream of blood down the old man's pants. He shook his head with despair. "What am I going to tell the kid?" he mumbled, fastening the poisoned puppy with the others.

They made two trips and dragged the dead dogs to the outskirts of town, past the Lebanese's house, past the empty fields, down into a dried-up ravine. Victor Julio covered them with a layer of dry branches, then doused the heap with the can of kerosene he had brought with him and set them afire. The dogs burned slowly, filling the air with the smell of scorched flesh and fur.

Panting, their throats raw with smoke and dust, the two men climbed out of the ravine. They didn't walk far before they collapsed under the shade of a blooming red acacia tree.

Victor Julio stretched out on the hard ground still cool from the night. His hands trembled as he held the walking stick securely over his stomach. He closed his eyes and tried to still his breathing, hoping it would dispel the pain constricting his chest. He wished he could sleep, lose himself in dreams.

"I've got to get going," Octavio said after a short while. "I've got some other jobs to do."

"Stay with me," the old man begged. "I have to tell the kid about her dog." He sat up and gazed imploringly at Octavio. "You can help me. Children so soon become afraid of me. She's one of the few who is friendly."

The wretched emptiness in Victor Julio's voice frightened Octavio. He leaned against the tree trunk and closed his eyes. He couldn't bear to see the fear and the loss reflected in the old man's face.

"Come with me to the plaza. Let everyone know you're the new man," Victor Julio pleaded.

"I won't stay in this town," Octavio said gruffly. "I don't like this business of killing dogs."

"It's not a matter of liking or disliking it," Victor Julio remarked. "It's a matter of fate." He smiled wistfully and let his gaze wander in the town's direction. "Who knows, you might have to stay here forever," he mumbled, closing his eyes again.

The silence was broken by the sound of angry voices. Down the road came a group of boys led by the oldest son of the Lebanese. They stopped a few paces away from the two men.

"You killed my dog," the Lebanese boy hissed, then spat on the ground inches away from Victor Julio's feet.

Propping himself on his cane, the old man rose. "What makes you think it was me?" he asked, trying to gain time. His hands shook uncontrollably as he searched for the bottle of rum in his sack. He stared at the empty bottle uncomprehendingly. He didn't remember having drunk the last drop.

"You killed the dog," the boys repeated in a chant. "You killed the dog." Cursing and jabbing him, they tried to grab his stick and his burlap sack.

Victor Julio backed away. Brandishing his cane, he swung it blindly at the jeering boys. "Leave me alone!" he screamed through trembling lips.

Momentarily startled by his rage, the boys stood still. Suddenly, as if they had only just noticed that Victor Julio was not alone, they turned to Octavio. "And who are you?" one of the boys yelled, looking from one man to the other, perhaps measuring the consequences of having to deal with both. "Are you with the old man? Are you his helper?"

Octavio didn't answer but swung the rope over his head, lashing it out in front of him like a whip.

Laughing and screaming, the boys dodged the well-aimed snaps. But when several of them were stung by the rope not only on their calves and thighs but also on their shoulders and arms, they backed away. They ran after Victor Julio, who, in the meantime, had fled toward the ravine, where the dogs were still burning.

Victor Julio turned his head. Terror dilated his pupils as he saw the boys approaching so close behind him. They no longer seemed human; they reminded him of a pack of barking dogs. He tried to run faster, but the searing pain in his chest slowed him down.

The boys picked up pebbles and threw them at him, just teasing him. But when the Lebanese boy reached for a good-sized stone, the rest of the boys, eager to outdo each other, selected even larger rocks. One of them hit Victor Julio on the head. He staggered. His vision blurred. The ground under his feet gave way, and he tumbled down the precipice.

The wind carried the old man's cry out of the ravine. Panting, their faces streaked with dust and sweat, the boys stood looking at each other. Then, as though someone had given a signal, they scurried in all directions.

Octavio ran down the steep slope and knelt by Victor Julio's inert body. He shook him vigorously. The old man opened his eyes. His breath came in spurts. His voice was only a faint muffled sound. "I knew that the end was near, but I thought it was only the end of my job. It never occurred to me it was going to be this way." His pupils flickered with an oddly bright gleam as he stared into his helper's eyes. Slowly, the light went out.

Octavio shook him frantically. "Jesus! He's dead!" he muttered, then made the sign of the cross. He raised his sweaty face toward the sky. A pale moon was clearly visible despite the blinding brightness of the sun. He wanted to pray but could not think of a single prayer. Only images came to his mind: a legion of dogs chasing the old man over the fields.

Octavio felt his hands grow cold and his body begin to tremble. He could run away again to another town, he thought. But then they might suspect him of having killed Victor Julio. He had better stay for a while, he decided, until things cleared up.

For a long time Octavio just kept staring at the dead man. Then, on an impulse, he picked up Victor Julio's cane lying nearby. He caressed it and rubbed the finely carved head against his left cheek. He felt that it had always belonged to him. He wondered if he would ever be able to make the stick dance.

7

Octavio Cantú had had his last treatment of the season. He put on his hat and rose from the chair. I noticed how the years had caved in his chest and wasted the muscles of his arms. His faded coat and pants were several sizes too big. Bulging sharply on the right-side pocket was a large bottle of rum.

"It always happens when she finishes my treatments, I put her to sleep," he whispered to me, fixing his sunken and discolored eyes on Mercedes Peralta. "I've talked to you too much today. Anyway, I can't figure out why you're interested in me."

A wide smile creased his face as he held his walking stick between his thumb and wrist. He moved his arm back and forth so skillfully the cane appeared to be suspended in midair. Without saying another word he walked out of the room.

"Doña Mercedes," I called softly, turning to her. "Are you awake?"

Mercedes Peralta nodded. "I'm awake. I'm always awake even when I'm asleep," she said softly. "That's the way I try to stay a jump ahead of myself."

I told her that since I had begun talking to Octavio Cantú I had been plagued by deep, nagging questions. Could Octavio Cantú have avoided stepping into Victor Julio's shoes? And why did he repeat Victor Julio's life so completely?

"Those are unanswerable questions," doña Mercedes replied. "But let's go to the kitchen and ask Candelaria. She's got more sense than the two of us together. I'm too old to have sense, and you're too educated."

With a beaming smile on her face, she took my arm and we walked to the kitchen.

Candelaria, engrossed in scrubbing the copper-plated bottoms of her precious stainless-steel pots and pans, did not hear or see us approach. She let out a piercing, startled scream when doña Mercedes nudged her arm.

Candelaria was tall, with sloping shoulders and wide hips. I couldn't tell her age. She looked as much thirty as she looked fifty. Her brown face was covered with tiny freckles, so evenly spaced they seemed to have been painted on. She dyed her dark curly hair a carrot red and wore dresses made from bold-colored printed cottons.

"Well? What are you doing in my kitchen?" she asked with feigned annoyance.

"The musiúa is obsessed with Octavio Cantú," doña Mercedes explained.

"My God!" Candelaria exclaimed. Her face expressed genuine shock as she looked up at me. "Why him?" she asked.

Baffled by her accusing tone, I voiced the questions I had just asked doña Mercedes.

Candelaria began to laugh. "For a minute I was worried," she said to doña Mercedes. "Musiús are weird. I remember that musiú from Finland who used to drink a glass of urine after his dinner to keep his weight down. And the woman who came all the way from Norway to fish in the Caribbean sea. To my knowledge, she never caught anything. But she had the boat owners fighting among themselves to take her out to sea."

Laughing uproariously, the two women sat down. "One never knows what goes on in the mind of a musiúa," Candelaria went on. "They are capable of anything." She laughed in spurts, each louder than the preceding one. Then she went back to scrubbing her pots.

"It looks like Candelaria thinks very little of your questions," doña Mercedes said. "I personally think that Octavio Cantú couldn't avoid stepping into Victor Julio's shoes. He had very little strength; that's why he was caught by that mysterious something I talked to you about; that something more mysterious than fate. Witches call it a witch's shadow."

"Octavio Cantú was very young and strong," Candelaria said all of a sudden, "but he sat too long under Victor Julio's shadow."

"What is she talking about?" I asked doña Mercedes.

"When people are fading away, especially at the moment they die, they create with that mysterious something a link with other persons, a sort of continuity," doña Mercedes explained. "That's why children turn out just like their parents. Or those who take care of old people follow into the steps of their wards."

Candelaria spoke again. "Octavio Cantú sat too long in Victor Julio's shadow. And the shadow sapped him. Victor Julio was weak, but upon dying the way he did, his shadow became very strong."

"Would you call the shadow the soul?" I asked Candelaria.

"No, the shadow is something all human beings

63

have, something stronger than their soul," she replied seemingly annoyed.

"There you are, Musiúa," doña Mercedes said. "Octavio Cantú sat too long on a link—a point where fate links lives together. He didn't have the strength to walk away from it. And, like Candelaria says, Victor Julio's shadow sapped him. Because all of us have a shadow, a strong or a weak one. We can give that shadow to someone we love, to someone we hate, or to someone who is simply available. If we don't give it to anyone, it floats around for a while after we die before it vanishes away."

I must have stared at her uncomprehendingly. She laughed and said, "I've told you that I like witches. I like the way they explain events, even though it's hard to understand them.

"Octavio needs me to ease his burden. I do that through my incantations. He feels that unless I intervene he will repeat Victor Julio's life detail by detail."

"It's advisable," Candelaria blurted out, "not to sit too long under anybody's shadow unless you want to follow in his or her footsteps."

PART TWO

8

I was anticipating the loud sounds that usually reverberated through the house every Thursday morning as Candelaria rearranged the heavy furniture in the living room. Wondering whether I had actually slept through the commotion, I walked down the silent corridor to the living room.

Shafts of sunlight filtered through the cracks in the wooden panels that covered the two windows facing the street. The dining table with its six chairs, the dark sofa, the stuffed armchairs, the glass coffee table, and the framed prints of pastoral landscapes and bullfighting scenes on the walls were exactly as Candelaria had arranged them the previous Thursday.

I walked out into the yard, where I found Candelaria, half-hidden behind a hibiscus bush. Her frizzy, red-dyed hair had been brushed out of her face and was held in place by bejeweled combs. Twinkling gold loops dangled from her earlobes. Her lips and nails were a glossy red and matched the colors of her brightly printed cotton dress. Her large eyes under lids that never opened all the way betrayed a dreaminess that was at odds with her sharp angular features and her crisp, almost brusque manner.

"What made you get up so early, Musiúa?" Candelaria asked. Rising, she tidied her wide skirt and the low-cut bodice of her dress that revealed a generous amount of her ample bosom.

"I didn't hear you move the furniture this morning," I said. "Are you going out?"

Without answering she hurried into the kitchen, her loose sandals slapping on her heels as she ran. "I'm behind with everything today," she declared, stopping momentarily to get her foot back into the sandal that had slipped off.

"I'm sure you'll catch up," I said. "I'll help you." I lit the wood in the cooking pit and set the table with the mismatched pieces of china. "It's just seven-thirty," I remarked. "You're only half an hour late."

As opposed to doña Mercedes, who was totally indifferent to schedules, Candelaria divided her day into precisely timed tasks. Although no one ever sat down for a meal at the same time, Candelaria fixed breakfast at exactly seven. By eight o'clock she was mopping the floors and dusting the furniture. She was tall enough that she had to stretch only her arms to reach the spider webs in the corners and the dust on the lintels. And by eleven o'clock the daily pot of soup was simmering on the stove.

As soon as that was accomplished, she tended to her flowers. Watering can in hand, she first walked up and down the patio, then the yard, sprinkling her plants with loving care. At two o'clock sharp she did the laundry, even if she only had one towel to wash. After the ironing was done, she read illustrated romances. In the evenings, she cut out magazine pictures and pasted them in photo albums.

"Elio's godfather was here last night," she whispered. "Doña Mercedes and I talked with him till dawn." She reached for the mortared corn cooked the evening before and began to knead the white dough for the corncakes we ate for breakfast. "He must be over eighty years old. And he still hasn't gotten over Elio's death. Lucas Nuñez blames himself for the boy's death."

"Who is Elio?" I asked.

"Doña Mercedes' son," Candelaria murmured, shaping the dough into round patties. "He was only eighteen when he died tragically. It was a long time ago." She brushed a strand of hair behind her ear, then added, "You'd better not mention to her that I told you she had a son."

She placed the corncakes on the grill spanning the cooking pit, then faced me, a devilish grin on her lips. "You don't believe me, do you?" she asked, but stopped me from responding by holding up one hand. "I have to concentrate now on the coffee. You know how fussy doña Mercedes gets if it isn't strong or sweet enough."

I regarded Candelaria suspiciously. She was in the habit of telling me the most outlandish stories about the healer, such as the time when doña Mercedes was apprehended by a group of Nazis during the Second World War and held captive in a submarine. "She's a liar," doña Mercedes had once confided. "And even if she's telling the truth she exaggerates it so much that it might as well be a lie."

Candelaria, thoroughly unconcerned about my suspicions, wiped her face on the apron she had tied around her neck, then with a swift, abrupt movement, she turned around and hurried out of the kitchen. "Watch over the corncakes," she cried out from the corridor. "I'm behind with everything today."

* * *

Around midday, Mercedes Peralta finally woke up after sleeping through Candelaria's Thursday commotion, which was noisier than usual because of the hurry.

Undecidedly, doña Mercedes stood at the door of her room, squinting her eyes to adjust to the brightness. She rested against the door frame for a moment before venturing out into the corridor.

I rushed to her side, and taking her arm, I led her to the kitchen. Her eyes were red. She had a frown and a sad look around her mouth. I wondered if she, too, had spent the night awake. There was always the possibility that Candelaria had indeed been telling the truth.

Seemingly preoccupied, she studied the plateful of corncakes, but instead of taking one, she broke off two bananas from the bunch hanging on one of the rafters. She peeled them, cut them into slivers, then daintily ate the bananas, one sliver at a time.

"Candelaria wants you to meet her parents," she said, delicately wiping the corners of her mouth. "They live in the hills, close to the dam."

Before I had a chance to say that I would be delighted, Candelaria came sauntering into the kitchen. "You'll love my mother," she affirmed. "She's small and skinny like you, and she also eats the whole day long."

Somehow, I had never thought of Candelaria as having a mother. With a rapt smile the two women listened attentively as I tried to make them understand what I meant by that. I assured them that categorizing certain people as the motherless type had nothing to do with age or looks but with some elusive, remote quality that I couldn't quite explain.

What seemed to delight Mercedes Peralta the most about my elucidation was that it failed to make any sense. She sipped her coffee pensively, then looked at me askance.

"Do you think I had a mother myself?" she asked. She closed her eyes, and puckering up her mouth, she moved her lips as if she were sucking from a breast. "Or do you believe I was hatched from an egg?"

She glanced up at Candelaria and in a serious tone pronounced, "The musiúa is quite right. What she wants to say is that witches have very little attachment to parents or children. Yet, they love them with all their might but only when they are facing them, never when they turn their backs."

I wondered if Candelaria was afraid I would mention Elio, for she stepped behind doña Mercedes, gesticulating wildly for me to remain silent.

Doña Mercedes seemed to be determined to read our thoughts; she first looked at me, then at Candelaria, with fixed unblinking eyes. Sighing, she wrapped her hands around her mug and sipped the rest of her coffee.

"Elio was only a few days old when his mother, my sister, died," she said, looking at me. "He was my delight. I loved him as though he were my own child." She smiled faintly, and after a short pause, she continued talking about Elio. She said that no one would have called him handsome. He had a wide sensuous mouth, a flat nose with sprawling nostrils, and wild kinky hair. But what made Elio irresistible to young and old alike were his big, black, and lustrous eyes, which shone with happiness and sheer well-being.

At great length doña Mercedes talked about Elio's eccentricities. Although he was to become a healer like herself, he rarely spent any time thinking about healing. He was too busy falling in and out of love. During the day, he chatted the hours away with the young women and girls who came to see her. In the evenings, guitar in hand, he went to serenade his conquests. He hardly ever returned before dawn except when he was unsuccessful in his amatory ventures. Then, he was back early and entertained her with his witty, but never vulgar, renditions of his failures and successes.

With morbid curiosity I awaited for her to talk about his tragic death. I felt disappointed when she glanced up at Candelaria. "Go and get me my jacket," she murmured. "It gets windy in those hills where your parents live." She rose and, leaning against my arm, shuffled out into the yard. "Today, Candelaria will surprise you," she confided. "There are all kinds of delightful quirks about her. If you were to know only half of them, you would probably faint with shock." Doña Mercedes chuckled softly like a child trying hard not to give away a secret.

9

Laughter, excited voices, and the blaring sound of jukebox music spilled from the small restaurants and bars that lined the street leading out of Curmina. Beyond the gas station, before the street joined the road, large trees on either side interlinked their branches to form arches, creating a dreamlike stillness.

On the road we passed solitary shacks made out of cane plastered over with mud. They all had a narrow doorway, a few windows, and a thatched roof. Some of the huts were whitewashed, others just mud colored. Flowers, mostly geraniums growing in discarded cooking pots and tin cans, hung from deep eaves. Majestic trees aglow with golden and blood-red blossoms shaded meticulously swept yards, where women were doing their wash in plastic tubs or spreading clothes to dry on bushes. Some greeted us with a slow smile; others with an imperceptible nod of their heads. Twice we stopped at a roadside stall, where children sold fruit and vegetables picked from their gardens.

Candelaria, sitting in the backseat of my jeep, gave me directions. We passed a cluster of huts in the outskirts of a small town, and within moments a blanket of fog enveloped us. A fog so thick I could barely see beyond the hood of the jeep.

"Oh Lord Jesus Christ," Candelaria began to pray. "Come down and help us get through this devilish fog. Please, Holy Mary, Mother of God, come here to protect us. Blessed Saint Anthony, Merciful Saint Theresa, Divine Holy Ghost, gather around to help us."

"You'd better stop it, Candelaria," doña Mercedes cut in. "What if the saints are indeed listening to you and answer your prayers? How are we going to get them all into the car?"

Candelaria laughed, then burst into song. Over and over she repeated the first few lines of an aria from an Italian opera.

"Do you like it?" she asked me, catching my glance in the rearview mirror. "My father taught it to me. My father is Italian. He likes opera and taught me arias by Verdi, Puccini, and others."

I glanced at doña Mercedes for confirmation, but she had fallen asleep.

"It's true," Candelaria insisted, then proceeded to sing a few lines from arias of different operas.

"Do you know them, too?" she asked after I had correctly guessed the opera to which some of them belonged. "Is your father Italian, too?"

"No." I laughed. "He's German. I don't really know much about operas," I confessed. "The only thing he taught me about music was that Beethoven was nearly a demigod. Every Sunday, for as long as I lived at home, my father played all of Beethoven's symphonies."

The fog lifted as abruptly as it had descended about us, unveiling chain after chain of bluish mountains. They seemed to extend forever across an emptiness of air and light. Following Candelaria's directions, I turned into a narrow dirt lane angling sharply from the road; it was barely wide enough for the jeep.

"Here it is," she cried out excitedly, pointing at the two-story house at the end of the lane. The whitewashed walls were yellow with age, and the once red tiles were gray and mossy. I parked, and we got out of the jeep.

An old man clad in a frayed T-shirt was leaning out of an upstairs window. He waved at us and then disappeared, his loud excited voice ringing through the silence of the house. "Roraima! The witches are here!"

Just as we reached the front door, a small, wrinkled woman stepped out to greet us. Smiling, she embraced Candelaria, then doña Mercedes.

"This is my mother," Candelaria proudly said. "Her name is Roraima."

After a slight hesitation, Roraima also embraced me. She was barely five feet and very lean. She wore a long black dress. She had thick black hair and the bright eyes of a bird. Her motions, too, were birdlike, dainty, and quick as she ushered us inside the dark vestibule, where a small light burned under a picture of Saint Joseph.

Beaming with contentment, she told us to follow her along the wide L-shaped gallery bordering the inside patio, where a lemon and guava tree shaded the open living-dining room and the spacious kitchen.

Mercedes Peralta whispered something in Roraima's ear, then continued down the corridor that led to the back of the house.

For a moment I stood undecided, then followed Candelaria and her mother up the stone stairs to the second floor, past a row of bedrooms, all of which opened onto the wide balcony running the length of the patio.

"How many children do you have?" I asked as we passed the fifth door.

"I have only Candelaria." The leathery wrinkles in Roraima's face deepened as she smiled. "But the grandchildren from Caracas come to spend their holidays here."

Aghast, I turned to Candelaria and stared into her dark, guarded eyes in which a glimmer of amusement was just discernible. "I didn't know you had any children," I said, wondering if this was the surprise doña Mercedes had hinted at that morning. Somehow it was a letdown.

"How can I have any children?" Candelaria retorted indignantly. "I'm a maiden!"

I burst into laughter. Her statement not only implied that she was unmarried but that she was also a virgin. The haughty expression on her face left no doubt that she was very proud of the fact.

Candelaria leaned over the railing, then she turned and looked up. "I've never told you that I have a brother. Actually he's only a half brother. He's much older than I. He was born in Italy. Like my father, he came to Venezuela to make his fortune. He has a construction company. He's rich now."

Roraima nodded her head emphatically. "Her half brother has eight children. They love to spend the summers here with us," she added.

In a sudden change of mood, Candelaria laughed and embraced her mother. "Imagine!" she exclaimed. "The musiúa can't conceive that I have a mother." With an impish smile she added, "And what's even worse—she doesn't believe that I have an Italian father!"

At that very instant, one of the bedroom doors opened, and the old man I had seen at the window stepped out onto the balcony. He was stocky, with sharp angular features that strongly resembled Candelaria's. He had dressed in a hurry. His shirt was buttoned up askew, the leather belt holding up his pants had not been fitted into the loops around the waist, and his shoe laces were untied. He embraced Candelaria.

"Guido Miconi," he introduced himself to me, then apologized for not welcoming us at the door. "As a child, Candelaria was as pretty as Roraima," he said, holding his daughter in a warm embrace. "Only when she grew up did she start to resemble me."

Clearly sharing a private joke, all three burst into laughter. Giving a satisfied nod, Roraima regarded her husband and her daughter with unabashed admiration. She took my arm and led me downstairs. "Let's join doña Mercedes," she suggested.

The yard, bordered by a stake fence, was enormous. At the farthest end stood an open hut with a thatched roof. Sitting in a hammock fastened to the crossbeam of the hut was Mercedes Peralta. She was sampling Roraima's homemade cheese. She congratulated Roraima on her success.

Guido Miconi stood irresolute in front of doña Mercedes; he seemed unsure whether to shake her hand or to put his arm around her. She smiled at him, and he embraced her.

We all sat around the hammock except for Roraima, who sat in it beside Mercedes Peralta. She asked her questions about me, which doña Mercedes promptly answered as if I were not there.

For a while I listened to their conversation, but soon the heat, the stillness of the air, and Guido Miconi's and the women's low voices interspersed now and then by faint giggles made me so drowsy I stretched out on the ground. I must have dozed off, for doña Mercedes had a hard time making me understand that I was to check with Candelaria about lunch. I had not heard Candelaria and her father leave.

I went inside the house. A deep soothing voice murmuring an incantation came from one of the bedrooms. Afraid that Candelaria was entertaining her father with one of my tapes of a healing session, I rushed upstairs. On a previous occasion she had played a tape and promptly erased it by pushing the wrong button.

I stopped short at the half-opened door. Speechless, I watched Candelaria massage her father's back and shoulders, while she softly mumbled an incantation. There was something about her stance—the concentrated, yet fluid beauty of her moving hands—that reminded me of Mercedes Peralta. I realized then that Candelaria was also a healer.

As soon as she finished massaging her father, she turned to face me, a glimmer of amusement in her eyes. "Did doña Mercedes ever tell you about me?" Her voice had a curious softness that I had never heard before. "She says that I was born a witch."

There were so many questions running through my mind, I was at a loss where to begin.

Candelaria, aware of my bewilderment, shrugged her shoulders in a sort of helpless gesture.

"Let's fix lunch," Guido Miconi offered, heading for the stairs.

Candelaria and I followed behind him. Suddenly, he turned around and faced me. "Mercedes Peralta is right," he said, then bent his head and stared fixedly at the lacy shadows of the guava tree on the brick patio. For a long time he just stood there shaking his head now and then, unsure what to say or do next.

He looked up, smiled faintly, then began to walk about the patio, his hands lightly touching flowers and leaves, his shiny eyes seeming not quite to take me in when they focused on me.

"It's a strange story," he said to me in an excited voice that made his Italian accent more pronounced. "Candelaria says that doña Mercedes wants me to tell it to you. You know that you're welcome here. I hope you come often, so we can talk."

I was at a loss. I looked at Candelaria, hoping for some kind of explanation.

"I think I know what doña Mercedes wants to do with you," Candelaria said. Taking my arm, she led me to the kitchen. "She likes you a lot, but she can't give you her shadow because she's got only one and she's giving it to me."

"What are you talking about?" I asked.

"I'm a witch," she replied, "and I'm following in doña Mercedes' footsteps. Only by following in the spiritual footsteps of a healer can you be a healer yourself. That's what's called a junction, a link. Doña Mercedes has already told you that witches call it a shadow.

"Shadows are true for everything," she continued, "and there is only one heir to anyone who has real knowledge. Victor Julio had real knowledge about killing dogs and made an unwitting link for Octavio Cantú. I've said to you that Octavio sat too long in Victor Julio's shadow and that doña Mercedes is giving me her shadow. By letting certain people tell you their stories, she is trying to put you, for an instant, under the shadow of all those people, so that you'll feel how the wheel of chance turns and how a witch helps that wheel move."

Unsuccessfully, I tried to tell her that her statements were throwing me into deeper confusion. She stared at me with bright, trusting eyes.

"When a witch intervenes, we say it's the witch's shadow that turns the wheel of chance," she said thoughtfully; then after pausing for a moment, she added,

"My father's story would fit, but I shouldn't be present when he tells his story to you. I inhibit him. I always have." She looked back at her father and laughed. Her laughter was like a crystalline explosion; it reverberated through the whole house.

Sleepless, Guido Miconi tossed in the bed and wondered if the night, made longer by Roraima's peaceful sleep, would ever end. An anxious expression crossed his face as he gazed at her naked body, dark against the white sheet, and at her face, hidden behind a tangled mass of black hair. Gently, he pushed the hair aside. She smiled. Her eyes opened slightly, shiny between the thick, stubby lashes, but she did not wake up.

Taking care not to disturb her, Guido Miconi rose and looked out the window. It was almost dawn. In a nearby yard a dog began to bark at a singing drunkard staggering down the street. The man's steps and song died away in the distance. The dog went back to sleep.

Guido Miconi turned away from the window and squatted to reach under the bed for the small suitcase he kept hidden there. With the key he wore on a chain around his neck, along with the medal of the Virgin, he opened the lock and fumbled for the wide leather pouch tucked in between his folded clothes. An odd feeling, almost a premonition, made him hesitate for a moment. He did not tie the pouch around his waist. He reached inside, retrieved a heavy gold bracelet, placed it on the pillow beside Roraima and put the pouch back into the suitcase.

He shut his eyes tightly. His mind went back to the day he immigrated to Venezuela—twenty years ago—tempted by the opportunities for work and the good pay. He had been only twenty-six years old. Certain that his wife and their two children would soon join him, he had remained in Caracas for the first few years. To save money, he had lived in cheap rooming houses conveniently close to the construction sites where he was working. Each month he sent part of his savings home.

After several years, he finally realized that his wife did not want to join him. He moved out of Caracas and accepted work in the interior. Letters from home reached him only sporadically, and then they stopped altogether. He no longer sent money. Instead, as so many of his co-workers did, he began to invest his salary in jewels. He was going to return to Italy a rich man.

"A rich man," Guido Miconi murmured, holding the leather pouch around his waist. He wondered why the words no longer evoked the familiar excitement.

He glanced at Roraima on the bed. He was already missing her. His mind went back almost a decade to that day he first saw Roraima in the courtyard of his cheap rooming house, where he was heating his spaghetti on a Primus cooker. She was hollow-eyed and wore a dress that was too large for her thin, slight frame; he thought her to be one of the children in the neighborhood who were always making fun of the foreigners, in particular, the Italian construction workers.

But Roraima had not come to mock the Italians. She had been hired to work at the boarding house. And at night for a few coins, she shared the men's beds. To the annoyance of his co-workers, she attached herself to Guido so devotedly that she refused to sleep with anyone else, no matter how much money they offered. One day, however, she disappeared. No one knew where she had come from; no one knew where she had gone.

Five years later he saw her again. For some inexplicable whim, instead of driving out with the crew to the barracks next to the site where a factory and a pharmaceutical laboratory were being built, he took a bus all the way into town. There, sitting in the bus depot, as if waiting for him, was Roraima.

Before he had quite recovered from his surprise, she called to a little girl playing nearby. "This is Candelaria," she pronounced, grinning up at him disarmingly. "She's four years old and she's your daughter."

There was something so irrepressibly childish in her voice, in her expression, he couldn't help but laugh. As frail and slight as he remembered her, Roraima looked like the sister rather than the mother of the child standing beside her.

Candelaria looked at him in silence. The veiled expression of her dark eyes made him think of someone very old. She was tall for her age. Her face was serious as only a child's could be. She shifted her gaze to the children she had been playing with. When she looked up at him again there was an impish gleam in her eyes. "Let's go home," she said, taking his hand and pulling him forward.

Unable to resist the firm pressure of her tiny palm, he went with her down the main street to the outskirts of town. They stopped in front of a small house fenced in by a row of corn stalks waving in the breeze. The cement blocks were unplastered, and the corrugated zinc sheets of the roof were held in place with large stones.

"Candelaria finally brought you here," Roraima stated, reaching for the small suitcase in his hand. "And to think that I almost stopped believing that she was born a witch." She invited him inside to a small hall that opened into a wide room, empty except for three chairs arranged against the wall. One step down was a bedroom partitioned off by a curtain. On one side beneath a window stood a double bed on which Roraima dropped his suitcase. On the other side hung a hammock in which the child went to lie down.

He followed Roraima along a short corridor into the kitchen and sat down at the wooden table in the middle of the room.

Guido Miconi took Roraima's hands in his and, as though clarifying matters to a child, he told her that what had brought him to town wasn't Candelaria but the dam that was going to be built in the hills.

"No, that's only on the surface. You came because Candelaria brought you here," Roraima stammered. "Now you'll stay here with us. Won't you?" Seeing that he remained silent, she added, "Candelaria was born a witch." With an encompassing wave of her hand, Roraima took in the room, the house, the yard. "All this belongs to her. Her godmother is a famous healer and gave her all this." Her voice dropped, and she muttered the words, "But that's not what she wanted. She wanted you."

"Me!" he repeated, shaking his head sad and baffled. He had never lied to Roraima about his family in Italy. "I'm sure her godmother is a good healer. But being born a witch! That's pure nonsense. You know that one day I will return to the family that I left behind."

A strange disturbing smile flittered across Roraima's face as she reached for the pitcher and for the turned-down glass on the table. She filled it, then held the glass out to him and added, "Miconi, this tamarind water has been bewitched by your daughter Candelaria. If you drink it, you'll stay with us forever."

For a second he hesitated, then burst into laughter. "Witchcraft is nothing but superstition." He emptied his glass in one long gulp. "That was the best refreshment I have ever had," he remarked, holding out the glass for more.

His daughter's faint coughing broke into his reveries.

He tiptoed to the other side of the partitioned-off room and anxiously bent over Candelaria sleeping in a hammock that hung from two rings cemented into the wall. A sad smile parted his lips as he peered into her little face, in which so often he had tried to discover a likeness to himself. He saw none. But oddly enough, there were times the girl made him think of his grandfather. It was not so much a resemblance but rather a mood, a certain gesture made by the child, which never failed to startle him.

She also had that same easy way with animals that the old man had had. She healed every donkey, cow, goat, dog, and cat in the neighborhood. She actually coaxed birds and butterflies to perch on her outstretched arms. His grandfather had had that same gift. A saint, people had called him in the small town in Calabria.

Whether or not there was anything saintly about Candelaria, he was no longer sure. One afternoon he had found the child lying on her stomach in the yard, her chin resting on her folded arms, talking to a sickly looking cat curled up a few inches in front of her. The feline seemed to be answering her, not with meowing sounds, but with short grunts that resembled an old man's laughter.

The instant they felt his presence, both Candelaria and the cat leapt up in the air, as if some invisible thread had pulled them. They landed right in front of him, a spooky smile on their faces. He had stood bewildered, as for a fleeting instant, their features appeared to be superimposed on each other's. He had been unable to decide whose face belonged to whom. Ever since that day he had kept wondering about what Roraima always said, that Candelaria was not a saint but a witch.

Softly, so as not to wake her, Guido Miconi caressed the child's cheek and then tiptoed to the small vestibule lit dimly by the dying light of an oil lamp. He reached for his jacket, hat, and shoes laid out the evening before and finished dressing. He held the lamp up to the mirror and studied his image. At forty-six, his gaunt, weatherworn face was still filled with that indestructible energy that had carried him through years of hard work. His hair, although gray streaked, was still thick; and his light brown eyes shone brightly beneath his bushy brows.

Cautiously, without stepping on the dog whining and twitching its legs in sleep, he let himself out the door. He leaned against the wall and waited until his eyes adjusted to the shadows. Sighing, he watched the early workers heading toward work like phantoms in the emptiness of the predawn darkness.

Instead of going to the southern end of town, where a truck waited to take the laborers to the construction site of the dam in the hills, Miconi headed toward the plaza, where the bus for Caracas was parked. The faint light inside the bus blurred the shapes of the few passengers dozing in their seats. He moved to the very back, and as he lifted his suitcase to the rack above him, he saw a shadow through the grimy window of the bus. Black and immense, the shadow stood out against the white wall of the church. He didn't know what made him think of a witch. Although he wasn't religious, he quietly began to pray. The shadow dissolved into a faint cloud of smoke.

The dimming of the lights in the plaza must have played a trick on his eyes, he thought, and chuckled. Roraima and Candelaria would have explained it differently. They would have said that he had seen one of those nocturnal entities that wander about at night. Beings that never leave any trace but use mysterious signals to announce their presence and disappearance.

The ticket collector's voice cut into his musings. Miconi paid his fare, asked about the best way to go to the port of La Guaira, and then closed his eyes.

Rattling and swaying, the bus crossed the valley, then slowly ascended the dusty winding road. Miconi sat up and looked back for one last time. The retreating rooftops, the white church with its bell tower, kept swimming through his tear-filled eyes. How he loved the sound of those bells. Now he will never hear them again.

After resting for a moment under the elusive shade of the blooming almond trees in the plaza, Guido Miconi resumed his walk up the steep, narrow street that ended in a flight of crooked steps carved into the hill. He climbed halfway up, then turned to gaze at the port below him: La Guaira, a city crowded in between the mountains and the sea, with its pink, blue, and buff-colored houses, its twin church towers, and its old customhouse overlooking the harbor like some ancient fort.

His daily excursions to this secluded spot had become a necessity. It was the only place where he felt safe and at peace. Sometimes he spent hours up here watching the large ships dropping anchor. He tried to guess by their flags or the color of their smokestacks to which country they belonged.

His weekly visits to the shipping offices in town were as essential to his well-being as gazing at the ships. It had been a month since he left Roraima and Candelaria, and he was still undecided whether he should return to Italy directly or by way of New York. Or, as Mr. Hylkema at the shipping office had suggested, perhaps see something of the world first and board one of those German freighters that sailed to Rio, Buenos Aires, across to Africa, and then the Mediterranean sea. But regardless of how enticing the possibilities, he couldn't bring himself to book his passage back to Italy. He couldn't understand why. And yet, in the depths of him he knew.

He climbed to the top of the steps and turned into a narrow twisting path that led to a clump of palm trees. He sat on the ground, his back against a trunk, and fanned himself with his hat. The stillness was absolute. The palm fronds hung motionless. Even the birds seemed to be floating effortlessly, like falling leaves pinned to the cloudless sky.

He heard a faint laughter echoing in the silence. Startled, he looked around. The tinkling sound reminded him of his daughter's laughter. And suddenly, her face materialized before his eyes. A fleeting image, unsubstantial, floating in some tenuous light; so pale, it seemed her face was surrounded by a halo.

With quick abrupt movements, as though he were trying to erase the vision, Guido Miconi fanned himself with his hat.

Perhaps it was true that Candelaria was born a witch,

he mused. Could the child be indeed the cause for his indecision to leave? he asked himself. Was she the reason for his inability to bring to mind the faces of his wife and children in Italy regardless of how hard he tried?

Guido Miconi rose and scanned the horizon. For an instant he thought he was dreaming as he saw a large ship emerge like some mirage through the shimmering heat. The vessel came closer, angling toward the harbor. In spite of the distance, he clearly recognized its green, white, and red smokestack.

"An Italian ship!" he exclaimed, throwing his hat up in the air. He was certain that he had finally broken the spell of Venezuela, and of Roraima and Candelaria, superstitious creatures who read omens in the flight of birds, the movements of shadows, the direction of the wind. He laughed happily. This ship approaching the harbor, like some miracle, was his liberation.

In his excitement he stumbled several times as he hurried down the crooked steps. He ran past the old colonial houses. He had no time to stop and listen to the sound of water splashing in the fountains and the songs of caged birds spilling out of open windows and doors. He was going to the shipping offices. He was going to book his passage home this very day.

A child's voice calling his full name brought him up short. Overcome by a sudden dizziness he closed his eyes and leaned against a wall. Someone gripped his arm. He opened his eyes, but all he saw were black spots whirling in front of him. Again he heard a child's voice call his name.

Slowly, his dizziness subsided. With his eyes still unfocused he glanced into the worried face of Mr. Hylkema, the Dutchman at the shipping office. "I don't know how I got here, but I want to speak with you," Guido Miconi stammered. "From the hill I've just seen an Italian ship approach the harbor. I want to book my passage home this very instant."

Mr. Hylkema shook his head in disbelief. "Are you sure?" he asked.

"I want to book my passage home," Miconi insisted childishly. "Right now!" Upon catching Mr. Hylkema's eyes on him, eloquent with meaning, he added, "I have finally broken the spell!"

"Of course you have." Mr. Hylkema patted him reassuringly on the shoulder and then steered him toward the cashier.

Looking up, Guido Miconi watched the tall, gaunt Dutchman move behind the counter. As usual, Mr. Hylkema was dressed in a white linen suit and black cloth sandals. A fringe of gray hair growing on one side of his head had been carefully combed and distributed over his naked skull. His face had been aged by the relentless tropical sun and, no doubt, by rum.

Mr. Hylkema brought out a heavy ledger and placed it noisily on the counter. He pulled up a chair, sat down, and began to write. "There are some of us who are meant to stay here," he said, then lifted his pen and pointed to Miconi. "And you, my friend, are never going to return to Italy."

Guido Miconi, not quite knowing what to make of his words, bit his lip.

Mr. Hylkema burst into a loud, toneless laughter, which sprung from the depths of his belly, moving up with a rumbling painful sound. But when he spoke his voice had a curious softness. "I was just joking. I'll take you to the ship myself."

* * *

Mr. Hylkema had gone with him to his hotel and helped him gather his belongings. After making sure he had a cabin all to himself, as he had requested and paid for, the Dutchman left him with the ship's purser.

Still dazed, Guido Miconi glanced around him, wondering why there was no one on the deck of the Italian ship anchored at pier 9. He reached for a chair beside a table on the deck, straddled it, and rested his forehead against the wooden back. He wasn't insane. He was in the Italian ship, he repeated to himself, hoping to dispel the realization that there was no one around. As soon as he had rested a moment, he'd walk down to another deck and confirm for himself that the crew and the rest of the passengers were somewhere in the ship. The thought restored his confidence.

Guido Miconi rose from his chair and, leaning over the railing, looked down at the pier. He saw Mr. Hylkema waving, looking up at him.

"Miconi!" the Dutchman shouted. "The ship is pulling anchor. Are you sure you want to go?"

Guido Miconi felt a cold sweat. An immeasurable fear took possession of him. He longed for his peaceful life, for his family. "I don't want to go," he shouted back.

"You have no time to get your luggage. The gangplank has been lifted. You must jump now. You'll land in the water. If you don't jump now, you'll never make it!"

Guido Miconi vacillated for an instant. In his suitcase were the jewels he had hoarded over the years, working with almost inhuman strength. Was all that going to be lost? He decided he still had enough strength to start all over again and jumped over the railing.

Everything blurred. He braced himself for the impact with the water. He was not worried; he was a good swimmer. But the impact never came. He heard Mr. Hylkema's voice saying loudly, "I think this man has fainted. The bus cannot leave until we take him out. Someone get his suitcase."

Guido Miconi opened his eyes. He saw a black shadow against the white wall of the church. He didn't know what made him think of a witch. He felt that he was being lifted and carried away. And then he had a devastating realization.

"I've never left. I've never left. It's been a dream," he kept repeating. He thought of his jewels in his suitcase. He was sure that whoever grabbed his suitcase would steal it, but the jewels no longer mattered to him, he had already lost them in the ship.

10

Mercedes Peralta accompanied me on my last visit to Guido Miconi's house. When we were about to return to town at the end of the day, Roraima took me by the hand and led me through a patch of canebrake up a narrow trail to a small clearing enclosed by yucca plants, whose flowers, straight and white, made me think of rows of candles on an altar.

"Do you like it?" Roraima asked, pointing to a seed bed roofed with a framework of thin, dry branches that were held at the corners by slender, forked poles.

"It looks like a doll's vegetable patch!" I exclaimed, examining the ground covered with feathery carrot shoots, tiny heart-shaped lettuce leaves, and curly, lacy parsley sprigs.

Beaming with delight, Roraima walked up and down the neatly ploughed rows in the adjacent field. Pieces of dry leaves and bits of twigs clung to her long skirt. Each time she pointed out the spot where she would plant a lettuce, a radish, a cauliflower, she turned toward me, her mouth arched in a faint, ethereal smile, her sharp eyes glinting between lids half-closed against the already low afternoon sun.

"I know that whatever I have is due to a witch's

intervention," she suddenly exclaimed. "The only good point that I have is that I know that."

Before I had a chance to take in what she had said, she approached me with her arms wide open in an expansive gesture of affection.

"I hope you don't forget us," she said and led me to my jeep.

Mercedes Peralta, seated in the front seat, her head reclining on the backrest, was sound asleep.

Leaning out from one of the upstairs windows was Guido Miconi, waving farewell in a gesture that was more a beckoning than a good-bye.

Shortly before we reached Curmina, Mercedes Peralta stirred. She yawned loudly, then absentmindedly looked out the window.

"Do you know what really happened to Guido Miconi?" she asked.

"No," I said. "All I know is that both Miconi and Roraima call it a witch's intervention."

Doña Mercedes giggled. "It certainly was a witch's intervention," she said. "Candelaria already told you that when witches intervene it's said that they do it with their shadows. Candelaria made a link, a junction for her father; she made him live a dream. Since she is a witch, she moved the wheel of chance.

"Victor Julio also made a link, and he also moved the wheel of chance, but since Victor Julio wasn't a witch, the dream of Octavio Cantú—although it is both as real and unreal as Miconi's dream—is longer and more painful."

"How did Candelaria intervene?"

"Certain children," doña Mercedes explained, "have the strength to wish something with great passion for a long period of time." She settled back in her seat and closed her eyes. "Candelaria was such a child. She was born that way. She wished her father to stay, and she wished it without a single doubt. That dedication, that determination, is what witches call a witch's shadow. It was that shadow that wouldn't let Miconi go."

We drove the rest of the way in silence. I wanted to digest her words. Before we went into her house, I asked her one final question.

"How did Miconi have such a detailed dream?"

"Miconi never wanted to leave, not really," doña Mercedes replied. "So that offered an opening to Candelaria's unwavering wish. The details of the dream itself, well, that part had nothing to do with the witch's intervention; that was Miconi's imagination."

PART THREE

11

I sat up as something brushed my cheek. Slowly, I raised my eyes toward the ceiling, searching for a gigantic moth. Ever since I had seen that bird-sized moth in the healing room, I had been obsessed with it. Nightly, the moth appeared in my dreams transforming itself into Mercedes Peralta. When I told her that I somehow believed my dream, she laughed it off as a figment of my imagination.

I settled back onto my lumpy pillow. As I was drifting back into sleep, I heard the unmistakable shuffle of Mercedes Peralta passing my door. I got up, put on my clothes, and tiptoed down the dark corridor. A soft laughter came from her working room. The amber glow of candlelight seeped through the opening of the carelessly drawn curtain. Overcome by curiosity I looked inside. Sitting at the table were Mercedes Peralta and a man, his face shaded by a hat.

"Won't you join us?" doña Mercedes called. "I was just telling our friend here that it wouldn't be long before you came looking for me."

"Leon Chirino!" I exclaimed as he turned toward me and pushed up the brim of his hat by way of greeting. He had been introduced to me during my unsuccessful séance participation as the man in charge of organizing the spiritual meetings. He was in his seventies, perhaps even in his eighties, yet his dark face had few wrinkles. He had big black eyes and sparkling white teeth, which ought to have been yellow from smoking cigars. There were white stubbles on his chin, yet his white, short-cropped hair was immaculately combed. His dark suit, wrinkled and baggy, looked as if he had slept in it.

"He's been working like a madman," doña Mercedes said as if reading my thoughts.

Although I had not been invited again to a séance, Mercedes Peralta had encouraged me to visit Leon Chirino at least once a week. Sometimes she accompanied me; sometimes I went alone. He was a carpenter by profession, yet his knowledge about the various shamanistic traditions practiced in Venezuela was astounding. He was interested in my research and spent hours going over my notes, tracing sorcerers' procedures to their Indian and African roots. He knew about all the Venezuelan spiritualists, witches, and healers of the eighteenth and nineteenth centuries. He spoke of them with such unaffected familiarity that he gave me the impression he had known them personally.

Mercedes Peralta's voice intruded on my reveries. "Would you like to come with us to fulfill a promise?" she asked me.

Disconcerted by her question, I gazed from one to the other. Their faces revealed nothing.

"We'll be leaving right away," she said to me. "We have a long night and a long day ahead of us." She rose and took my arm. "I've got to prepare you for the trip."

It took her no time to get me ready. She hid my hair under a tight, knitted sailor's cap and darkened my face with a black vegetable paste. And she made me swear that I would not speak to anyone or ask questions.

Ignoring my suggestion that we take my jeep, Mercedes Peralta scrambled into the backseat of Leon Chirino's old Mercury. With its crumpled fenders and battered chassis, the car looked as if it had been salvaged from a junk yard.

Before I had a chance to ask about our destination, she ordered me to hold and take good care of her basket, which was filled to capacity with medicinal plants, candles, and cigars. Sighing loudly, she made the sign of the cross and promptly fell asleep.

I did not dare disturb Leon Chirino with conversation; he seemed to need all his concentration to keep his car rolling. The dim headlights barely illuminated the area right in front of us. Bent slightly forward, he tensely gripped the wheel, as if he could thus help the car over the dark hills. When it balked on the steep upgrades, he spoke softly to it, urging it forward. Downhill, he let the car go, taking the curves in almost complete darkness, and at such a reckless speed, I feared for our lives. Dust billowed through the glassless windows and through the gaps in the cardboard that concealed the rusted holes in the floor.

Smiling triumphantly, he finally brought the car to an abrupt halt. He turned off the headlights. Doña Mercedes stirred in the backseat.

"We've arrived," Leon Chirino said softly.

Quietly, we got out of the car. It was a dark, cloudy night. Not a star shone in the sky. Whatever was out there stretched in front of us like a black void. I stag-

gered clumsily after doña Mercedes, who seemed to
have no problem seeing in the darkness.

Leon Chirino took me by the arm and guided me.
I heard muffled laughter all around me. There seemed
to be other people, but I couldn't see any of them.

Finally, someone lit a kerosene lantern. In the faint,
wavering light I was able to make out the silhouette
of four men and doña Mercedes crouching in a circle.
Leon Chirino took me a few feet away from the group.
I felt totally incapacitated. He helped me to sit down
and then propped me against something that looked
like a rock protruding from the ground. He handed
me the lantern and instructed me to hold on to it and
shine it on whatever I was told to. Then he gave me
two canteens; the largest one was filled with water,
the smaller one with rum. I was supposed to hand
them to the men whenever they asked for them.

Silently and quite effortlessly, two men began to
dig the loose dirt with long shovels. They deposited
the dirt in a neat pile next to the hole. At least a half
hour elapsed before they stopped and asked for the
canteen with rum. While they drank and rested, Leon
Chirino and another man began to dig.

Taking turns, the men worked, drank either rum or
water, and rested. Within an hour they had dug a hole
deep enough for a man to disappear in it. The instant
one of the men hit something hard with his shovel
they stopped working. Léon Chirino asked me to shine
the light inside the hole but not to look at it.

"This is it," said one of the men. "Now we can all
dig around it." He and his partner joined the others in
the hole.

I was dying with curiosity but did not dare break
my promise. I wished I could at least talk to doña

Mercedes, sitting not too far from me. Immobile, she seemed to be in a deep trance.

The men worked feverishly in the hole. At least half an hour elapsed before I heard Leon Chirino's voice telling doña Mercedes that they were ready to open it.

"Musiúa, light a cigar from my basket and hand it to me," she ordered. "And also bring me my basket."

I lit a cigar, and as I rose to bring it to her, Leon Chirino whispered from the bottom of the hole. "Crouch, Musiúa! Crouch."

I stooped and handed doña Mercedes the cigar and the basket.

"Don't look into the hole for anything in the world!" she whispered in my ear.

I moved back to where I had been sitting, fighting the nearly invincible desire to shine the lantern into the hole. I knew with absolute certainty that they were digging out a trunk filled with gold coins. I could hear the dull sound of the shovels hitting what seemed to be a large and heavy object.

Fascinated, I watched doña Mercedes retrieve a black candle and a jar with black powder from her basket. She lit the black candle, propped it on the ground next to the hole, and then ordered me to turn off the lantern.

The black candle gave out an eerie light. Doña Mercedes sat on her calves next to the candle. Obeying some unvoiced command, the men stuck their heads out of the hole one by one right in front of her. Each time a head appeared, she poured some of the black powder into her cupped hands and then rubbed each head as if it were a ball. As soon as she was done with the heads, she smeared the black powder on the men's hands.

My curiosity reached its peak when I heard the cracking sound of a lid being opened.

"We've got it," Leon Chirino said, popping his head out of the hole.

Doña Mercedes handed him the jar with the black powder, another one filled with a white powder, and then she blew out the black candle.

Once again we were engulfed by total darkness. The groaning and heaving sounds of the men rising from the hole only accentuated the unnatural silence. I huddled against doña Mercedes, but she pushed me away.

"It's done," Leon Chirino whispered in a strained voice.

Doña Mercedes relit the black candle. I could barely make out the shapes of the three men carrying a large bundle. They deposited it behind the mound of dirt. I was watching them so intently that I almost fell forward into the pit when I heard doña Mercedes' voice telling Leon Chirino, who was still inside the hole, to fasten the nails quickly and climb out.

Leon Chirino emerged right away, and doña Mercedes massaged his hands and face, while the other three men picked up their shovels and filled the hole. As soon as they were done, doña Mercedes placed the lit candle in the center of the filled-up hole. Leon Chirino threw the last shovel of dirt over it and put out the flame.

Someone relit the kerosene lamp, and immediately the men went to work; they arranged the ground so perfectly that no one could have guessed that a hole had been dug. I watched them for a while, but I lost interest, all my curiosity was focused on the now visible bundle wrapped in a tarpaulin.

"No one will ever know," one of the men said and chuckled softly. "Now, let's get out of here. It'll be daylight soon."

We all walked over to the bundle. I led the way with the light. In my eagerness to find out what it was, I tripped over it. The tarpaulin slid a bit, revealing a woman's foot clad in a black shoe.

Unable to restrain myself, I pulled the tarpaulin and shone the light on the exposed bundle. It was the corpse of a woman. My fright and revulsion were so intense I did not even scream—as I wanted and meant to. All I could manage was a faint croak, and then everything went black.

I came to, lying on doña Mercedes' lap in the backseat of Leon Chirino's car. Pressed firmly against my nose was a handkerchief soaked with a mixture of ammonia and rose water. It was doña Mercedes' favorite remedy. She used to call it a spiritual injection.

"I always knew you were a coward," she commented and began to massage my temples.

Leon Chirino turned around. "You're very daring, Musiúa," he said. "But you still don't have the strength to back it up. You will though. Some day, you will."

I was not in the mood for comments. My fright had been too great for comfort. I accused them of malice for not warning me about their doings.

Doña Mercedes said that everything they did was premeditated and that part of that premeditation was my total ignorance. It gave them a sort of protection against the desecration of a tomb. The flaw was my greedy interest to find out what was under the tarpaulin.

"I told you that we were going to fulfill a promise," doña Mercedes said to me. "We have done the first part. We have unearthed a corpse, now we have to bury it again." She closed her eyes and fell asleep.

I scrambled into the front seat.

Humming softly, Leon Chirino turned the car onto a dirt road that led to the coast.

It was already morning when we reached an abandoned coconut grove. Cued perhaps by the smell of the sea breeze, Mercedes Peralta awoke. She yawned loudly, then sat up. Leaning out the window, she seemed to breathe in the sound of the distant waves.

"This is a good place to park," Leon Chirino stated, stopping at the foot of the straightest and tallest palm tree I had ever seen. Its heavy silvery fronds appeared to be sweeping the clouds from the sky.

"Lorenzo Paz's house isn't far from here," Leon Chirino went on, helping doña Mercedes out of the car. "The walk will do us good." Smiling, he handed me her basket to carry.

We turned away from the sea and set out along a well-trodden path that cut across a thick grove of tall bamboo bordering a stream. It was cool and dark inside the grove, and the air had taken on the green transparency of leaves. Leon Chirino walked way ahead of us, his straw hat down over his ears, so that the wind would not carry it away.

We caught up with him by a short narrow bridge. Leaning over the rustic balustrade made out of freshly cut poles, we rested for a moment and gazed at a group of women washing their clothes, pounding them on flat river stones. A shirt slipped out of someone's hands, and a young girl jumped into the water to catch it. Her thin dress swelled out like a balloon, then molded itself to her breasts, stomach, and the gentle curve of her hips.

The straight dirt road on the other side of the bridge led to a small village, which we did not approach. Instead, we turned onto a side road along a neglected maize field. Hardened corn husks hung forlornly on withered stalks; they rustled like crumpled newspapers in the faint breeze. We came to a small house; its walls had been recently painted, and the tile roof had been partially redone. Banana trees, their fronds almost transparent in the sunlight, stood on either side of the front door like so many guards.

The door was ajar. Without knocking or calling out, we walked straight in. A group of men squatting on the brick floor with their backs against the wall lifted their rum-filled glasses in greeting, then continued their conversation in low, unhurried voices. Dust bars of sunlight beamed in through a narrow window, adding to the stale heat and intensifying the pungent odor of kerosene and creosol. In the far corner, propped on two crates, stood an open coffin.

One of the men rose and, holding my elbow gently, led me to the coffin. The man was slight but strongly built. His white hair and wrinkled face indicated age, yet there was something youthful about the graceful slant of his cheek-bones and the mischievous expression in his tawny brown eyes.

"Have a look at her," he whispered, bending toward the dead woman lying in the rough, unpainted coffin. "See how beautiful she still is."

I stifled a scream. It was the same woman we had unearthed last night. I moved closer and examined her carefully. Despite the gray-greenish tint to her skin that not even the heavy makeup could disguise, there was something alive about her. She seemed to be smiling at her own death. On her finely chiseled nose rested a pair of wire-rimmed, glassless spectacles. Her garish, red-painted lips were slightly parted, revealing her strong white teeth. A red robe trimmed with white had been wrapped around her long body. To her left lay a staff, to her right, a red-and-black wooden devil's mask fitted with two menacing, twisted ram's horns.

"She was very beautiful and very, very dear to me," the man said, straightening a fold in the robe.

"It's incredible how beautiful she still is," I agreed with him. Afraid he might stop talking, I held back my questions.

As he continued fussing with the woman's red robe, he gave me a detailed report on how he and his friends had unearthed her from her grave in the cemetery near Curmina and brought her to his house.

Suddenly, he looked up, and realizing that I was a stranger, he examined me with unrestrained curiosity.

"Oh, dear me! What kind of a host am I?" he exclaimed. "Here I'm talking and talking, when I haven't offered you anything to drink or to eat." He took my hand in his. "I'm Lorenzo Paz," he introduced himself.

Before I had a chance to say that I could not possibly swallow a thing, he ushered me through a narrow doorway that led to the kitchen.

Mercedes Peralta, standing by a kerosene stove that was perched on top of a waist-high stone hearth, was stirring a concoction made from the medicinal plants she had brought with her. "You'd better bury her soon, Lorenzo," she said. "It's far too hot to keep her above ground any longer."

"She'll be fine," the man assured her. "I'm certain her husband paid for the best embalmment job available in Curmina. And to be on the safe side, I sprinkled the coffin with quicklime and wrapped strips of cloth soaked in kerosene and creosol around her body." He looked at the healer beseechingly. "I've got to be sure her spirit has followed us here."

Nodding, doña Mercedes continued stirring her concoction.

Lorenzo Paz half filled two enamel mugs with rum. He handed one to me, the other to doña Mercedes. "We'll bury her as soon as it cools down," he promised and then went back to the other room.

"Who was the dead woman we unearthed last night?" I asked doña Mercedes and then sat down on a bundle of dried palm fronds stacked against the wall.

"For someone who spends most of her time studying people, you're not very observant," she remarked, laughing softly. "I pointed her out to you some time ago. She was the pharmacist's wife."

"The Swedish woman?" I asked aghast. "But why . . . ?" The rest of my words were drowned out by the roaring laughter of the men in the other room.

"I think they've just found out you were the one holding the light last night," doña Mercedes said and went into the other room to laugh with the men.

Unaccustomed to drinking liquor, I fell into a drowsy state not far from actual sleep. The men's voices, their laughter, and moments later, the rhythmic pounding of a hammer reached me as if they were coming from far away.

12

Late in the afternoon after the men had left for the cemetery with the coffin, doña Mercedes and I went to the village.

"I wonder where all the people are?" I asked. Except for a young girl standing in a doorway with a naked baby astride her hip and a few dogs lying in the shade of the houses, the place was deserted.

"At the cemetery," doña Mercedes said, leading me toward the church across the plaza. "It's the day of the dead. People are weeding the graves of their deceased relatives and saying prayers for them."

It was cool and shadowy inside the church. The last threads of sunlight spilling through the tinted-glass windows in the nave illuminated the statues of saints in the niches along the walls. A life-size crucifix, with its ripped, twisted flesh and its drooping, bleeding head in vivid color, dominated the altar. To the right of the crucifix stood the statue of the blissful-faced Virgin of Coromoto draped in a blue, star-embroidered, velvet cape. To the left was the cross-eyed figurine of Saint John, with his narrow-brimmed hat at a rakish angle and a red flannel cape, torn and dusty, flung casually over his shoulders.

Doña Mercedes blew out the flames of seven candles that were burning on the altar, put them in her basket, and lit seven new ones. She closed her eyes and, folding her hands, recited a long prayer.

The sun was only a glimmer behind the hills when we walked out of the church. The crimson and orange clouds trailing across the sky toward the sea gilded the late afternoon in a golden twilight. By the time we arrived at the cemetery it was dark.

The entire village seemed to have come out to commune with their dead. Men and women praying in soft voices were crouched beside graves ringed with lit candles.

We walked along the low wall encircling the cemetery to a secluded spot where Lorenzo Paz and his friends were resting. They had already lowered the coffin into the ground and covered it with dirt. Their faces, sculpted into abstract masks by the surrounding candlelight, could have been the ghostly forms of the dead beneath us. As soon as they spotted Mercedes Peralta, they began to pound the makeshift cross firmly into the ground at the head of the grave. Then, the men disappeared, swiftly and soundlessly, as if they had been swallowed up by the darkness.

"Now we have to lure Birgit Briceño's spirit here," doña Mercedes said, retrieving the seven candles she had taken from the church's altar and the same number of cigars from her basket. She stuck the candles in the soft ground on top of the grave. As soon as she had them all lit, she put a cigar in her mouth. "Watch carefully," she mumbled, handing me the rest of the cigars. "The instant I finish smoking this one, you must have the next cigar ready for me, already lit."

Taking deep drags she blew the smoke into the four cardinal directions. She huddled over the grave, and smoking uninterruptedly, she recited an incantation in a low raspy voice.

The tobacco smoke no longer seemed to come out of her mouth but directly from the ground. Like a fine mist, it grew around us, enveloping us like a cloud. Fascinated, I just sat there, handing her cigar after cigar, listening to her melodious, but incomprehensible, chanting.

I edged closer to her as she began to move her left arm over the grave. I thought she was shaking a rattle, but I could see nothing in her hand. I could only hear the clattering sound of seeds or, perhaps, small pebbles moving rapidly in her hand. Tiny sparks, like fireflies, escaped from in between her closed fingers. She began to whistle a strange tune that soon became indistinguishable from the rattling noise.

Out of the cloud of smoke emerged a tall bearded figure wearing a long robe and a Phrygian cap. I held my hand over my mouth to muffle my giggles. I believed that either I was still under the influence of the rum I had had earlier or the pallbearers were playing some kind of trick, all part of the day's festivities for the dead.

Totally absorbed, I watched the figure move out of the circle of smoke toward the wall surrounding the cemetery. The vision lingered there, a wistful smile on its face. I heard soft laughter, so quiet, so unearthly, it might have been part of Mercedes Peralta's chanting.

Her voice became louder. The sound seemed to come from the four corners of the grave, each side repeating the words like an echo. The smoke dispersed; it rose toward the palm trees and vanished into the night. For a long time, doña Mercedes remained huddled over the grave, mumbling softly, her face barely visible in the light of the burned-down candles.

She turned toward me, the trace of a smile on her lips. "I lured Birgit Briceño's spirit here but not to her grave," she said. Holding on to my arm, she stood up.

I wanted to ask her about the strange vision, but something in the empty expression of her eyes compelled me to silence.

Lorenzo Paz, leaning against an enormous boulder, was waiting for us outside the cemetery. Without saying a word he rose and followed us down the narrow path leading to the beach. A half-moon shone brightly on the bleached-out driftwood scattered about the wide stretch of sand.

Doña Mercedes ordered me to wait by an uprooted tree trunk. She and Lorenzo Paz walked down to the shoreline. He took off his clothes, then waded into the water and vanished amid the rolling phosphorescent whitecaps edged in silver shadows.

He was gone for quite some time until a wave, shimmering with moonlight, washed him up on the beach.

Mercedes Peralta retrieved a jar from her basket and poured its contents over his prostrated form in the sand. Kneeling beside him, she rested her hands on his head and murmured an incantation. Gently, she massaged him, her fingers barely touching his body, until a faint halo appeared around him. Swiftly, she rolled him from side to side, her hand describing oddly circular movements in the air, as if she were gathering shadows and wrapping them around him.

Moments later she came up to where I was sitting.

"Birgit Briceño's spirit was clinging to him like a second skin," she said, sitting beside me on the tree trunk.

Shortly, Lorenzo Paz, fully dressed, walked toward us. Doña Mercedes, with a movement of her chin, motioned him to sit in front of her on the sand. Pursing her lips, she made loud smacking noises, and her rapid, drawn-in breaths became muffled growls in her throat as she recited a long prayer.

"It will be a long time before Birgit Briceño's ghost will forget," she said. "Dying continues long after the body is in the ground. The dead lose their memories ever so slowly."

She turned toward me and ordered me to sit in the sand beside Lorenzo Paz. His clothes smelled of candle smoke and rose water.

"Lorenzo," doña Mercedes addressed him, "I'd like you to tell the musiúa the story of how you bewitched Birgit Briceño."

He regarded her with a puzzled air, then turned around and faced the sea; his head slightly cocked, he seemed to be listening to a secret message from the waves. "Why would she like to hear nonsensical stories about old people?" he asked her without looking at me. "The musiúa has her own stories. I'm sure of that."

"Let's say that I ask you to tell her," doña Mercedes said. "She's examining the many ways through which the wheel of chance can be made to turn by human means. In your case, an object turned the wheel for you, Lorenzo."

"The wheel of chance!" he said, a wistful tone in his voice. "I remember it all as if it happened only yesterday." Seemingly bemused, he prodded a pebble with the tip of his shoe and stretched out flat on the sand.

From his rocking chair behind the counter of the dim, smoke-filled bar, Lorenzo watched the group of men leaning over the billiard table in the corner. He shifted his gaze to the old mantel clock on the shelf, marking the time under a glass bell. It was almost dawn. He was about to rise and remind the men of the late hours, when he heard the unmistakable sound of Petra's shuffling feet from back of the house. Promptly, he sat down again. A wicked grin spread slowly over his face. He would let his aunt deal with the men. No one in town escaped her admonitions; they listened to them regardless of how vile and outrageous they were.

"Those damn clinking billiard balls won't let a soul sleep," she complained in a croaky voice as she stepped into the room. "Don't you have wives waiting for you? Don't you have work to go to in the morning, like any good Christian?" She gave the men no time to recover from their surprise but continued in the same indignant manner. "I know what's the matter with you. You're already regretting that you brought those pagan Christmas trees into your homes and that you permitted your children to act in a Christmas play."

She crossed herself and faced one of the men. "You are the mayor," she said. "How can you allow such things! Have you all turned Protestant?"

"God forbid, Petra," the mayor said, making the sign of the cross. "Don't make a mountain out of a molehill. What's the harm in a tree and a play? The children like it."

Grumbling something unintelligible, she turned to

go, then stopped short. "Shame on don Serapio! He's more foreign than a true foreigner. And shame on that real foreign wife of his. Thanks to them most children in town will not get their presents from the Three Wise Men on the sixth of January, as every good Christian should." She reached for a pack of cigarettes on the counter. "Now they will get them on Christmas day," she went on, "from some fellow called Santaclos. It's a disgrace!"

Leaning against the door, she stared at the mayor menacingly, oblivious that the ever present cigarette in her mouth had fallen onto the floor. She reached for the half-empty bottle of rum next to the billiard table and left the room muttering to herself.

Lorenzo, grinning behind the counter, clearly remembered the day when a truck loaded with singularly fragrant trees arrived in town. Don Serapio, the pharmacist, had called them Christmas trees. He had ordered them from Caracas, together with the appropriate decorations and records of European Christmas songs.

Not to be outdone by each other, don Serapio's friends quickly followed his example and paid a great deal of money for the brittle trees so that they could be prominently displayed in their living rooms.

To the great chagrin of the older relatives living in those homes, the trees were placed next to, and in some instances even in place of, the traditional nativity scenes.

With their windows wide open, so every passerby could see in and hear such unknown tunes as "Silent Night" and "O Tannenbaum," the women decorated the scraggly branches with glass balls, garlands, gold and silver tinsel, and cotton snow.

The rattling of the beaded curtain shattered Lorenzo's reveries. He waved to the men as they left the bar, then put the bottles back on the shelves. His glance was caught by a mask crammed behind the cheap religious statuary of virgins, saints, and mute-suffering Christs. The figurines had been given to him over the years by his poorer customers to pay for their drinks. He pulled out the mask. It was a devil's mask with huge ram horns. A man from Caracas had left it behind. He, too, had been unable to pay for the glasses of rum he had consumed.

Upon hearing Petra clanking her pots and pans in the kitchen, he put the mask back on the shelf. Instead of locking up the bar, he took his rocking chair outside on the sidewalk. The wide branches of the ancient samans on the plaza stood outlined against the pale dawn sky.

Leisurely, he rocked himself back and forth. Through half-closed lids he watched the old men who never slept beyond dawn. They sat in front of their doors, talking, recollecting every minute detail of their bygone days in ever increasing vividness.

A melody floated through the stillness. Across the street, Birgit Briceño, the pharmacist's wife, was looking out from her window directly at Lorenzo, her face resting on her folded arms. Her radio was on. He wondered if she had also not slept or if she had simply risen early.

Her face was a perfect oval. And the corners of her small, sensual, beautiful mouth were set in a gesture of defiance and boldness. Her yellow hair was braided around her head, and her cold blue eyes seemed to sparkle as she smiled at him.

He nodded at her in silent greeting. He was always dumbstruck in her presence, for she had been for him, since the day he first saw her, the picture of beauty. She's the reason I've reached the age of forty and never married, he mused. To him, all women were desirable and irresistible, but Birgit Briceño was more than irresistible, she was indeed unattainable.

"Why don't you come and watch the Christmas play tonight, Lorenzo? Tonight is Christmas Eve," Birgit Briceño shouted from across the street.

The old men, dozing in front of their doors, suddenly perked up and turned their heads toward the bar owner. Grinning expectantly, they waited for his answer.

So far, Lorenzo had consistently declined don Serapio's invitations. He couldn't abide the pharmacist's air of self-importance, nor his insistence in trying to convince every friend and acquaintance that he was the most influential man in town and that it fell upon him to give an example of what civilized living was all about.

However, regardless of how insufferable he found the man, Lorenzo couldn't resist his wife's summons. In a loud voice, he promised Birgit Briceño that he would come that evening. He then took his rocking chair inside and went to sleep in his hammock at the back of the house, pleased and full of confidence in himself.

Dressed in a white linen suit, Lorenzo walked around his bedroom, testing his new patent leather shoes. It was a large room crowded with heavy ornate mahogany pieces that had once stood in the parlor, which his father had converted into a bar years ago. Lorenzo sat on the bed, took off his shoes and socks, and put on his cloth sandals.

"I'm glad you aren't that vain," Petra commented, shuffling into the room. "There's nothing worse than having uncomfortable feet. It makes a person downright insecure." Her little dark eyes shone with approval as she examined his suit. "You'll never entice Birgit Briceño by ordinary means, though," she pronounced, catching his glance in the mirror. "That foreigner will respond only to witchcraft."

"Really?" Lorenzo mumbled, shrugging his shoulders with studied indifference.

"Isn't that the reason you went to see a witch? To get a love potion for that musiúa?" she challenged him, crossing her spindly arms across her flat chest. Realizing that he wasn't about to answer, she added, "Well then, why don't you follow the witch's advice?"

Lorenzo laughed and regarded his aunt thoughtfully. She had an uncanny way of knowing what was on his mind, and her assessments were always accurate.

Petra had moved into the house upon his father's death. He had been ten years old then. Not only had she taken care of him all these years, but she had also managed the bar until he had been capable of doing so himself.

"Birgit Briceño will respond only to witchcraft," Petra repeated obstinately.

Lorenzo examined himself in the mirror. He was too short and stocky to look dignified. His cheekbones were too pronounced, his mouth too thin, his nose too short to be handsome. Yet, he loved women unabashedly, and he knew that women loved men who loved them that way. But to have Birgit Briceño, he would need more than that. And he wanted her more than anything in the world.

He had never doubted the power of witchcraft. The

witch's recommendation on how to seduce the foreign woman, however, was far too outlandish. "Love potions are for people who don't have the strength to go directly to the spirit of things," she had said to him. "Anything can grant you your wish, your most earnest wish, if you're strong enough to wish your wish directly into the spirit of a thing. You have a devil's mask; ask the mask to seduce Birgit Briceño." He decided it was all too vague. He was too practical; he relied only on something that was concrete.

"You know what?" he said, facing his aunt. "Birgit Briceño herself has invited me to her house."

"She probably invited half the town," Petra replied cynically. "And the uninvited half will be there, too." She rose and, before shuffling back to her room, added, "I didn't say you couldn't get Birgit Briceño. But mark my words. It won't be through ordinary means."

He had discarded the witch's advice because he did not want merely to seduce the Swedish woman; he wanted her to love him, even if only for an instant. In his moments of euphoria he thought he would not be satisfied with less than one hour.

The front door and the windows of the Briceños' house were wide open. The tall fir tree in the living room, lit by a myriad of colorful lights, could be seen in all its splendor from the plaza.

Lorenzo walked inside the house. The place looked like a train station. Rows of chairs faced a raised platform that had been set up in the patio. The stuffed leather armchairs, couch, and Moroccan stools from the living room had been moved out into the gallery next to the willow furniture. Boys and girls dashed about barefoot, their mothers in tow, trying to put last minute touches on their costumes.

"Lorenzo!" don Serapio called out the instant he caught sight of him from the wide open living room. Although he was tall and thin, don Serapio had quite a paunch, and whenever he stood, his legs were slightly spread. He adjusted his thick horn-rimmed glasses and patted Lorenzo cordially on the shoulder. "We're about to serve coffee," he said, steering him toward his guests, the elite of the town. Among them were the doctor, the mayor, the barber, the school principal, and the priest. They all had the same expression on their faces: utter perplexity at seeing Lorenzo in don Serapio's house.

The pharmacist seemed genuinely pleased to have the elusive bar owner among his guests.

Lorenzo greeted everyone, then edged his way to the door and almost collided with Birgit Briceño as she stepped into the room.

"Well!" she exclaimed, her smile taking them all in. "We have the children ready to start the play. But first, come and join your wives for cookies and coffee." Taking her husband's arm she led the way to the dining room.

Lorenzo could not take his eyes off her. She was tall and strongly built, yet he thought there was something vulnerable, almost frail about her long neck and her delicate hands and feet.

As though aware of his scrutiny, she looked at him. She hesitated for a moment, then poured coffee into two minute, gold-rimmed cups and brought them over to where he stood. "There is also rum," she said, wistfully eyeing the bottle at the far end of the table, "to which only the men help themselves."

"I'll take care of that, right away," Lorenzo said, finishing his coffee in one gulp. He reached for the bottle, filled his cup with the rum, then casually exchanged her empty cup with his.

Grinning, she reached for a cookie, nibbled at it, and sipped her rum daintily. "There are always surprises in store for me," she said, her eyes suddenly sparkling, her cheeks flushed.

Lorenzo was oblivious to everything except her. He had not realized that don Serapio was talking until she made a subtle gesture of annoyance. "I'd better get back to the children," she said.

In a slow pedantic voice, the pharmacist was denouncing the Venezuelan tradition of Christmas revelers, who each night played their drums and sang improvised Christmas carols. Not only was it annoying, he stressed, to hear the incessant beating of drums, but it was downright disgusting to see young men reeling through the streets from all the rum they had been given as a reward for their songs.

An expression of pure mischief spread slowly over Lorenzo's face as he recalled his last visit to the witch. "I don't believe what you're telling me," he had said, "because I don't know who could grant me such a monumental wish."

"Trust me," she had replied. "There is no way to know who grants these wishes. But they do happen. And when you least expect it." She had insisted that he already possessed the item that would cast a spell on Birgit Briceño: a devil's mask. "All I can add is that you must wear the mask in triumph, and it will grant you your wish."

The witch had told him that it was vital for him to

choose his time well, for the mask's magic would work only once.

Certain that more than a coincidence was involved in his spotting the mask that morning, Lorenzo walked casually out into the yard. He made sure no one saw him, then dashed into a side street and slipped into his house through the back door.

He tiptoed to the bar, lit a candle, and reached for the mask on the shelf. Hesitantly, he ran his fingers over its red-and-black-painted surface. The carver had put something diabolical into his creation, Lorenzo thought. He had the odd feeling that the eye slits, half-hidden behind bushy brows made from sisal fibers, were accusing him for his neglect. And the mouth, with the long fangs of some wild animal at each corner, grinned fiendishly, daring him to dance with the mask on.

He held it over his face. His eyes, nose, and mouth fitted so well into the mask, he almost believed it had been made for him. Only his cheekbones rubbed slightly against the smooth wood inside. He tied the rawhide straps behind his head and covered them with the long sisal fibers, dyed purple, green, and black, hanging down the back.

Lorenzo did not hear Petra shuffling into the room. Startled, he leapt into the air when she spoke.

"You'll have to change your clothes," she declared and handed him a pair of pants and a patched shirt. "Take off your sandals, the devil goes barefoot." She looked around, afraid someone might overhear, then added, "Remember, the devil commands without uttering a word."

Quietly, the same way he had come in, Lorenzo slipped out the back door. He deliberated for an instant, wondering which way to turn when he heard a group of revelers playing their drums down the street. Protected by the shadows, Lorenzo kept close to the walls as he approached them.

"The devil!" one of them shouted upon seeing Lorenzo, then excitedly ran up and down the street, announcing that the devil had come to town.

Four young men detached themselves from the group and surrounded the devil, their hands moving loosely and gracefully as they began to beat on their drums. One of them sang an impromptu verse, proclaiming that they were at the devil's command for the night.

Lorenzo felt a shiver run up his spine. It filled him with a restlessness he could not control. Slowly, he lifted his muscular arms, and his feet moved, on their own accord, to the rhythm of the drums.

Windows and doors opened as they cavorted through the streets toward the plaza, followed by an ever increasing crowd. As if the devil had requested it, the lights in the plaza and in the surrounding houses went out for three or four seconds. The music stopped. Momentarily paralyzed, the crowd watched the devil go into the Briceños' house.

He leapt upon the platform in the patio just as rockets, lit by someone outside, shot up in the air. Red, blue, green, and white lights exploded against the sky, then fell dizzily to earth, a shower of faint golden sparks.

Spellbound, the guests stood transfixed, their eyes on the devil and the drummers that had followed close behind him. As if hearing some silent music, he danced in the middle of a circle of quiet drummers, his body slightly stooped over, his red-and-black mask gleaming, his horns menacingly pointing to heaven.

Then all at once like thunder came the sound of the drums, turning the prolonged silence into a rumble that extended to every corner of the house.

The devil, seeing Birgit Briceño leaning against the dining-room door, jumped down from the platform, grabbed the bottle of rum on the table, and handed it to her.

Laughing, she took the bottle, then proudly tossed her head back and drank.

Confident of his power, the devil danced around her, moving with consummate grace, his back stiff, only a suggestion of movement in his hips.

With hands outstretched, her face rapt, Birgit Briceño responded to the drums as if in a trance.

Don Serapio, his face contorted behind the thick, horn-rimmed glasses, sat huddled in the depths of an armchair that suddenly looked too wide for him.

The guests, mingling with the crowd that had come in from the plaza, began to dance. Slowly, their hips swayed modestly, their movements deliberately restrained.

Lorenzo, surrounded by an ever increasing number of dancing women, who all wanted to hold him, to touch him, to reassure themselves that he was made of flesh and blood, lost sight of Birgit Briceño. He broke free from the women's eager hands and hid behind a door. Making sure he had not been followed, he dashed to the back of the house, peeking into every room he passed.

The sound of joyful laughter brought him to an abrupt halt. Leaning against the arch that separated the laundry area from the backyard stood a tall, corpulent figure clad in black boots, a long red robe trimmed with white, and a red Phrygian cap fastened on top of a curly wig.

Lorenzo moved closer to the oddly attired person. "Birgit Briceño," he mumbled under his breath, gazing up into her clear, bold eyes framed by wire-rimmed spectacles that had no glass in them.

"Santaclos!" she corrected, a wide grin parting her lips, hidden by a shaggy beard and mustache. She reached for a burlap sack on the ground stuffed with packages and a staff leaning against the wall.

"I was going to wait until tomorrow and surprise the children who took part in the Christmas play with gifts," she explained, "but I can't pass up this opportunity." Her smile took on a sly, conspiratorial edge. "You are with me, aren't you?" she asked, and her eyes shone with a wicked gleam as she bent down to look into the slits of his mask.

Lorenzo bowed to her, then reached for the burlap sack, flung it over his shoulder, and motioned her to follow him.

He led her out to the backyard onto a side street toward the plaza, where a few old people, several women, and their small children had gathered to watch the party at the Briceños' house from across the street.

"There goes the devil!" a little girl shrieked. Calling to the other children to follow her, she ran toward the middle of the plaza. They stopped abruptly. Silently, the children stood in front of the two figures, their eyes wide with fear and curiosity.

"That's the devil," the little girl said, pointing to Lorenzo. "And who are you?" she demanded of the tall figure. "Why are you dressed like that?"

"I'm Santaclos and I bring presents," Birgit Briceño

said, pulling out a package from her burlap sack. Smiling, she handed it to the child.

"Do you have presents for us, too?" the other children asked, dancing around them.

Laughing, Birgit Briceño placed the packages into their eager little hands. A bewildered little girl held a box tightly against her chest and shouted excitedly, "Santaclos and the devil are going to dance together!"

The children's delighted shrieks attracted a crowd in a matter of moments. Some musicians among them began to play their instruments and beat their drums.

"Let's dance away from your house," Lorenzo whispered into Birgit Briceño's ear. "And when we get to a side street, we'll slip away."

Lorenzo looped a bandanna around her waist and held the ends firmly. Their bodies twisted and trembled in a fiery, rhythmical embrace.

Afraid to loose his grip on the ends of his bandanna, he ignored the other women's explicit invitations to dance with them. In the eyes of everyone, he was engrossed in his dancing, but the moment he heard another group of musicians coming down the street, he grabbed the startled Birgit Briceño by the hand and pulled her through the multitude. Before anyone realized what had happened, the devil and Santaclos had vanished.

They ran until they were out of breath. And when they heard the crowd laughing and thumping just around the corner, Lorenzo lifted Birgit Briceño in his arms and walked through the front door into the home of one of his friends and customers. He saw him in the living room amid a small group of people. It did not occur to Lorenzo that he might be intruding upon a family reunion. All he could think of was that he had to convince his friend to lend him his car.

"What a night," Birgit Briceño sighed, a beaming smile parting her lips. "That crowd almost got us." Pulling off the wig, beard, and mustache, she threw them out the window. She unfastened the cushions from under her robe and flung them on the backseat. "Where are we going?" she asked, searching the darkness outside.

Lorenzo chuckled behind his mask and continued driving toward the small house he owned near the sea.

Giggling, she relaxed in her seat. "I smell the sea breeze," she murmured shortly, breathing in deeply. "I was born in a Swedish fishing village," she said. "The people I come from have always been buried at sea or by the sea, and the only regret I have in life is that I won't. Serapio already owns a plot in the cemetery in town."

Puzzled by her odd concern, he stopped the car.

"Can the devil's mask grant me my wish to be buried by the sea?" she asked with such a serious, determined expression on her face that he could only nod in agreement.

"A promise like that is sacred," she said. The look in her eyes made it clear that for her their understanding was total. She leaned back in her seat. She was still, yet a strange, almost mischievous smile played around her mouth. "And I, on my part, promise to love the bearer of the wish-granting mask all this night," she whispered.

He would have settled for an instant of love. Next to an instant, a night was an eternity.

13

For days on end, I had pondered the meaning of the stories I had heard. I thought I understood what was meant by a link, or a witch's shadow, or the wheel of chance; but, I still wanted doña Mercedes or Candelaria to clarify things.

I had accepted from the beginning that I was not there to interpret what I was experiencing in terms of my academic training, however, I could not help seeing things in terms of what I had learned in the nagual's world.

Florinda would have explained it all in terms of *intent:* a universal, abstract force responsible for molding everything in the world we live in. Being an abstract force, its molding power is ordinarily outside the reach of man, yet under special circumstances it allows itself to be manipulated. And that is what gives us the false impression that people or things grant us wishes.

Compared to Florinda—and I could not avoid making the comparison—doña Mercedes and Candelaria were more simple pragmatists. They did not have an overall encompassing understanding of their actions. They understood whatever they did, as mediums, witches, and healers, in terms of separate, concrete events loosely connected with one another. For instance, doña Mercedes was giving me concrete examples of ways of manipulating something nameless. The act of manipulating it, she called a witch's shadow. The result of that manipulation she called a link, a continuity, a turn of the wheel of chance.

"It was certainly the mask that granted Lorenzo's wish," doña Mercedes said with absolute conviction. "I've known other, very similar instances of things granting wishes."

"But tell me, doña Mercedes, which is the important factor, the thing itself or the person who has the wish?"

"The thing itself," she replied. "If Lorenzo hadn't had that mask, he could've spent his life panting over Birgit Briceño; and that would've been all his wish amounted to. A witch would say that the mask, not Lorenzo, made the link."

"Would you still call it a witch's shadow, even if there was no witch involved?"

"A witch's shadow is only a name. All of us have a bit of a witch in us. Lorenzo is definitely not a spiritualist or a healer, yet he has a certain power to bewitch. Not enough, though, to make a link, to move the wheel of chance; but with the aid of the mask, it was a different story."

PART FOUR

14

A faint noise startled me. I tried to move, but my left arm, flung behind my head, was stiff from lack of circulation. I had fallen asleep in Mercedes Peralta's room after becoming thoroughly exhausted from taking an inventory of her dried medicinal plants.

I turned my head upon hearing a voice call my name. "Doña Mercedes?" I whispered. Except for the sound of the knots of the healer's hammock, squeaking as they rubbed over the metal rings, there was no answer. I tiptoed over to the corner. No one was in the hammock. Yet, I had the distinct feeling that she had just been in the room and that somehow her presence still lingered about.

In the grips of inexplicable anxiety, I opened the door, then ran down the dark silent corridor; I crossed the patio to the kitchen and out into the yard. There in the hammock that hung between two soursop trees lay doña Mercedes enveloped in tobacco smoke, like a shadow.

Slowly, her face emerged from the smoky dimness. It was more like an image in a dream. Her eyes glittered with a peculiar hollow depth.

"I was just thinking about you," she said. "About what you're doing here." She pulled up her legs to get out of the hammock.

I told her that I had fallen asleep in her room and had been frightened by the sound of her empty hammock.

She listened in silence, a worried expression on her face. "Musiúa," she said sternly, "how many times have I told you never to fall asleep in the room of a witch? We're very vulnerable while asleep."

Unexpectedly, she giggled and covered her mouth, as though she had said too much. She signaled me to come closer and to sit on the ground near the edge of her hammock. She began to massage my head. Her fingers traveled with an undulating movement down to my face.

A soothing numbness spread across my features. My skin, muscles, and bones seemed to dissolve under her deft fingers. Totally relaxed and at peace, I fell into a drowsiness that was not quite sleep. I was half-conscious of her gentle touch, as she continued to massage me. Finally, I lay faceup on the nearby cement slab.

Silently, doña Mercedes stood over me. "Watch, Musiúa," she suddenly cried out, looking up at the full moon racing through the clouds. Hiding, rising, emerging, the moon seemed to tear the clouds in its rush. "Watch," she cried out again, throwing a clump of gold medals fastened to a long gold chain into the air high over her head. "When you see the chain again, you'll have to return to Caracas."

For an instant the dark clump seemed to be suspended against the full moon emerging from behind a cloud. I did not see it fall. I was too preoccupied wondering what had prompted her to mention that I had to go back to Caracas. I asked her about it; she remarked that it was foolish of me to assume I was going to stay in Curmina forever.

15

The persistent sharp call of a cicada on the branch above my head was more like a vibration punctuating the stillness of the hot and humid night. I turned on my stomach on the mat in the patio and waited for the woman who had been appearing to me at the same spot every night.

Doña Mercedes, dozing in a nearby hammock, had decided to keep me company that night, breaking with her presence the singularity of those appearances. She had established from the beginning that as long as no one else was with me or watched me, my contacts with the spirit would remain superpersonal events. If, however, someone else was present, the entire matter would become public property, so to speak.

I had acquired by then a certain expertise in smoking cigars. At first, I had expressed to doña Mercedes my concern about the irritating effect of the heat on the delicate tissue inside the mouth. She had laughed my fear away, assuring me that the smoke of ritual cigars was actually cool and soothing.

After practicing for a short while, I had to agree with her; the smoke was indeed cool; the tobacco seemed mentholated.

Doña Mercedes' decision to accompany me that

night was triggered by Candelaria's doubts that I was strong enough to hold a full séance by myself. To them, a full séance meant that at one point the medium has absolutely relinquished all voluntary control of her person and the spirit can express itself through the medium's body.

Earlier that day, doña Mercedes had explained to me that my presence in her house was no longer tenable. Not because she or Candelaria were in any way at odds with me or cross with me, but because she had nothing of value to give me. She assured me that both Candelaria and herself felt nothing but the deepest affection for me. Had she liked me less, she would have been satisfied with letting me watch her treat the sick and pretend that I was her helper. It was her affection for me that forced her to be truthful. What I needed was a link, and she had none for me. She could only make one for Candelaria. However, since the spirit had chosen me to be an intermediary or, perhaps, even a true medium, she had to honor that choice. So far, she had done so by indirectly helping me make nightly contacts with the apparition.

"The fact that the spirit of my ancestor has chosen you," she had said, "makes you, Candelaria, and me sort of relatives."

Candelaria had told me then that she had had contact with the same spirit since childhood. But, following a medium's tradition of total secrecy, she could not possibly elaborate on that.

Doña Mercedes stirred in her hammock and crossed her arms behind her head. "Musiúa, you better squat and start smoking," she said in a soft, relaxed tone.

I lit a cigar, puffing at it in short even spurts and murmured the incantation she had taught me. The smoke and the sound were definitely the agents that brought the apparition every time. I heard a soft rustle. Doña Mercedes also heard it, for she turned at the same instant I did. A few feet away, squatting between Candelaria's giant terra-cotta flower pots, was the woman.

Doña Mercedes crouched beside me and took the cigar from my mouth. She puffed at it, mumbling an incantation, a different one from mine. I felt a tremor in my body; an invisible hand gripped me by the throat. I heard myself making whizzing, gurgling noises. To my amazement, they sounded like words said by someone else with my own vocal cords. I knew instantly—although I did not understand them—that they were words of yet another incantation. The apparition hovered over my head, and then it disappeared.

Next, I found myself with doña Mercedes and Candelaria inside the house. I was soaked in perspiration and felt physically exhausted. And so were the two women. However, my exhaustion was not a debilitating one. I felt extraordinarily light and exhilarated.

"How did I get here?" I asked.

Candelaria consulted doña Mercedes with a questioning look and then said, "You had a full séance."

"This changes everything," doña Mercedes said in a faint voice. "The spirit of my ancestor has made a link for you. So, you must stay here until the spirit lets you go."

"But why did the spirit choose me?" I asked. "I'm a foreigner."

"There are no foreigners for the spirits," Candelaria answered. "The spirits only search for mediums."

16

Mercedes Peralta sat hunched over the altar, mumbling an incantation. Faint with hunger and fatigue, I kept glancing at my watch. It was nearly six o'clock in the evening. I fervently wished that the large woman sitting by the table would be doña Mercedes' last patient for the day.

There had been no explanation for her seeing more than two sick persons a day, but for the last four Saturdays doña Mercedes had seen as many as twelve in one day.

They were mostly women from the nearby hamlets who took advantage of their weekly trip to the market and stopped by to see the healer. There were always those who sought help for such specific ailments as headaches, colds, and female disorders. The great majority, however, came to be relieved of their emotional problems. Unrequited love, marital difficulties, strife with in-laws, growing children, and problems at work and in the community were the most frequently discussed topics. Graying hair, loss of hair, the appearance of wrinkles, and bouts of bad luck were among the more frivolous complaints. Doña Mercedes treated each person, whatever his or her problem, with the same genuine interest and efficiency.

She would first diagnose the ailment with the aid of her nautical compass or by interpreting the pattern of the cigar's ashes on the plate. If the person's imbalance was caused by psychological turmoil— she called it spiritual—she would recite a prayer-incantation and give a massage. If the person was suffering from a physical ailment, she would prescribe medicinal plants and a follow-up.

Her artful use of language and her great sensitivity to each person's minute change in mood prompted the most reluctant man or woman to open up and talk candidly about his or her intimate concerns.

Mercedes Peralta's voice startled me. "You really messed up this time," she addressed the large woman sitting in front of the table. Shaking her head in disbe-lief, she once again examined the cigar's ashes, which she had collected on a metal plate on the altar. "You're a fool," she declared, holding the plate under the wom-an's face, expecting the woman to recognize in the soft, gray-greenish powder the nature of her ailment. "You really are in trouble this time."

Flushing with apprehension, the woman looked from side to side, as if she were trying to find a way to escape. She puckered up her lips like a child.

Doña Mercedes rose, moved to where I sat on a stool in my usual corner, and in a formal tone pro-nounced, "I would like you to write down the treatment my client is to follow."

As usual, I listed first the prescribed herbs, flower essences, and dietary restrictions. Then, I wrote out a detailed account of when and under what circum-stances the patient was to take the herbal infusion and the purifying baths. With doña Mercedes' permission, I never failed to make a carbon copy for myself. And finally at her urging, I read out loud several times what I had written. I was certain that it was not only to reassure doña Mercedes herself that I had listed everything correctly but mainly to benefit the patient in case she was illiterate.

With the instructions clutched in her hand, the woman rose and faced the altar. She put some bills under the statue of the Virgin, then solemnly promised that she would follow doña Mercedes' instructions.

Doña Mercedes stepped over to the altar, lit a candle, and kneeled to pray to the saints that her judgments would be correct.

I mentioned that I knew doctors who prayed a great deal.

"What good doctors and healers have in common is abiding respect for their patients," she declared. "They trust the great force that is out there to guide them. They can summon that power through prayer, meditation, incantations, tobacco smoke, medicines, and equipment."

She reached for the carbon copies of all the instructions I had written out that day, then counted the pages. "Did I really see that many persons today?" she asked, seemingly uninterested in hearing my answer. A faint smile parted her lips as she closed her eyes and leaned back in her uncomfortable-looking chair. "Go and bring me all your notebooks on all my clients but not the ones on the persons who are telling you their stories. I want to see how many people I've treated since you got here." She got up and walked with me to the door. "Bring everything to the patio. I want Candelaria to help me," she added.

It took me almost an hour to gather all my materials. With the exception of my diary, I carried everything to the patio, where doña Mercedes and Candelaria were already waiting for me.

"Is that it?" doña Mercedes asked, eyeing the bundles of paper I had placed on the ground right in front of her.

She did not wait for my answer but ordered Candelaria to stack the papers and index cards by the steel drum at the far end of the patio. As soon as she had done so, Candelaria came to sit beside me on the mat. We both faced doña Mercedes, who was once again lying in her hammock.

"I've already told you that you are here under the auspices of the spirit of my ancestor," doña Mercedes said to me. "Since last night you are a medium chosen by that spirit. And mediums don't keep papers about healing. The very idea is hideous."

She rose from her hammock and walked to where my bundles of notes were. Only then did it dawn on me what she intended to do. She broke the string bindings with a knife and dropped handfuls of paper into the steel drum. Mesmerized, I watched the smoke rise from the drum. I had not noticed before that there was a fire inside it.

Eager to save some of my work, I jumped up. Candelaria's words stopped me from running to the drum.

"If you do that, you must leave right away." She smiled and patted the mat beside her.

In that instant I understood everything. There was nothing I could have done.

17

After an entire day's work, doña Mercedes fell soundly asleep in her chair.

I watched her for a while, wishing I could relax that easily, then I quietly put back the various bottles, jars, and boxes in the glass cabinet. As I tiptoed past her on my way out, she suddenly opened her eyes. She turned her head slowly and listened, her nostrils flaring as she sniffed the air.

"I almost forgot," she said. "Bring him in, right away."

"There isn't anybody," I replied with absolute certainty.

She raised her hands in a helpless gesture. "Just do what I tell you," she said softly.

Certain that she was going to be wrong this time, I stepped outside. It was nearly dark. No one was there. With a triumphant smile on my face I was about to walk back into the room when I heard a faint cough.

As if he had been conjured up by doña Mercedes' assertion, a neatly dressed man emerged from the shadows in the corridor. His legs were disproportionately long. His shoulders, in contrast, seemed small and looked frail under his dark coat. He vacillated for an instant, then lifted a cluster of green coconuts in a slight salute. In his other hand, he held a custom-made machete. "Is Mercedes Peralta in?" he asked in a deep, raspy voice, interspersed by a harsh cough.

"She's waiting for you," I said, holding the curtain aside for him.

He had short, stiff, curly hair, and the space between his brows was creased in a deep frown. His dark, angular face exuded an unyielding hardness, matched by the fierce, relentless expression in his eyes. Only at the corners of his well-shaped mouth lingered a certain softness.

He stood irresolute for a moment, then a faint smile spread slowly over his face as he approached doña Mercedes. He dropped the coconuts on the ground and, adjusting his pants at the knees, squatted by her chair. He selected the biggest coconut on the cluster and, with three expert cuts of his short machete, removed the top. "They are just the way you like them," he said. "Still soft and very sweet."

Doña Mercedes brought the fruit to her lips and, in between her noisy slurps, remarked how good the milk was. "Give me some of the inside," she demanded, handing the fruit back to him.

With one sure blow, he halved the coconut and then loosened the soft, gelatinous pulp with the tip of his machete.

"Prepare the other half for the musiúa," doña Mercedes said.

He stared at me long and hard, then without a word he scraped the remaining half of the coconut with the same meticulous care and handed it to me. I thanked him.

"And what brings you here today?" doña Mercedes

asked, breaking the awkward silence. "Do you need my help?"

"Yes," he said, pulling a cigarette case from his pocket. He lit a cigarette with a lighter. After taking one long drag, he returned the case to his pocket. "The spirit is all right. It's this damned cough that's getting worse. It doesn't let me sleep. I also have this headache. It doesn't let me work."

She invited him to sit down, not opposite her where her patients usually sat, but on the chair by the altar. She lit three candles in front of the Virgin, then casually inquired about the coconut plantation he owned somewhere along the coast.

He turned around slowly and gazed into her eyes. She coaxed him with a movement of her head. "This musiúa helps me with my patients," she said to him. "You can talk as if she weren't present."

His eyes caught mine for a moment. "My name is Benito Santos," he said and swiftly looked back at doña Mercedes. "Does she have a name?"

"She says her name is Florinda," doña Mercedes answered before I had time to say anything. "But I call her Musiúa."

She watched him intently, then positioned herself behind him. With slow easy movements, she rubbed an unguent on his chest and shoulders for nearly a half hour.

"Benito Santos," she said, turning toward me, "is a powerful man. He comes to see me from time to time; always for a headache or a cold or a cough. I cure him in five sessions. I use a specially made unguent and an eloquent prayer offered to the spirit of the sea."

She continued massaging him for a long time. "Is

the headache gone?" she asked, resting her hands on Benito Santos' shoulders.

He did not seem to have heard her question. He stared with unseeing eyes at the flickering candles. He began to talk about the sea and how ominous it was at dawn, when the sun rises from the dim lusterless water. In a monotonous, almost trancelike murmur, he spoke about his daily noon excursions into the sea. He had never learned to swim, only to float.

"Pelicans circle around me," he said. "Sometimes they fly very low and look directly into my eyes. I'm certain they want to know if my strength is waning."

With his head bowed, he remained silent for a long time, then his voice faded to an even lower, hard-to-understand murmur. "At dusk, when the sun is behind the far away hills and the light no longer touches the water, I hear the voice of the sea. It tells me that someday it will die, but while it lives, it is relentless. I know then that I love the sea."

Mercedes Peralta pressed her palms over his temples, her fingers spanning his head. "Benito Santos," she said, "is a man who has overcome guilt. He's old and he's tired. But even now he is relentless like the sea."

Benito Santos came to see doña Mercedes for five consecutive days. After finishing each of his daily treatments, she always asked him to tell me his story. He never answered her and totally ignored me. Finally, at the end of his last appointment, he abruptly turned and faced me. "Is that your jeep out there in the street?" he asked. Without giving me time to answer, he added, "Drive me back to the coconut plantation, please."

We drove in silence. Just prior to reaching the coast,

I assured him that he did not have to honor doña Mercedes' request.

He shook his head emphatically. "Whatever she asks is sacred to me," he said dryly. "I just don't know what to say or how to say it."

I paid countless visits to Benito Santos under the pretext of getting coconuts for doña Mercedes. We talked a great deal. But he never warmed up to me. He always stared at me defiantly until I turned my eyes away. He made it perfectly clear that he was talking to me only because Mercedes Peralta had requested it. He certainly was, as she had described him, hard and relentless.

Clutching his machete firmly in his hand, Benito Santos stood motionless in the hot noon sun. It scorched his back, stiff from cutting cane for a week. He pushed back the brim of his hat to cool his forehead. His eyes followed the group of weary men walking across the empty, harvested sugarcane fields on their way into town.

For the last day and night everyone had worked without rest. Like him, the men would have no jobs to go to on Monday. It had been the last sugarcane crop before the tractors were to flatten and parcel off the land. The owner of those fields had held out the longest. But finally, like all the other planters in the area, he had been forced to sell his property to a land-developing company in Caracas.

The valley was to be converted into an industrial center. Germans and Americans were going to build pharmaceutical laboratories. Italians were not only going to construct a shoe factory but bring their own workers from Italy as well.

"Damn foreigners," Benito Santos swore, spitting on the ground. He didn't know how to read or write, and he had no skills. He was a sugarcane cropper. All he knew was how to wield a machete. Dragging the long blade on the ground, he approached the hacienda's courtyard, then turned to the small bungalow, where the foreman had his office. A group of men, some standing, some squatting under the shade of the building's wide overlapping roof, eyed him suspiciously as he stepped into the office.

"What do you want?" the short, potbellied foreman sitting behind a gray metal desk asked. "You got paid, didn't you?" he added impatiently, wiping the sweat off his neck with a neatly folded white handkerchief.

Benito Santos nodded. He was a taciturn man, almost gruff. It was hard for him to speak, to ask a favor. "I heard that the sugarcane has been transported to a mill in the next town," he stammered, his eyes fixed on the foreman's massive neck bulging over the collar of his starched shirt. "I've been around mills before. I'm wondering if you could hire me to work there."

Leaning back in his chair, the foreman regarded Benito Santos through drooping lids. "You live around here, don't you? How would you be getting to the next town? It's more than fifteen miles from here."

"By bus," Benito Santos mumbled, looking furtively into the man's eyes.

"Bus!" The foreman laughed scornfully, stroking his thin, neatly trimmed mustache. "You know well that the bus only leaves when it's full. You'd never get there before noon."

"I'll make it," Benito Santos said desperately. "If you give me the job, I'll make it somehow. Please."

"Listen," the foreman snapped. "I hired anyone capable of cutting down sugarcane regardless of age or experience because we had a deadline to meet. It was made perfectly clear to every man hired that this was a six-day job. At the mill we already have more people than we need." The foreman began to shuffle through the papers on his desk. "Don't waste any more of my time. I'm a busy man."

Benito Santos stepped into the courtyard, making sure not to trample on the tufts of grass growing between the stones. The mill, at the far end of the yard, already looked abandoned even though it had been in use only a few days ago. He knew he would never see its like in the valley again.

The loud honking of a truck jolted him. Quickly, he stepped aside, lifting his hand for a ride into town. He was enveloped in a cloud of dust.

"You got to walk, Benito Santos," someone shouted from the moving vehicle.

Long after the dust had settled he could still hear the shouts and laughter of the workers on the truck. His fingers curled tightly around the handle of his machete. Slowly, they relaxed again. He pulled his hat well over his forehead to shade his eyes from the bright sun glazing the blue of the sky.

Benito Santos didn't follow the main road into town but cut across the empty fields until he reached a narrow trail. It led toward the southern end of town, where the Saturday open-air market was situated. He walked slower than usual, aware of the hole in one of his shoes and the flapping sole of the other, which stirred the dust on the ground before him. From time to time, he rested under the dark cool shade of the mango trees growing on either side of the path; dispiritedly, he watched the fleeting green outline of lizards darting in and out of the bushes.

It was way past noon when he reached the market. The place was still bustling with people. Vendors, their voices already hoarse, advertised their merchandise with the same enthusiasm they had displayed earlier that morning. And the customers, mostly women, haggled shamelessly over the prices. Benito Santos walked past the Portuguese farmers' stands, where the now limp vegetables lay in disarray; past the meat and dry-fish stalls, where flies swarmed around and mangy dogs waited with endless patience for a piece of meat to fall on the ground. He grinned at the hired children, who were standing behind the fresh-fruit stalls, packing rotten fruit in paper bags instead of letting the customers choose from the merchandise on display.

He fingered the money in his pocket: six days' wages. He deliberated whether he should buy food for his wife, Altagracia, and their small son now or later. "Later," he said out loud. There was always the chance that he would get a better deal if he haggled with the merchants just before they were ready to pack up.

"Get your food while you have the money, Benito Santos," an old woman who knew him well shouted. "The beans and the rice won't get any cheaper."

"Only women wait for the afternoon bargains," a merchant taunted him, making obscene gestures with a plantain.

Benito Santos stared at the grinning faces of the Lebanese peddlers, standing behind their gaudy stalls, advertising cheap dresses, costume jewelry, and perfumes. Rage made the veins in his temples swell and stiffened the muscles on his neck. The humiliating incident in the foreman's office was vivid in his mind. The scornful laughter of the workers on the truck still rang in his ears. The machete was as light as a knife in his hand. With tremendous effort he turned around and walked away.

A cold sweat bathed his body. His mouth was dry. He felt a tingling in his stomach that was not hunger. He would have his rum now, he decided. He couldn't wait until he got home. He needed the rum to dispel his anger, to dispel his gloom, his despondency.

Purposefully, he headed toward the main entrance of the market, where trucks and packtrains of donkeys waited to be reloaded with the produce that wasn't sold. He crossed the street, then stepped inside the small dark store at the corner and bought three pint bottles of the cheapest rum.

He sat down under the shade of a tree, facing the trucks and the donkeys. He didn't want to miss the moment the merchants began to pack up. Sighing contentedly, he leaned against the tree trunk. He took off his hat and wiped the sweat and the dust from his haggard face with his sleeve. Carefully, he opened one of the bottles and downed the first pint in one long gulp. Gradually, the rum dulled the tension in his stomach; it eased the pain in his stiff back and sore legs. He smiled. A vague feeling of well-being drifted through his head. Yes, he mused, it was better to sit there, enjoying his rum, than to go home and listen to Altagracia's incessant nagging. He was slow to anger, but today he had had as much as he could take.

Through drooping lids, Benito Santos watched the people gathered in a circle near the market's entrance. It was the same crowd that came every Saturday afternoon from the nearby hamlets to bet on the cockfights. Drowsily, he let his gaze wander to the two men squatting beneath a tree directly across from him. He wasn't much interested in cockfights, yet his attention was caught by the two roosters the men held in their hands. They bounced them up and down to strengthen their legs. With an oddly gentle gesture, the men ruffled the birds' feathers and then shoved them against each other to rouse their spirits.

"That's a fine-looking bird," Benito Santos said to the man holding the dark rooster with the golden-tipped feathers.

"He certainly is," the man agreed readily. "He'll be in the last fight this afternoon. The best birds are saved for the last fight," the man added proudly, brushing the rooster's feathers. "You ought to bet on him. He'll be the winner today."

"You're sure?" Benito Santos asked casually, taking out another bottle of rum from his paper bag. He took a long gulp, then meandered through the crowd of excited men squatting around a sand pit. They made room without looking at him, their eyes fixed on the center of the arena where two birds were locked in deadly combat.

"Your bets! Gentlemen, your bets!" a man shouted, his voice silencing the noisy crowd for a moment. "Your bets for the last fight! For the real fight!"

Eagerly the men exchanged their dirty bills for the colored markers indicating the amount of their bets.

"Are you sure your rooster is going to win today?" Benito Santos asked the owner of the bird with the golden-tipped feathers.

"He sure is!" the man exclaimed, planting rapturous kisses on the bird's scarred crest.

"Afraid to bet, Benito Santos?" asked one of the workers who had been cutting cane with him during the week. "You'd better buy some food for your old woman if you don't want trouble tonight," he added mockingly.

Benito Santos chose a marker and without hesitation bet the rest of his wages on the cock with the golden-tipped feathers. He was certain he would double his money. He would be able to buy not only rice and beans but meat and more rum. There might even be enough money to buy his son his first pair of shoes.

Benito Santos, as excited as the rest of the spectators, shouted his approval as the owners raised their birds high over their heads. They sucked the sharp, deadly spurs on the roosters' legs as evidence that there was no poison on them. The men mumbled sweet nothings to their birds, and then, at the command of the referee, they placed them in the center of the sand pit.

The combatants viewed each other angrily but refused to fight. The crowd shouted, and a wicker cage was lowered over the roosters. Excitedly the men goaded the birds to attack. The roosters trembled with rage, and their plumage spread out beneath their shaved, bloodshot necks.

The cage was lifted. The cocks jumped at each other, skillfully avoiding pecks and blows of wings. But soon they were engaged in a deadly wing-beating, head-thrusting, leg-kicking explosion of fury. The white cock's feathers were red with blood, either from its own wounds or from the deep gash on its opponent's neck.

Silently, Benito Santos prayed for the bird he had bet on to win.

At a signal from the referee, the open-beaked, hard-breathing roosters were lifted from the pit. With mounting anxiety Benito Santos watched the owner of the golden-feathered bird blow on its wounds. Soothingly, he talked to the rooster, caressing and fussing over it.

At the referee's command, the birds were once again placed in the center of the circle. The white-feathered bird instantly took a well-aimed jump and sunk its spurs into its opponent's neck. Its triumphant crow shattered the silence of the audience as the golden-tipped rooster toppled over dead.

Benito Santos smiled bitterly, then laughed behind a grimace that struggled to hold back his tears. "At least I've got my rum," he mumbled, then gulped down the rest of his second bottle. With trembling fingers he wiped his chin dry. He walked away from the crowd, heading toward the hills. The empty cane fields stretching endlessly before him shimmered in the bright afternoon sunlight. The yellow dust of the road raised by his shoes settled like fine, golden powder on his arms and hands.

Slowly, he went up a steep hill. Wherever there was a tree, he crossed the road and rested in its shade.

He opened his last bottle of rum and took one long gulp. He didn't want to see his wife. He couldn't bear to look into her accusing eyes. He scanned the hills around him and let his gaze rest on the green slopes on the other side of the road where a high ranking general in the government had his farm.

Benito Santos took another swallow. The rum filled him with a vague hope. Perhaps they might give him a job at the general's place. He could cut the green, irrigated alfalfa grown specifically for the horses. Hell! He had a skill! he thought. He was a sugarcane cropper. Cutting cane or alfalfa was all the same. He might even be able to ask for an advance. Not much. Just enough to buy some rice and beans.

He almost ran down the hill, then up the newly paved road leading to the general's farm. He was so excited by the possibility of getting a job that he didn't even see the two soldiers by the wide open gate.

"Where do you think you're going?" one of them stopped him, pointing his rifle to a sign on the road. "Can't you read? No trespassing beyond this point. This is a private road."

Benito Santos was so winded his throat hurt with each breath. He looked from one soldier to the other, then addressed the second soldier, who was leaning against a large boulder next to the sign. He looked older and friendlier. "I'm in desperate need of a job," he murmured.

Silently, the soldier shook his head; his eyes fixed on Benito Santos' stiff black hair sticking through his torn straw hat. His worn, rolled-up khaki pants and shirt clung damply to his tall, gaunt frame. "There are no jobs in this place," he said in a sympathetic tone. "There isn't anyone around here to hire you, anyway."

"There must be someone there with the horses," Benito Santos insisted. "Maybe I could help. Just for a couple of hours every day."

The guards looked at each other, then shrugged and grinned mischievously. "Ask for the German in charge of the horses," the younger-looking man said. "He might help you."

For a moment Benito Santos wondered what the

soldiers could be laughing about. But he felt too grateful to let it worry him. Afraid they might change their minds and call him back, he hurried along the straight paved road cut into the hill.

He stopped short in front of the general's house. Undecided, he stood looking at the two-story building. It was all white with a long balcony supported by massive columns. Instead of calling out, he tiptoed toward one of the downstairs windows. It was open, and the air gently fluttered the gauzy curtain. He wanted to have a quick look and see what it was like inside. He had heard that the luxurious furnishings had been brought over from Europe.

"What are you doing here?" a loud, heavily accented voice asked from behind him.

Startled, Benito Santos almost dropped his bottle of rum as he turned around. Wide-eyed, he regarded a wiry, middle-aged man with blond, closely cropped hair. He must be the German the soldiers had told him to see, he thought, looking into the man's restless eyes. They were the color of the sky and shone hard under fiercely jutting brows.

"Do you have a job for me?" Benito Santos asked. "Any kind of job."

The man moved closer to Benito Santos and stared at him menacingly. "How dare you come here, you drunkard?" he spat out, his voice cold with contempt. "Get out of here before I set the dogs on you."

Benito Santos' gaze became unsteady, his eyelids twitched. He felt like a beggar. He hated to ask for a favor. He had always worked the best he could. His tongue felt heavy. "Just for a couple of hours." He held out his hand so the man could see the cracks and calluses. "I'm a hard worker. I'm a cane cutter. I could cut some grass for the horses."

"Get out!" the German yelled. "You're drunk."

Benito Santos walked slowly, dragging the tip of his machete on the ground. The road before him seemed longer than ever, as though it stretched itself deliberately to delay his arrival home. He wished he had someone to talk to. The monotonous drone of the insects made him feel even more desolate.

He crossed the dry gully to his shack. He remained outside for a moment, deeply breathing in the late-afternoon air, letting the gentle breeze cool his flushed face.

He had to stoop to enter his shack. It had no windows, only an opening in the front and one in the back, which he closed at night with a piece of cardboard propped up with a stick.

The heat was stifling inside. The sound of the hammock's ropes rubbing against the wood and Altagracia's uneven breathing irritated him. He knew she was seething with wrath. He turned to look at his son sleeping on the ground. He wore a discolored rag, which barely covered his small chest. He couldn't remember whether the boy was two or three years old.

Altagracia rose from her hammock, her eyes fixed on the bag in his hand. She planted herself in front of him and demanded in a harsh, shrill voice, "Where is the food, Benito?"

"The market was already packed up by the time I got there," Benito Santos mumbled, moving over to the cot in one corner of the shack, the paper bag held tightly in his hand. "I'm sure there are still some beans and rice left here."

"There is nothing here as you well know," Altagracia said, trying to grab the paper bag. "You sure had time to get drunk." Her face with its yellowish, sagging skin was flushed. Her sunken, usually lifeless eyes shone with anger and despair.

He clearly felt the accelerated pounding of his heart. He didn't have to give her an explanation. He didn't owe anyone an explanation.

"Shut up, woman," he yelled. He lifted the bottle and drank the rest of the rum without drawing a breath. "I worked the whole night cutting cane. I'm tired." He threw the empty bottle through the opening of the shack. "I want some peace and quiet now. I want no woman shouting at me. Take the boy and get the hell out of here."

Altagracia grabbed him by the arm before he had a chance to lower himself on the cot. "Give me the money; I'll buy the food myself. The boy needs to eat." She ripped open his pocket. "No money?" she repeated, in a daze, looking uncomprehendingly at him. "Didn't you get paid today? You couldn't have spent six days' wages on rum." Shouting obscenities, she pulled his hair and pounded her clenched fists against his aching back and chest.

He felt drunk, not with rum, but with rage and hopelessness. He saw the gleam of fear in her eyes as he raised his machete. Her scream filled the air, then there was silence. He looked at her still form on the ground, at her tangled mass of hair soaked in blood.

He felt something tugging at his pants. His small son held on to his leg with such strength he was certain the child would never let him free. Possessed by an irrational fear, he tried to shake him loose, but the boy would not let go. His eyes were those of his mother, dark and deep, filled with that same accusing light. His temples began to throb under the boy's unblinking stare. With blind fury, he raised the machete once more.

Never in his life had he felt such an agonizing desolation. Never before had he been so clear-headed either. For a moment it was as if he had had another life, a more meaningful life—a life with a greater purpose—and was now looking into the nightmare that his existence had become. Then, more aware than he had ever been, he soaked some rags in the nearly empty can of kerosene and set his shack on fire.

He ran as far as he could and then stopped. Motionless, he stood gazing at the empty fields at the foot of the hills, at the faraway mountains in the distance. In the morning those mountains were the color of hope. Beyond them was the sea. He had never seen the sea. He had only heard that it was immense.

Benito Santos waited until the mountains, the hills, and the trees were no more than shadows. Shadows, like the memories of his childhood. He felt he was again walking with his witch mother through the narrow streets of his village amid the crowd of the faithful behind some procession at nightfall with candles winking through the darkness. "Holy Mary, Mother of God, pray for us sinners, now and at the hour of our death. Amen." His voice drifted away with the wind and the thousands of small sounds shrouding the hills. He shivered with fear and took off again in a wild run. He ran until he could no longer breathe. He felt himself sinking into the soft ground. The earth was swallowing him; it was soothing him with blackness. And Benito Santos knew that this was the last day of his useless life. He had at last died.

* * *

He opened his eyes to the sound of a woman's wailing. It was the night breeze, rustling through the leaves around him. How he had wished to remain forever in darkness. But he knew that nothing would ever be that easy for him. He rose, picked up his machete, and headed toward the road that led to the mountains. A clear light came down from the sky. It spread around him; it even gave him a shadow. The clear light made the air thinner, easier to breathe.

He had no place to go. Nothing to look forward to. He felt no profound emotion. There was only a vague sensation, a vague hope that he might get to see the sea.

18

"It's time for you to go," Candelaria said. "You shouldn't be working on Sundays." She pulled the plug of my tape recorder.

At that very instant, doña Mercedes stepped into the kitchen. She frowned, noticing that I was still in my robe. "Why aren't you ready?" she asked me.

"I know why," Candelaria said. Her voice held a curious softness, and a glimmer of amusement shone in her eyes. "She doesn't want to collect Benito Santos' coconuts. She's afraid of him."

Before I had a chance to deny her accusation, she was gone from the room.

"Is that true, Musiúa?" doña Mercedes asked, pouring herself a cup of coffee. "I haven't noticed that you held any ill-feelings toward him."

I assured her that I did not. However, I couldn't help feeling that what Benito Santos had done to his wife and his child was abominable.

"His story has nothing to do with morality or justice," she interrupted me. "It's the story of a violent, desperate man."

I protested because I deeply resented that he had looked after only himself. I talked almost hysterically about the despair and the hopelessness of women and children.

"Stop it, Musiúa." With her finger she poked me on my chest next to my collarbone. It felt as if she were pushing me with an iron tip. "Don't give in to your false sense of order. Don't be a musiúa that comes from a foreign country to find flaws; that kind of person would feel offended by Benito Santos and miss what I am trying to show you. I want to place you under the shadow of the people I've selected to tell you their stories.

"The story of Benito Santos' last day of his useless life sums up all his existence. I asked him to tell it to you with all the details he could remember. And I have also sent you to see for yourself his coconut grove by the sea, so you would verify that the wheel of chance did turn."

It was hard for me to explain my feelings to doña Mercedes without moralizing. I did not want to, but I could not help myself. She gave me an all-knowing smile.

"The value of his story," she said all of a sudden, "is that without any preparation, he made a link himself; he made the wheel of chance move.

"Witches say that sometimes one single act makes that link."

Doña Mercedes pushed herself up from the chair she had been sitting on and, holding firmly to my arm, walked out of the kitchen toward her room.

At her door, she stopped and looked at me. "Benito Santos killed his wife and child. That act moved the wheel of chance; but what made him end up where he is now—by the sea—was his desire to see the sea.

"As he must have told you, it was a vague desire,

yet it was the only thing he had after committing an act of such violence and finality. So, the desire took hold of him and drove him.

"That is why he has to remain faithful to that desire that saved him. He has to love the sea. He comes to me so that I can help him maintain his unwavering course.

"It can be done, you know. We can make our own link with one single act. It doesn't have to be as violent and desperate as Benito Santos' act, but it has to be as final. If that act is followed by a desire of tremendous strength, sometimes, like Benito Santos, we can be placed outside of morality."

PART
FIVE

19

It was late in the afternoon when doña Mercedes and I left the house and walked up the street to Leon Chirino's house. Leisurely, we went past the old colonial houses near the plaza and peeked inside the open windows. The rooms were dark, yet we could make out the shadows of old women counting rosary beads as they said their silent afternoon prayers.

We rested on a bench in the plaza, surrounded by old men sitting on crude wooden chairs propped against tree trunks. We waited with them for the sun to disappear behind the hills and for the evening breeze to cool the air.

Leon Chirino lived on the other side of town at the foot of a shack-covered hill. His house, made of unplastered cement blocks, had an extensive yard and was encircled by a high wall.

The small wooden gate in the wall was unlocked, as was the front door. Without bothering to knock or to call out we went through a large living room and headed straight for the back patio, which had been converted into a workshop. Under the bright glare of a single bulb, Leon Chirino was sanding a piece of wood. He spread his hands in a gesture of invitation and pleasure and invited us to sit on the bench across from his working table.

"I guess it's time to get ready," he said, brushing the sawdust off his kinky white hair and the wood-shavings from his clothes.

Expectantly, I looked at doña Mercedes, but she merely nodded. A secret light shone in her eyes as she turned to Leon Chirino. Without a word she rose and shuffled down the corridor bordering the patio toward the back of the house.

I was about to follow, when Leon Chirino stopped me short. "You'd better come with me," he said, switching off the light. He spat through his teeth, accurately aiming at one of the dried-up flower pots in the corner.

"Where is doña Mercedes going?" I asked.

He shrugged impatiently and guided me in the opposite direction to a narrow alcove that separated the living room from the kitchen. Against one wall of the small enclosure stood an earthenware water filter; against the other, a refrigerator.

"Would you like one of these?" He held up a bottle of Pepsi he had removed from the icebox. Not waiting for my reply, he opened the bottle and casually added, "Doña Mercedes is making sure there are enough cigars."

"Is there going to be a séance?" I asked, taking the bottle from his hand.

Leon Chirino turned on the light in the living room, then moved to the high window facing the street. He reached for a wooden panel, and before placing it in the window sill, he looked back over his shoulder, his eyes shining, one hand stroking his chin. His smile, slightly crooked, was devilish.

"There certainly is going to be one," he said.

Sipping the Pepsi, I went to sit on the couch by the window. The lack of furniture made the room appear larger than it actually was. Other than the couch, there was only a tall cabinet crammed with books, snapshots, bottles, jars, cups, and glasses and several wooden chairs lined up against the walls.

Mumbling something unintelligible, Leon Chirino turned off the light, then lit the candles that stood on the carved ledges beneath the various pictures of saints, Indian chieftains, and black slave leaders adorning the ochre-painted walls. "I want you to sit here," he ordered, placing two chairs in the middle of the room.

"On which one?"

"Whichever you prefer." Grinning broadly, he unfastened my wristwatch, put it in his pocket, then went to the cabinet and took out a small jar. It was half-filled with mercury. In his dark hands it looked like the giant pupil of a live monster.

"I understand that you're a full-fledged medium," he said, placing the jar in my lap. "The mercury will keep the spirit from gravitating toward you. We don't want the spirit near you. It's too dangerous for you." He winked and hung a silver chain necklace with a medal of the Virgin around my neck. "This medal is guaranteed to be a protection," he assured me.

Closing his eyes, he joined his hands in prayer. As soon as he had finished, he warned me that there was no way of knowing whose spirit would visit us during the séance. "Don't let go of the jar and don't remove the necklace," he admonished, pulling up the rest of the chairs to form a circle in the middle of the room.

He blew out all the candles except the one burning beneath the picture of *El Negro Miguel*—a famous slave leader who had headed the first slave uprising in Venezuela. Then he said another short prayer and silently left the room.

The candle had almost burned down when he returned. Urging me to keep my eyes fixed on the jar in my lap, he sat beside me. Overcome by curiosity, I looked up several times when I heard people come into the room and sit on the chairs. In the uncertain light I failed to recognize a single face.

Mercedes Peralta was the last one to come in. She removed the candle from the ledge and distributed the hand-rolled cigars. "Don't talk to anyone before or after the séance," she whispered in my ear as she held the flickering flame to my cigar. "No one else besides Leon Chirino knows you are a medium. Mediums are vulnerable."

She sat down opposite me. I closed my eyes and puffed skillfully, as I had done countless times in doña Mercedes' patio. I became so engrossed in that act that I lost track of time. A soft moan arose from the smoky darkness. I opened my eyes and saw a woman materialize in the middle of the circle of chairs, a hazy figure. Slowly, a reddish light spread all over her until she seemed to be aglow.

The manner in which she carried herself, the way she was dressed—black skirt and blouse—the familiar way she tilted her head to one side, made me think it was Mercedes Peralta. However, the longer I observed her, the less sure I was.

Wondering whether I was going through one of the inexplicable visions I had had in the patio, I clutched the mercury jar in my hands and rose from my chair. I stood transfixed as the woman became transparent. I found nothing frightening about her transparency; I simply accepted that it was possible to see through her.

Without any warning the woman collapsed in a dark heap on the ground. The light inside her seemed to have been turned off. I was totally reassured that she was not an apparition when she took out a handkerchief and blew her nose.

Exhausted, I sank into my chair. Leon Chirino, sitting on my left, nudged me with his elbow, gesturing me to keep my attention on the center of the room. There, in the circle of chairs, where the transparent woman had been, stood an old, foreign-looking woman. She stared at me, her blue eyes wide open, frightened, bewildered. Her head jerked back, then forward, and before I could make any sense of the vision, it faded. Not suddenly but slowly, it floated about.

It was so quiet in the room that for an instant I thought everyone had gone. On the sly, I glanced around me. All I saw was the glow of cigars. They couldn't possibly be smoking the same cigars doña Mercedes had distributed, I thought. I had finished mine a long time ago. As I leaned forward to attract Leon Chirino's attention, someone placed a hand on my shoulder.

"Doña Mercedes!" I exclaimed, recognizing her touch. With my head bent I waited for her to say something. When she didn't, I looked up, but she was not there. I was alone in the room. Everyone else had left. Frightened, I stood up and ran toward the door, only to be stopped by Leon Chirino.

"Frida Herzog's spirit roams around here," he said. "She died on the steps of this hill." He moved toward the window and opened the wooden panels. Like a ghostly apparition the smoke swirled out of the room, dissolving into the night air. Leon Chirino faced me and once again repeated that Frida Herzog had died on the steps of that hill. He walked around the room carefully inspecting the shadowy corners, perhaps to make sure that no one was there.

"Was Frida Herzog the old woman I saw?" I asked. "Did you see her, too?"

He nodded, then mumbled once again that her spirit was still roaming around. He brushed his forehead repeatedly, as if he were trying to rid himself of a thought or, perhaps, the image of the frightened old woman.

The stillness in the room became unsettling. "I'd better catch up with doña Mercedes," I said softly and opened the door.

"Wait!" Leon Chirino stepped forward and grabbed my arm. He lifted the silver necklace over my head and took the jar containing the mercury from my hand. "During a séance, chronological time is suspended," he murmured in a slow, tired voice. "Spiritual time is a time of equilibrium that is neither reality nor a dream. Yet, it is a time that exists in space." He emphasized that I had been plummeted into an event that had happened a long time ago. "The past has no time sequence," he continued. "Today can be joined up with yesterday, with events of many years ago." He fastened my watch around my wrist. "The best thing is not to talk about these matters. What happens is vague and elusive and not meant to be put into words."

Anxious to catch up with doña Mercedes, I agreed with him halfheartedly. Leon Chirino, however, determined to keep me in his house, repeated again and again that Frida Herzog had died on the hills right behind his house.

"I saw doña Mercedes turn transparent," I interrupted him. "Did you see that, too?"

He stared at me, as though he had not expected me to ask about her. But the next moment he was laughing. "She wanted to dazzle you," he said brimming with pride. "She's a perfect medium." Half-smiling, he closed his tired eyes. He seemed to be savoring some treasured vision. Then gently he pushed me outside and, without a sound, closed the door behind me.

For a moment I stood bewildered outside Leon Chirino's door. I knew I had lost track of time during the séance, but somehow I couldn't believe that the whole night had gone by and that I had failed to hear the rain. Yet, it was dawn and there were puddles on the sidewalk.

A parrot screeched somewhere in the distance. I looked up. Across the street, standing like a shadow by the eucalyptus tree that marked the cement steps leading up the shack-covered hill, was Mercedes Peralta. I ran toward her.

Anticipating my questions, she touched my lips with her finger, then bent low and picked up a small, freshly broken branch lying on the ground. It was still wet with the night's rain. She shook it; the scent of eucalyptus, imprisoned in hundreds of drops, showered on my head.

"We better get going," she said, but instead of heading home, she led me up the hill.

The air smelled of mildewed cardboard. There was no one around. The shacks appeared to be abandoned. Halfway up, we turned onto one of the paths that spread like branches from the wide steps and stopped in front of a yellow-painted house roofed with sheets of corrugated tin.

The unlocked front door opened directly into what seemed to be a bedroom. A narrow, neatly made-up bed stood in the middle of the room. Hairy ferns growing in animal-shaped flower pots rested on stools. Bamboo cages with canaries in them hung from the ceiling. Pants, jackets, and crisply ironed shirts dangled from wrought-iron hooks fastened on the yellow walls.

A man emerged from behind a brightly patterned curtain that I first mistook for a wall decoration.

"Efrain Sandoval!" I exclaimed, wondering what the man from whose store I purchased my notepads and pencils was doing in that place. I was well acquainted with him and his German-born wife, who by speech and manner was more Venezuelan than a born native. Together with their two daughters they lived near the plaza above the stationery-radio-TV shop he owned.

He was in his forties, but his slight build and his delicately featured face made him look much younger. His slanted dark eyes fringed by long, curly lashes shone brightly. He appeared to be amused by some secret thought. As always, he was immaculately dressed; but that morning, his whole being reeked of cigar smoke.

"Were you at the séance?" I asked him in an involuntary tone of incredulity.

Gesturing me to be quiet, he invited us to sit on the bed. "I'll be right back," he promised, vanishing behind the curtain. Shortly, he reappeared, carrying a bamboo tray heavy with food, plates, and cutlery. He cleared off one of the stools and placed the tray on it, and with the flamboyant movements of a maître d', he served us black beans, rice, fried plantains, spicy shredded meat, and coffee.

In nervous anticipation I looked from one to the other, expecting a discussion of the spiritualists' meeting.

"The musiúa is about to burst with curiosity," doña Mercedes announced, a devilish glint in her eyes. "She wants to know why you live up here, when you have such a nice home above your store in town. I would like you to tell her why."

"You would?" Efrain Sandoval asked indifferently as he ate the last of the beans on his plate. He chewed slowly, stalling for time. He rose, walked over to the window, and opened it. For a second or two, he gazed at the pale dawn sky, then turned and stared at me. "I guess you must have a good reason for wanting to know about me?" he added in a questioning tone.

"She does," doña Mercedes answered. "So don't be put off when she comes to your store to pester you for your story."

Efrain Sandoval smiled sheepishly, tilted his stool, and leaned against the wall. He let his gaze wander about the room. There was a remote expression in his eyes; he seemed no longer aware of our presence.

"But what's the point of telling her?" he finally asked without looking at doña Mercedes. "It's not an earth-shaking story. It's rather banal."

"That's the very point of it," she said. "The musiúa has heard all kinds of stories by now. Yours is of particular interest because you never did anything to make it happen. You were just there, placed by a higher order."

"I still don't see how the story of Frida Herzog is going to help the musiúa," Efrain Sandoval insisted.

"Let her worry about that," Mercedes Peralta said dryly. She rose from the bed and motioned me to do likewise.

Efrain Sandoval looked as though he was going to argue the point. Instead he nodded. "As you already know, I have a large house in town," he said, turning toward me. He opened his arms wide. "Yet, I also live here where I can feel the presence of Frida Herzog, who unwittingly gave me everything I have." He moved toward the window, but before closing it he glanced uncertainly at doña Mercedes and asked, "Are you going to give me a cleansing today?"

"Of course." She laughed. "Don't mind the musiúa. She has seen me doing this before."

Efrain Sandoval seemed to vacillate for a moment, then, apparently afraid that there might not be enough time, he promptly took off his coat and lay face up on the bed.

Mercedes Peralta retrieved a small bottle, a white handkerchief, two candles, and two cigars from her dress pocket. Meticulously, she lined them up on the floor at the foot of the bed. She lit one of the candles then a cigar and inhaled deeply. Wrapped in smoke, the murmured words of her incantation tumbled out of her mouth with each exhalation. A wicked smile flittered across her face as she reached for the white handkerchief and the little bottle, half-filled with a mixture of perfumed water and ammonia. She poured a generous amount on the handkerchief and folded it into a perfect square.

"Breathe!" she commanded, and in one swift, well-aimed motion she held the handkerchief under Efrain Sandoval's nose.

Mumbling incoherently, he twisted and turned in an

effort to sit up. Tears rolled down his cheeks, and his moving lips tried in vain to form a plea. Doña Mercedes held him in place quite effortlessly by simply increasing the pressure of her hand over his nose. Soon, he gave up struggling. He crossed his arms over his chest and lay still, utterly exhausted.

Doña Mercedes lit a second cigar. Mumbling a soft prayer, she asked the spirit of Hans Herzog to protect Efrain Sandoval. The last few puffs of smoke she blew into her cupped hands and then ran her fingers over his face, his folded arms, all the way down his legs.

Startled upon hearing a strange sound, I looked around me. The room was filled with smoke, and out of that haze a form appeared, no more than a shadow or a billow of smoke that seemed to be hovering beside the bed.

Efrain Sandoval's deep sleep, punctuated by loud snoring, broke the spell. Mercedes Peralta rose, put all her paraphernalia, including the cigar stubs, into her pocket, then turned to the window and opened it. Pointing her chin to the door, she motioned me to follow.

"Will he be all right?" I asked once we were outside. I had never attended such a short session.

"He'll be fine for another year," she assured me. "Every year, Efrain Sandoval attends a spiritualists' meeting to renew himself." She made a wide sweeping gesture with her arms. "Frida Herzog's spirit roams around here. Efrain believes it has brought him luck. That's why he has chosen to keep this shack while his family lives in town. It isn't true, but his belief doesn't harm anyone. In fact, it brings him relief."

"But who is Frida Herzog?" I asked. "And who is

Hans Herzog? You definitely asked his spirit to protect Efrain."

Doña Mercedes put her hand over my lips. "Musiúa, have patience," she said, bemused. "Efrain will tell you in time. All I can say is that the one who moved the wheel of chance for Efrain wasn't Frida Herzog. She had no reason to. It was actually a ghost who did it. The ghost of Hans Herzog."

Doña Mercedes leaned heavily against me as we walked down the hill. "I can hardly wait to get into my hammock," she mumbled. "I'm dead tired."

Afraid that someone might tamper with or perhaps even steal his moped, Efrain pulled it up onto the sidewalk and into the hallway of the new two-story building owned by his employer, Frida Herzog.

The Finnish woman and her children who lived in the bottom apartment watched him resentfully. They considered the hallway their front porch. He shrugged his shoulders apologetically and climbed the stairs to Frida Herzog's apartment.

He had worked for the Herzogs since he was an adolescent. It was Hans Herzog who had bought him the moped. The years he worked for him had flown by so fast, Efrain had not even felt them. He had liked his job as an all-around helper and delivery boy in Hans Herzog's poultry business, but what he had enjoyed the most was his employer's gentility and his grand sense of humor. Efrain never had the feeling that he was working but rather that he went to the office every day to get a lesson in the art of good living.

Over the years he had become more like an adopted

son or a disciple of Hans Herzog than an employee. "I thank you, Efrain," he used to tell him, "a man of my nature needs, at a certain age, an unbiased audience, a captive ear."

Hans Herzog had immigrated from Germany before the war, not to make a fortune, but in search of fulfillment. He married late in life because he considered marriage and parenthood a moral necessity. He called them the controlled strains of paradise.

When Hans Herzog had a stroke, it was Efrain who tended him day and night. He could not speak anymore, but he communicated with Efrain just the same through the intensity of his eyes. In his last moments, he made a frantic effort to say something to Efrain; he failed. So he shrugged his shoulders and laughed. And died.

Now, Efrain worked for the man's widow but not in the same capacity and certainly not with the same pleasure. She had sold the poultry business; it reminded her of her husband, she said, but she kept Efrain as an employee because he was the only one who knew how to drive the moped.

Noticing that the door to Frida Herzog's apartment was ajar, he pushed it open without knocking and stepped into the tiny hall that led to the living room.

The room, cluttered with beige upholstered furniture, was divided from the dining area by a grand piano. Glassed-in bookcases stood on either side of an enormous fireplace, which Frida Herzog lit once a year on Christmas Eve.

Efrain moved back a few steps so he could see himself completely in the gilded mirror hanging above the mantel piece. He was in his midtwenties, yet his small wiry frame and his boyish, somehow immature, beardless face, made him look sixteen. With pain-staking absorption he combed his curly hair and adjusted his tie and the cologne-scented handkerchief in his breast pocket. Being poor was no reason to look untidy, he thought, and he glanced over his shoulder to make sure the back of his coat was smooth and unwrinkled.

Whistling, he crossed the room and stepped out onto the wide balcony. Potted rubber trees, orchids, ceiling-high ferns, and bird cages partially hid Frida Herzog. Stout and solidly built, she sat at her desk, a white wrought-iron table with a heavy, opaque glass top.

"I've been waiting for you since nine o'clock," she said by way of greeting. The angry expression in her blue eyes was magnified by the thick, horn-rimmed glasses posted menacingly on her prominent nose.

"What peace! What coolness one breathes in this veritable heaven!" Efrain exclaimed in a tone of exaltation. He knew that flattering Frida Herzog about her jungle always put her in a good mood. "Even at noon your canaries sing like angels." Imitating the call of the birds, he took off his coat and hung it carefully over the back of a chair.

"Never mind the birds," she said crossly, motioning him to sit across from her. "I pay you a salary, and I expect you to be here on time."

"I was held up by prospective clients," he said importantly.

She regarded him doubtfully, dabbing at the tiny drops of perspiration on her upper lip and forehead with a delicately embroidered handkerchief. "Did you take any orders?" She gave him no opportunity to answer but pushed several of the slender white boxes on the table toward him. "Check these," she grumbled.

Undaunted by her bad mood, he cheerfully informed her that the orders were as good as written up and signed. Then, almost reverently, he opened the white boxes before him and gazed in awe at the bulky, silver-plated ballpoint pens lying luxuriously in the dark blue velvet-lined cases. He uncapped one pen, unscrewed its top, and carefully inspected a small rectangular piece of metal and rubber resting on a minute ink pad. It was a seal. To lift it out, he pressed the hollow end of the pen's cap on the perfectly fitting mount projecting from the metal plate. He stamped the box, screwed the seal back, and capped the pen. He did the same with the other pens; he made sure this way that the customers' names and addresses were spelled correctly.

"How many times do I have to tell you that I want no fingerprints on the pens?" Frida Herzog snapped, grabbing the pen from his hands. She polished it with her handkerchief and slipped it back inside the box. "Now wrap them!"

He gave her a hostile glance and did as she ordered. "Do you also want me to glue the address labels on them?" he asked as soon as he finished wrapping the last one.

"Yes. Do that." She handed him six neatly typed labels from a small, metal filing box. "Make sure to apply the glue evenly."

"What?" Efrain retorted irritably. He had not understood a word she said. Her accent, barely noticeable under ordinary circumstances, flared up whenever she was angry or afraid, making it difficult to understand what she was saying.

Frida Herzog spoke slowly, enunciating each word carefully as she repeated, "Apply the glue evenly all the way to the corners of the labels." She looked at him sternly and added, "I want the labels to stay glued."

"If looks could kill, I would be dead," he mumbled, bringing both hands to his head in a mock gesture of agony. Then he smiled at her entrancingly as he cursed her under his breath.

"What did you say?" Frida Herzog asked, her accent so thick that the words came out slurred.

"I said that it won't take me any time at all to do what you want." He loosened his blue-striped tie and the collar of his stiffly starched shirt, then reached for the gourd-shaped glue container on the table and squeezed a small amount of glue on each label. Meticulously, he spread it evenly with the rubber-tipped nozzle all the way to the corners and then pasted the labels to the small, perfectly wrapped, marked boxes containing the ballpoint pens.

"That's nicely done, Efrain." A hint of approval momentarily played upon Frida Herzog's plump, rosy face. She never got over being surprised at the neat way he adhered the labels exactly in the middle of the boxes. She couldn't have done it better herself.

Encouraged by her compliment, he decided to ask about the pen she had promised him. Although he had already given up hope of ever receiving one from her, he nevertheless reminded her at every opportunity. Each time she had a different excuse for not honoring her promise. "When are you going to give me a pen?" he repeated, his voice high and urgent.

Frida Herzog stared at him in silence, then shifted forward in her chair and planted her elbows firmly on the table. "Haven't I told you before of the difficulties I have had in convincing the manufacturer of the pens to give me the dealership for this area? Don't you realize that to be my age"——she never said how old she was——"and to be a woman is a great handicap?" She paused for a moment, then with a touch of pride in her tone, added, "Just because I am doing so well selling pens doesn't mean I'm in a position to give them away."

"One pen won't break you," Efrain insisted.

"Your pen! Your pen! Is that all you ever think of?" Indignation made her voice quiver. She thrust her face forward, only inches away from his. Her eyes didn't even blink as they held his fixed.

Mesmerized, he just kept staring at her blue eyes in which a glimmer of madness was just discernible.

Perhaps sensing she had gone too far, she shifted her gaze away. Slowly, her expression softened. In a coaxing tone she went on to say that she was certain that together they could sell thousands of pens. They would sell them not only in town and in the surrounding hamlets but all over the country. "Be patient, Efrain," she entreated, leaning even closer toward him. "When business expands, we'll both get rich!" She slumped back in her chair and ran her hand affectionately over the small, gray filing box.

"But all I want is a pen, you crazy old idiot," Efrain mumbled despairingly.

Frida Herzog didn't hear him. Dreamily, she gazed at her bird cages, a sad, faraway look in her eyes.

"I work very hard," Efrain said in a loud clear voice. "Not only have I been delivering pens for you, but I've gotten nearly all your customers myself." He ignored her attempt to interrupt him. "And you won't even give me a pen."

"I'm not saying that you haven't done well," she said peevishly. "All I'm trying to do is make you understand that at the beginning of any business venture, sacrifices have to be made." She paced about the balcony, her voice rising sharply as she continued. "Very soon I'll not only give you a pen and a commission but make you a partner." She came to stand in front of him. "I'm a businesswoman. I can envision these pens in every household all over the country. Efrain, we'll sell a pen to every literate person in this country."

She moved away from him and leaned over the railing. "Just look at those hills!" she cried out. "Look at those shacks!" With a sweep of her arm that made the wide sleeves of her housecoat flutter, she took in the whole panorama before her. A radiant smile parted her lips as she turned to face him. "Just think of all those shacks in the hills. What opportunities! We'll sell pens to the illiterates as well. Instead of having to make an X every time they need to sign a document, they can instead stamp their name on any paper that needs their signature." She clapped her hands in childish delight, then sat beside him and reached into her pocket. "This," she declared holding up her own gold-plated pen, "is the ideal answer for everyone's problem!" Gingerly, she unscrewed the pen, hooked the tiny seal onto the cap's hollow end, and stamped the back of each of the boxes on the table. Proudly, she read her name and address printed in minute, purple letters. "There are hundreds of people living in those shacks. I just know they'll all want one of these pens." She touched his arm. "Efrain, as of today I'll pay you a commission on every pen you sell in those hills."

"They can't afford one," he reminded her sarcastically.

"I'll do something I've never done before," she

declared bombastically. "I'll let them have the pens on credit." With a sweeping motion, she distractedly scooped the small pen boxes—including her gold pen—into Efrain's worn leather satchel. "You'd better go now."

A look of sheer incredulity spread across his face. He looked up at her, wondering if she had noticed her mistake, then nonchalantly reached for his satchel. "I'll see you tomorrow," he said.

"You only have six pens to deliver this afternoon," she reminded him. "I'll be expecting you back by five o'clock. These pens have already been paid for. You won't have to wait around for the money."

"It's the middle of the day," Efrain protested. "You can't expect me to go in this heat. Besides, I've got to eat first. I also need money to cover my traveling expenses." Noticing her blank expression, he clarified, "I need to get gas for the moped."

She handed him some small change. "Don't forget to ask for a receipt," she said, glaring at him over her glasses.

He shrugged with displeasure. "Stingy idiot. This won't even fill the tank," he said and hissed under his breath.

"What did you call me?" Frida Herzog snapped.

He bit back the insult that rose to his lips. "This isn't enough to fill the gas tank," he said, slipping the coins in his pocket. He took out his comb and, ignoring her disapproving expression, ran it through his unruly black hair.

"Four of the deliveries are within walking distance," she admonished. "There is no need to run the moped around town. I've walked those distances myself and even farther. If I can do it at my age, I would certainly expect a young man like you could do it."

Whistling softly, he adjusted his tie and put on his coat. With a casual wave of his hand he turned and walked out into the living room. A loud sigh escaped his lips. His eyes widened, expressing both surprise and admiration.

Sitting in one of the bulky armchairs, her bare legs hanging over the armrest, was Antonia, Frida Herzog's only daughter. She didn't cover her legs but looked at him with tender concern—the way women look at babies—and then smiled provocatively.

She was a small, pretty woman in her midtwenties; but her worn-out, haggard expression and the air of despair about her made her look much older. She was gone most of the time. Much to her mother's embarrassment, Antonia took off with men every chance she got, only returning periodically to visit. No wonder the old woman was in such a foul mood, Efrain thought. He felt a surge of passion for Antonia and wished he could stay and talk to her; but knowing that Frida Herzog could hear them from the balcony, he merely puckered his lips and blew Antonia a soundless kiss before he walked out the front door.

Frida Herzog stood motionless by the balcony railing. She blinked repeatedly. The burning sun and the vibrant air made her eyes tear. Heat waves billowed in the nearby foothills, transforming the multicolored shacks into a hazy flickering collage.

Not too long ago those hills had been green. Almost overnight, squatters had transformed them into shanty towns. Like mushrooms after a heavy rain, the shacks

had just popped up one morning, and no one had dared
to pull them down.

Her glance strayed to Efrain's noisy moped sput-
tering along in the street below. She hoped that he
would first call on the two secretaries at the
pharmaceutical laboratory who had been so enthu-
siastic about the pens. Frida Herzog was certain that
once the two girls showed off their dazzling new pens
to their co-workers, orders would be coming in
promptly.

Chuckling to herself, she turned and gazed across
the balcony into the living room where her daughter
sat. She heaved a deep sigh and disappointedly shook
her head from side to side. There was no way to make
Antonia understand that she didn't want bare legs on
the beige, raw silk–covered armchairs. She had had
such high hopes for her beautiful daughter. Antonia
could have married any number of rich men. It was
beyond Frida Herzog's comprehension why the girl
had married a penniless, unambitious salesman, who
one day just walked out on her. She couldn't remember
whether it had been during lunch or dinner when he
got up from the table and never returned.

With an air of resignation, Frida Herzog stepped
into the living room, forcing her lips into a pleasant
smile.

"Really! Efrain is getting more impudent every day,"
she said, sitting in the armchair opposite Antonia. "I'm
afraid that if I give him a pen, he'll quit work. That's
all he's interested in."

"You know what he's like," Antonia said. She didn't
look up but continued to buffer her long, well-cared-
for nails. "So, all Efrain wants is a pen. What's wrong
with that?"

"He should buy one!" Frida Herzog snapped spitefully.

"Really, Mother," Antonia chided. "Those silly trinkets are way too expensive. Obviously, he can't afford one."

"Don't make me laugh," Frida Herzog snorted. "I pay him well. If he wouldn't waste his money on clothes, he could—"

Antonia's words stopped her in midsentence. "Those pens are only a fad," she stated, "and Efrain knows it, too. In a few months or perhaps only weeks, people will no longer want them."

Frida Herzog straightened in her chair as if her spine had been pulled up. Her face was red with anger. "Don't you dare tell me that," she yelled. "This pen will go on forever!"

"Calm down, Mother. You can't believe that," Antonia said in a conciliatory tone. "Why do you think you're selling pens in this godforsaken place? Don't you realize it's because no one in Caracas wants them any longer?"

"That's not true," Frida Herzog shouted. "Some day I'll have the dealership for the entire region, maybe even for the whole country. If I were the manufacturer of the pens, I would be trying to expand internationally. That's what I would do. Create an empire."

Antonia laughed, then turned toward the mirror above the mantel piece. Streaks of premature gray laced her dark blond hair. There were wrinkles on either side of her mouth. Her large blue eyes would have been beautiful had it not been for their hard, embittered expression. Not age, but exhaustion and despair were beginning to rob her face and body of its youth.

"Efrain has skills you haven't yet discovered," Antonia said. "No one can equal him in finding ways to make money. But to think you can get rich on pens! That's a joke. Why can't you simply use him in what he's best at?"

A contemptuous grin spread over Frida Herzog's face. "Use him at what he's best at! You think that I don't know what you have been up to in the last few months. I might be a little deaf, but I'm not stupid." Seeing Antonia was about to rise, she hastily added, "You never had any class. Making out with Efrain! You should be ashamed of yourself. He's a mulatto, or whatever! He's colored."

Her anger spent, Frida Herzog leaned back in her armchair and closed her eyes. She wished she could retract her words, yet when she spoke again, her voice was still querulous. "Isn't there anything you want out of life?"

"I want to marry Efrain," Antonia said softly.

"Over my dead body!" Frida Herzog yelled. "I'll disinherit you. I'll throw you out of this house." She gasped for air. "Let me tell you, I'm going to take his moped away and fire him."

But Antonia no longer heard her. She had left the living room, slamming the door behind her.

For a few seconds Frida Herzog gazed at that door through which her daughter had disappeared, expecting her to return at any moment. Her eyes felt heavy with tears that would not fall. Silently, she headed toward her bedroom down the hall.

She sat in front of the kidney-shaped dressing table. With trembling fingers, she took off her glasses and examined herself in the mirror. She ought to get a new permanent, she thought, combing her fingers through her wispy gray hair. Her eyes, encircled by dark shadows, were sunken. Her skin, once as smooth and white as fine porcelain, had aged inexorably, eroded by the relentless tropical sun.

Tears flooded her eyes. "Oh God," she said softly. "Don't let me get ill and die in this foreign place."

She heard soft steps outside; no doubt Antonia had been listening by the door. She was too tired to worry about it. She lay on the bed and dozed in a half-pleasant sleep, lulled by the gentle sound of a Mozart sonata. The thought that Antonia was actually playing the grand piano filled her with intense joy. The girl had always played so well.

It was almost four when Frida Herzog awoke. As usual after a nap, she felt refreshed and in good spirits. She decided to wear the polka-dot silk dress and the matching shoes Antonia had given her for Christmas.

The sun, already halfway down the sky, filled the living room with shadows. She looked out across the balcony at the brightly colored shacks on the distant hills. They appeared to be so much closer in the afternoon light. She went to the kitchen and prepared her afternoon tray: coffee, sugar, cream, and a plateful of poppy-seed pastries.

"Antonia," she called affectionately, as she sat down in one of the armchairs. She listened for the familiar clicking of heels on the hard tile floor before pouring the coffee. She called again, but there was no answer. She must have gone out, Frida Herzog decided, unfolding a white linen napkin on her lap.

It was close to five when she checked the time on her gold wristwatch. Efrain should be back any minute now, she thought. Perhaps he had been telling the truth and had indeed found her a new client. Although she never voiced it, she had long ago recognized that despite his lack of ambition, he was good at dealing with people. Too bad she would have to let him go. She would have a hard time finding a replacement for him, but she couldn't possibly consent to having him around when she knew Antonia's plans for him. The thought that her daughter might have wanted only to upset her crossed her mind. She couldn't really believe that Antonia would marry that boy.

By six o'clock Frida Herzog was so restless that she called the two secretaries at the laboratory and the owner of the clothing store near the plaza. The pens had not been delivered.

Dumbstruck, she stared at the telephone, then stepped out on the balcony, and with nervous hands, she turned over every item on her desk. "He took my pen!" she shrieked. She headed for the front door and hurried down the stairs out into the street. She neither saw the startled faces of the neighbors gossiping on the sidewalk nor heard their greetings as she dashed around the corner. Only upon reaching the foot of the hill did she stop to rest. Wishing she had put on more comfortable shoes instead of high heels, she slowly climbed the wide dirt path leading to the shacks.

She had never been to Efrain's house, but she knew more or less where it was. She had heard about the dangers of those shanty towns, where no stranger dared to go. Even the police were reluctant to pursue criminals that chose to hide in those hills. She was not afraid. Who would want to harm an old woman? She felt quite reassured upon noticing that not all the dwellings were shacks. Some were made of cement blocks, and a few were even two stories high.

She paused frequently to catch her breath, to quiet her rapidly pounding heart. People stared at her curiously. Barefoot, half-naked children stopped their games and giggled as she walked by. Just before reaching the top of the hill, she turned around and gazed at the town below. A gentle breeze cooled her flushed face.

Bathed in the mellow, diffused glow of the twilight, still vibrant with the afternoon heat, the town had never looked more beautiful. Overcome by an odd, undefinable premonition of doom, her eyes searched for the silhouette of her building.

A girl's friendly voice dispelled her feelings. "Do you need any help?" she asked, regarding her curiously. "Are you lost?"

"I'm looking for Efrain Sandoval's house," Frida Herzog responded. So absorbed had she been in locating her building, she hadn't noticed that it was almost night. "Can you tell me where Efrain lives?" She repeated her question several times, while the girl kept staring at her, a blank expression on her face. It was obvious that she had not understood a word she was saying.

"You have gone too far," an old man squatting nearby informed her politely. He was barely outlined by the faint light escaping from the unevenly hammered boards of a shack. "Go down a bit and turn left onto the walkway. It's the yellow house. You can't miss it. It looks like a canary." There was a worried look in his eyes as he watched her unsteady steps down the hill. "You'd better go home though," he called after her. "There are a lot of drunks around at this time, and they get into fights."

But Frida Herzog didn't hear his warning words.

They were drowned by the angry shouts of men and the sound of hurried, thudding steps. Before she had a chance to turn and see what was happening, she felt a sharp blow. The ground seemed to move underneath her, and she crashed through a makeshift railing put up to mark, rather than safeguard, a vertical drop. For an instant, she saw in horror how the rock-covered ground below advanced to meet her. There were voices, some loud, some soft, and then there was only silence and darkness.

Efrain awoke with a start. He had had an uncanny dream. As he had done so many times before in his sleep, he had again talked with Hans Herzog. His friend was urging him to take matters in his own hands and marry Antonia. Together they should take a tour around the world. Efrain had laughed; he told his friend that he would rather hear one of his stories about those foreign places. Hans Herzog had refused, saying that it was time for Efrain to see those places himself.

Although he was accustomed to the vividness of his dreams of Hans Herzog, this particular one had been so suggestive; it had left a lingering sense of reality, which Efrain could not dispel. To this day he had doggedly refused to admit that his friend and employer was dead. After all, he saw him and talked to him every night in his dreams.

Efrain lit the kerosene lamp on the table by his bed and opened the bottle of beer he had put on a stool. He poured it into a tall glass and blew the foam from the rim before taking a long gulp. He didn't mind that the beer was warm.

"To taking matters in my own hands!" he toasted, removing the gold-plated pen from his satchel. Chuckling contentedly, he unscrewed the seal, hooked it onto the cap's hollow end, and stamped his arm repeatedly.

A week ago he had decided to take matters in his own hands and arranged with an engraver at a jewelry store to make him an exact replica of the seal but with his name on it. Efrain had no doubt that luck had intervened in his favor. How else could he explain this startling coincidence: the day he was to pick up the stamp bearing his name and address, Frida Herzog, by mistake, had put her own gold-plated pen in his satchel, along with the six he was to deliver.

He poured the rest of the beer in his glass and sipped contentedly. Perhaps some unconscious part of Frida Herzog had wanted him to have the pen. He liked to believe that.

An insistent knocking on his door intruded on his thoughts.

"Efrain!" someone called, the voice urgent. "An old foreign lady who was looking for you has been knocked down by a drunk."

"Frida Herzog!" Grabbing the satchel from the table he rushed outside toward the crowd gathered at the bottom of the hill.

"It can't be," he repeated, pushing the people aside. She was sprawled on the ground. He kneeled down by her. The dim light of a kerosene lamp cast a yellowish gleam on her face. He tried to say something, but not a word passed his lips. All he could do was stare into her pale blue eyes. Without her glasses, which lay smashed beside her, her eyes looked wide, watchful, almost childlike. The suggestion of a frown hovered around her lips, slightly parted to reveal her white teeth. He felt that there was something she wanted to say.

"I've got the pens," he said reassuringly, taking the six boxes from the satchel. He held them close to her face. "I couldn't deliver them today," he lied, "because I got involved with filling out some order forms for you. We have four new clients."

Her frown deepened. Her lips moved, mumbling something about his being fired from the job and about Antonia. Her eyes grew wider, her pupils dilated, and then life ran out.

"I work for her," Efrain said to no one in particular. "Life is so strange. Only this morning she gave me this most beautiful pen," he explained, removing the gold-plated pen from his pocket. With precise, careful movements he hooked the seal to the pen's cap and pressed it against his forearm. "Efrain Sandoval. The Canary Shack. Curmina," he read his name and address in a loud clear voice. "And I can arrange for any of you to buy one of these precious pens on credit."

20

It was Sunday morning, and I was sitting with doña Mercedes in the plaza, waiting for Candelaria to come out of church. Only one hour earlier, I had had my last meeting with Efrain Sandoval.

On a nearby bench was a well-dressed, dignified old man, reading out loud from a Caracas newspaper. He read in a grave voice, absorbed in what seemed important to him; he never noticed the smiles of the people around him.

Across the street, a disheveled old man came out of a bar that was already open. He put on his hat, and clutching a bottle in a plastic sack tightly under his arm, he walked down the street, coughing and wheezing.

With an inexplicable feeling of sadness I glanced at doña Mercedes. She was wearing sunglasses, and I couldn't see the expression in her eyes as she looked straight ahead of her. She folded her arms across her chest and hugged herself as if touched by a sudden cold wind.

She listened attentively as I tried to tell her how I had understood so far all the stories I had heard.

"You are showing me the different ways to manipulate that force that Florinda calls *intent*," I said.

192

"To make it move is not the same as to manipulate it," she corrected me, still hugging herself. "And I'm trying much more than that. As I said, I'm putting you temporarily under the shadow of those people so that you can feel the wheel of chance moving. Without that feeling, everything you're doing will be empty. You must follow the ups and downs of the person who is telling you his tale; for an instant you must be under his shadow."

"How about Efrain Sandoval? He certainly had nothing to do with what happened to him. Why should I be placed under his shadow?" I asked.

"Because the wheel moved for him. He didn't move it himself, yet it's his life that changed. I wanted you to feel that change, to feel that movement of the wheel.

"As I've already mentioned to you, a ghost, the spirit of Hans Herzog, moved it for him. Just as Victor Julio, at the moment of dying, moved the wheel of chance and ruined the life of Octavio Cantú, Hans Herzog moved that wheel after he was dead and enriched the life of Efrain Sandoval."

Doña Mercedes took off her glasses and looked straight into my face. She opened her mouth to add something, but instead she smiled and rose from the bench. "Mass will be over any moment now," she said. "Let's wait for Candelaria at the church door."

PART
SIX

21

"Musiúa, are you there?" Mercedes Peralta whispered, opening the door to my room noiselessly. Outlined by the weak beam of my reading light, she was the picture of a witch, with her long black dress and her wide-brimmed felt hat that hid half of her face.

"Don't turn on the light," she said as I reached for the switch. "I can't bear the brightness of a bulb." She sat on my bed. Her brow was set tightly in concentration as she smoothed out the wrinkles in my blanket. She looked up and fixed her unblinking eyes on my face.

Self-consciously I ran my fingers over my cheeks and chin, wondering whether there was something wrong.

Giggling, she turned toward the night table and began neatly stacking my small, thin notepads. "I must go to Chuao right now," she finally said, her voice low and grave.

"Chuao?" I repeated. "At this hour?" Seeing her emphatic nod, I added, "We'll get stuck in the mud if it rains." Chuao was a village near the coast, at least an hour's drive from Curmina.

"It will rain," she casually admitted. "But with your jeep we won't get stuck." She sat hunched over the night table, biting her lower lip, deliberating whether to say more. "I have to be there tonight by midnight," she murmured in a tone that betrayed urgency rather than desire. "I have to get some plants that will be available only tonight."

"It's past eleven," I pointed out, checking the illuminated dial of my wristwatch. "We'll never make it by midnight."

Grinning, doña Mercedes reached for my jeans and shirt hanging at the front of the iron bedstead. "We'll make your watch stop counting the hours." A faint smile lit up her face; her eyes, trusting and expectant, held mine. "You'll take me, won't you?"

Heavy raindrops drummed on the jeep the moment we left town. Within seconds the rain came in a solid sheet, dense and dark. I slowed down, unable to see, irritated by the squeaking of the wipers clearing an arc of glass that was instantly blurred again. The trees fringing the road waved indistinctly beside and above us, giving the impression that we were driving through a tunnel. Only the intermittent solitary bark of a dog indicated that we had passed another shack.

The rainstorm ended with the same abruptness with which it had begun, yet the sky remained overcast. The clouds hung oppressively low. I kept my eyes glued to the windshield, intent on avoiding the frogs, which, momentarily blinded by the headlights, jumped across the road.

All at once, as if they had been erased from the sky, the clouds vanished the moment we turned onto the road that led to the coast. The moon shone brightly upon a flat landscape where an occasional tree swayed gently in the breeze, its leaves shining silvery in the unreal light.

I stopped in the middle of a crossroad and got out of the jeep. The air, warm and humid, smelled of the mountains and the sea.

"What made you stop here, Musiúa?" Mercedes Peralta asked, her voice full of bewilderment as she got out and stood beside me.

"I'm a witch," I explained, looking into her eyes. I knew that if I'd told her that I just wanted to stretch my legs, she wouldn't believe me. "I was born in a place like this," I went on, "somewhere between the mountains and the sea."

Mercedes Peralta frowned at me, then a humorous, delighted twinkle shone in her eyes. Giggling uncontrollably, she sat on the wet ground and pulled me down with her. "Perhaps you weren't born like a normal human being; maybe a *curiosa* lost you on her way across the sky," she said.

"What is a *curiosa?*" I asked.

She regarded me cheerfully and explained that *curiosas* were witches who were no longer concerned with the obvious aspects of sorcery: symbolic paraphernalia, rituals, and incantations. "*Curiosas,*" she whispered, "are beings preoccupied with things of the eternal. They are like spiders, spinning fine, invisible threads between the known and the unknown." She took off her hat, then lay on her back, flat on the ground, with her head precisely in the middle of the crossroad, pointing north. "Lie down, Musiúa," she urged me, stretching her arms toward the east and the west. "Make sure the top of your head touches mine and that your arms and legs are in the same position as mine."

It was comfortable lying head to head on the crossroad. Although separated by our hair, I had the feeling our scalps were fused together. I turned my head sideways and to my great amusement noticed how much longer her arms were than mine. Seemingly aware of my discovery, doña Mercedes moved her arms closer to mine.

"If someone sees us, they'll think we're crazy," I said.

"Perhaps," she conceded. "However, if it's people who usually walk by this crossroad at this time of the night, they will run away in fright, thinking they have seen two *curiosas* ready for flight."

We were silent for a moment, but before I asked her about the *curiosas'* flight, she spoke again.

"The reason I was so interested to know why you stopped at the crossroad," she said, "was that there are people who swear they have seen a *curiosa* lying naked on this very spot. They say that she had wings growing out of her back and that they saw her body become translucent white as she took off into the sky."

"I saw your body turn transparent at the séance for Efrain Sandoval," I said.

"Of course you did," she retorted with an amused casualness. "I did that just for you because I know that you'll never be a healer. You're a medium and, perhaps, even a witch but not a healer. I should know it, I'm a witch myself."

"What makes one a witch?" I asked in between fits of giggles. I did not want to take her seriously.

"Witches are creatures not only capable of moving the wheel of chance," she replied, "but also capable of making their own link. What would you say if at this moment we took off flying, joined at our heads?"

For a second or two, I had the most terrifying apprehension. Then, a feeling of utter indifference invaded me.

"Repeat any of the incantations the spirit of my ancestor taught you," she commanded. "I'll say it with you."

Our voices merged into a single harmonious sound, filling the space around us, enveloping us into a giant cocoon. The words rose into a deep continuous line, carrying us up and up. I saw the clouds advancing at me. We began to turn like a wheel until everything was black.

Someone was shaking me vigorously. I woke up with an unexpected jolt. I was sitting behind the steering wheel of my jeep. And I was driving! I had no recollection of walking back to the car.

"Don't fall asleep," doña Mercedes said. "We'll crash and die like two fools."

I stepped on the brakes and turned off the ignition. The thought that I had been driving asleep made me tremble with fear.

"Where are we going?" I asked. My voice sounded an octave lower.

She smiled and made a gesture of exasperation, raising her eyebrows. "You get tired too easily, Musiúa," she said. "You're too little. But, I think that's your best feature. If you were bigger, you would be unbearable."

I insisted on knowing our destination. I meant it in terms of physical locale, so that I could drive with a sense of direction.

"We are going to meet Leon Chirino and another

friend," she informed me. "Let's go. I'll give you directions as you drive."

I started the jeep and drove in silence. I was still drowsy.

"Is Leon Chirino a medium and a healer?" I asked shortly.

She laughed softly but did not answer. "What makes you think that?" she asked after a long moment.

"There's something quite inexplicable about him," I said. "He reminds me of you."

"Does he now?" she asked mockingly, then in a sudden serious tone she admitted that Leon Chirino was a medium and a clairvoyant.

Lost in thought, I did not hear her directions and was jolted when she yelled. "You passed it! You've got to back up now," she admonished, pointing to a tall *bucare* tree. "Pull up there!" She smiled, then added, "We have to walk from here on."

The tree marked the entrance to a narrow path. The ground was covered with small flowers. I knew them to be red, but they appeared black in the moonlight. *Bucares* hardly ever grow by themselves; usually, they are found in groves, shading coffee and cacao trees.

Following a narrow, overgrown trail bordered by other *bucare* trees, we headed toward a cluster of hills looming darkly before us. There were no other sounds than Mercedes Peralta's uneven breathing and the crackling of twigs being crushed under our feet. The path ended in front of a low house bordered by a wide clearing of hard-packed earth. Its mud walls, plastered over a cane frame, were badly weathered. The roof was partially covered with zinc sheets and dried palm fronds. Deep eaves extended to make a wide porch.

The front had no windows, only a narrow door through which a faint light escaped.

Doña Mercedes pushed the door open. Flickering candles cast more shadows than light in a sparsely furnished room. Leon Chirino, sitting on a straight-backed chair, stared at us with an expression of surprise and delight. Haltingly, he stood up, embraced the healer warmly, and guided her to the chair he had just vacated.

He greeted me and jokingly shook my hand. "Let me introduce you to one of the greatest healers around," he said. "Second only to doña Mercedes herself."

But before he could continue, someone cried out, "I'm Agustín."

Only then did I notice the low-hanging hammock in the corner. A small man lay in it. His body was half-twisted, one foot touching the ground, so that he could rock the hammock back and forth. He didn't seem particularly young, nor was he old. He was perhaps in his thirties, yet his hollowed cheeks and sharp bones made him look like a starved child. The most remarkable thing about him was his eyes. They were light blue, and in his black face they shone with a dazzling intensity.

Awkwardly, I stood in the middle of the room. There was something eerie about the uncertain light of the candles playing with our shadows on the walls, gauzy with cobwebs. The Spartan furniture—a table, three chairs, two stools, and a cot, all meticulously arranged against the wall—imparted an unlived-in atmosphere to the room.

"Do you live here?" I asked Agustín.

"No. I don't," he said, approaching me. "This is

my summer palace." Pleased with his joke, he threw his head back and laughed.

Embarrassed, I moved toward the nearest stool and screamed as something sharp scratched my ankle. A hideous, dirty-looking cat stared up at me.

"There is no need to yell the place down," Agustín said and gathered the scrawny feline in his arms. It began to purr the instant he rubbed its head. "She likes you. Do you want to touch her?"

I shook my head emphatically. It wasn't so much the fleas and the mangy bare spots scattered over its yellowish fur that I minded, but its piercing yellow-green slitted eyes that never left my face.

"We better go if we want to get the plants in time," Leon Chirino said, helping doña Mercedes to her feet. He unhooked the oil lamp hanging from a nail behind the door, lit it, and then signaled us to follow him.

A low-arched doorway covered by a plastic curtain led into a back room that served as a kitchen and storage area. One side of the room opened to a large plot filled with short, stubby trees and tall shrubs. In the faint light of the lantern, it looked like an abandoned fruit orchard.

We squeezed through a gap in the seemingly impenetrable wall of bushes and found ourselves in a desolate landscape. The hillside, with its recently burned underbrush and charred stumps, looked frighteningly grotesque in the moonlight.

Without a sound, Leon Chirino and Agustín vanished.

"Where did they go?" I whispered to doña Mercedes.

"They went ahead," she said vaguely, pointing into the darkness.

Shadows, animated by the oil lamp she carried,

zigzagged beside and ahead of us on the narrow path leading into the thicket. I saw a light in the distance, gleaming through the bushes. Like a glowworm, it appeared and disappeared in quick succession. As we came closer to it, I felt sure I could hear a monotonous chant mingling with the distinct sound of buzzing insects and of leaves stirring in the breeze.

Mercedes Peralta turned off the oil lamp. But before the last glimmer died out, I saw her billowing skirt settle near a crumbling low wall, about twelve feet from where I stood. A glowing cigar illuminated her features. A diaphanous, shimmering radiance escaped through the top of her head. I called out her name, but there was no answer.

Fascinated, I watched a misty cloud of cigar smoke hover directly above me in a circle. It didn't disperse the way smoke would, but stayed fixed in midair for a long moment. Something brushed my cheek. Automatically, I brought my hand to my face and then in utter astonishment gazed at my fingertips; they were phosphorescent. Frightened, I ran toward the low wall where I had seen doña Mercedes sit down. I had barely moved a few steps, when I was intercepted by Leon Chirino and Agustín.

"Where are you going, Musiúa?" Leon Chirino asked mockingly.

"I have to help doña Mercedes collect her plants."

My response seemed to amuse them. They chuckled. Leon Chirino patted me on the head, and Agustín daringly grabbed my thumb and squeezed it as if it were a rubber pump.

"We have to wait here patiently," Agustín said. "I've just pumped patience inside you through your thumb."

"She brought me here to help her," I insisted.

"Sure," he said reassuringly. "You have to help her but not with her plants." Taking my arm, he guided me toward a fallen tree trunk. "Let's wait for doña Mercedes here."

Leaves hung from Mercedes Peralta's forehead, silvery green and shining. Quietly, she fastened the oil lamp on a branch, then squatted on the ground and proceeded to sort the plants she had collected into separate piles. Verbena roots were prescribed for menstrual pains. Valerian roots soaked in rum were an ideal remedy for nervousness, irritability, anxiety, and nightmares. *Torco* roots, soaked in rum, cured anemia and yellow fever. *Guaritoto* roots, basically a male remedy, were prescribed for bladder difficulties. Rosemary and rue were used mainly as disinfectants. *Malva* leaves were applied on skin rashes, and *Artemisia* boiled in sugarcane juice eased menstrual pains, killed parasites, and reduced fevers. *Zabila* cured asthma.

"But you grow all these plants in your yard," I said puzzled. "Why did you come here to collect them?"

Agustín grinned gleefully. "Let me tell you something, Musiúa," he whispered, bringing his head close to mine. "These plants have grown out of corpses." He made a sweeping gesture with his hand. "We are in the middle of a cemetery."

Alarmed, I looked around. There were neither tombstones nor mounds to indicate that we were in a graveyard, but I hadn't seen any tombstones in the other cemetery either.

"Our ancestors are buried here," Agustín said and crossed himself. "On nights like this, when a full moon alters the distance of graves and paints white shadows at the foot of trees, one can hear a pitiful moaning and the rattling of chains. Men carrying their cutoff heads wander about. They are the ghosts of slaves who, after having dug a deep hole to bury their masters' treasures, were decapitated and interred with the gold. But there is no need to be frightened," Agustín hastened to add. "All they want is a bit of rum. If you give them some, they will tell you where the treasures are buried.

"There are also ghosts of friars who died blaspheming and now want to confess their sins, but there is no one to hear them. And there are the ghosts of pirates who came all the way to Chuao in search of the Spaniards' gold." He chuckled, then added in a confidential tone, "There are also the lonely ghosts, who whistle at passersby. These are the simplest of them all. They don't ask for much. All these lonely ghosts want is for someone to say an Our Father for them."

Mercedes Peralta, a root poised in one hand, slowly lifted her head. Her dark eyes held mine in their gaze. "Agustín has an inexhaustible supply of stories," she said. "Each tale he garnishes to the limit."

Agustín rose. The way he stretched his body and limbs gave the impression that he was boneless. He plopped down in front of doña Mercedes and buried his head in her lap.

"We better get going," she said, stroking his head tenderly. "I'm sending the musiúa to your place in a few days."

"But I treat only children," Agustín stammered, looking up at me with a sad, apologetic face.

"She doesn't need a healing." Doña Mercedes laughed. "All she wants is to watch you and to hear your stories."

22

I sat up with a jolt. Something had plopped down on my bed by my feet with a forceful thump. The dog sleeping nearby raised its head, pricked its ears, but hearing nothing other than my mumbled imprecations, put its muzzle back on its forepaws. For a moment, I was totally disoriented as to where I was. But when I heard doña Mercedes' soft, yet persistent, murmur, I realized I was in the house of Leon Chirino's brother, in a small town an hour's drive from Curmina. I was on the cot they had set up for me in the kitchen. I had driven Leon Chirino and doña Mercedes there in the middle of the night, for they had to conduct a private séance for his brother.

Closing my eyes, I settled back on the lumpy pillow and abandoned myself to the comforting sound of the healer's voice. I felt the sound wrap itself around me. I was definitely falling asleep when another thumping noise woke me up again.

The musty blanket I was covered with was all bunched up around my neck. I half rose to straighten it out and screamed upon seeing Agustín's cat perched on my knee.

"Why do you always shriek when you see my pet?" His voice coming from the darkness was full of gentle mockery. Agustín, sitting cross-legged at the foot of my cot, reached for his cat. "I've come to protect you from the dog," he explained, his dazzling blue eyes fixed on my face. "Dogs don't really sleep at night. If you open your eyes in the darkness you can see how a dog watches you all night long. That's why they are called watchdogs." He laughed at his own joke.

I opened my mouth to speak to him, but no sound crossed my lips. I reached out, but Agustín and the cat wavered indistinctly before my eyes until they finally faded away. Perhaps they are all outside, I thought, and stepped into the yard, still shrouded by the shadows of dawn. There was no one about. I looked at my wristwatch. Only two hours had passed since doña Mercedes, Leon Chirino, and I had arrived. Realizing that I had had far too little sleep, I went back to my cot, pulled the blanket over my head, and dozed off.

I awoke to the sound of voices and music and the scent of coffee. Leon Chirino, bent over the kerosene stove, was listening to the radio as he strained freshly made coffee through a flannel sieve.

"Did you have a good sleep?" he asked, motioning me to sit down by him.

I joined him at a big, square table covered with brand-new oilcloth. He half filled two cups with coffee and added to each a generous amount of cane liquor.

"For strength," he said, pushing the steaming porcelain cup toward me.

Afraid to get drunk, I took a few hesitant sips. The cup had golden edges and painted roses on its surface.

He replenished his own cup with more coffee and cane liquor.

"Doña Mercedes says that you're clairvoyant," I

said. "Can you tell me what fate has in store for me?"
I hoped that my abrupt question would elicit a candid
response.

"My dear," he said in that charming forbearance
older people show when addressing someone much
younger. "I'm an old friend of doña Mercedes. I live
with her ghosts and her memories. I share her solitude." He spat through his teeth, then taking two cigarettes from the pack on the table, he put one behind
each ear. "You'd better go and see Agustín," he advised. "He starts early. Let me show you the way into
town."

"You really haven't answered my question," I said
undaunted by his eagerness to get me out of the house.

A sardonic, bemused expression appeared on his
face. "I can't tell you what's in store for you," he
affirmed. "Clairvoyants have glimpses of things they
don't understand and then make up the rest."

He took my arm and practically pulled me outside.
"Let me show you the way to Agustín's house," he
repeated. He pointed to a trail winding down the hill.
"If you follow this path, you'll reach town. Anyone
there will tell you where Agustín lives."

"What about doña Mercedes?" I asked.

"We'll come and get you in the evening," he replied,
then bent toward me and in a conspiratorial whisper
he added, "Doña Mercedes and I will be busy the
whole day with my brother's business."

The twittering of bluebirds in the trees and the fra-
grance of the ripe mangoes, shimmering amid the dark
foliage like clumps of gold, filled the air. A well-
trodden path winding down the slope ran into a wide

dirt-packed street and branched off again into the hills at the other end of the hot, sunlit town.

Women sweeping the cement sidewalks in front of their brightly painted houses paused for an instant to return my greeting as I walked by.

"Can you tell me where the healer Agustín lives?" I asked one of the women.

"I sure can," she replied, resting her chin on her hands cupped over the end of the broom handle. In a loud voice—no doubt for the benefit of her curious neighbors—she directed me to the green stucco house at the very end of the street. "It's the one with the big antenna on the roof. You can't miss it." She lowered her voice to a murmur and in a confidential tone assured me that Agustín could cure anything from insomnia to snakebites. Even cancer and leprosy were not too much for him. His young patients always got well.

I knocked repeatedly on Agustín's front door, but there was no answer.

"Just walk right in," a young girl shouted, leaning out a window across the street. "Agustín can't hear you. He's way in the back."

Following her advice, I stepped through the front door that opened into the inside patio. I peeked into each of the three rooms I passed, which also opened onto the patio. Except for a hammock in each of them, the first two rooms were empty. The third one was the living room. Calendars and magazine pictures decorated the walls. A row of straight-backed chairs and a plastic-covered couch faced an enormous television set.

Farther back was the kitchen. Beyond the kitchen through an alcove was yet another room. I saw Agustín there, seated at a large table. As I approached, he rose smiling and stood scratching his head, his other hand thrust deep into the pocket of his worn khaki pants. His white shirt had patches, and the cutoff sleeves were frayed at the unhemmed cuffs.

"This is my working room!" he exclaimed proudly, extending his arm about in a circle. "I've got everything in here. And I'm about to open. My patients come through the side door. That door brings both of us luck."

The room, well lit and ventilated by two windows facing the hills, smelled of disinfectant. There were rows of unvarnished, unpainted shelves on all the walls. On the shelves, neatly arranged and all properly labeled, stood various-sized flasks, bottles, jars, and boxes filled with dried roots, bark, leaves, and flowers. These boxes were not only identified by their common names but also by their scientific Latin nomenclature.

The table was hand carved and faced the open windows. Bottles, bowls, pestles, books, and two scales were lined up on the highly polished surface. A cot and the three-foot-tall crucifix hanging in a corner with its votive candle burning on a triangular ledge beneath it indeed confirmed that I had stepped into the working room of a healer, not an old-fashioned apothecary.

Without much ado, Agustín brought in another chair from the kitchen and invited me to observe him at work. He opened the lucky side door he had pointed out earlier. There were three women and four children in the adjacent room.

The hours passed swiftly. He treated each patient by first examining a jar filled with the child's urine that had been brought in by the mother. Prompted by each woman's account of her child's symptoms, Agustín proceeded to "read the waters." The odor, the color, and the kind of microbes, or filaments, as he preferred to call them and which he claimed to see with the naked eye, were all carefully considered before he arrived at a diagnosis. Fevers, colds, indigestion, parasites, asthma, rashes, allergies, anemia, and even measles and smallpox were among the most prevalent illnesses Agustín claimed to recognize after a thorough "reading of the waters."

In respectful silence, each woman waited for Agustín to invoke the help of Christ before he prescribed the appropriate medication. He mixed his own herbal concoctions. Being familiar with, and a believer in, modern pharmacopoeia, Agustín was inclined to supplement his own remedies with milk of magnesia, antibiotics, aspirins, and vitamins, which he had repacked and rebottled in his own containers. Like Mercedes Peralta, he charged no set fee but left it to the judgment of his clients. That is, they paid whatever they could afford.

Our late lunch of chicken and pork empanadas, brought to us by a woman in the neighborhood, came to an abrupt end when a man carrying a small boy walked into the kitchen. The child, perhaps six or seven years old, had cut the calf of his leg while playing in the field with his father's machete.

In his calm, sure manner, Agustín carried the child to the cot in his working room and undid the makeshift, blood-soaked bandage. First he bathed the deep gash with rosemary water, and then with peroxide.

It was hard to tell whether the child was being hypnotized by Agustín's soothing touch, as he massaged the anxious little face, or by his soft voice, as he recited an incantation. But in a matter of moments, the boy was asleep. And then Agustín began the most important part of his treatment. To stop the bleeding, he applied to the wound a poultice of leaves that had been soaked in clear sugarcane liquor. Then he prepared a paste that, he claimed, would heal the wound in less than ten days and leave no scar.

Invoking the guidance of Christ, Agustín sprinkled a few drops of a milky substance on an abalone shell. With slow, rhythmic motions he began to grind the shell with a broad wooden pestle. A half hour elapsed before he had little less than a half teaspoon of a greenish, musky-smelling substance.

He examined the cut once more, pressed the wound closed with his fingers, and carefully spread the paste over the gash. Mumbling a prayer, he expertly bandaged the leg with strips of white cloth. A satisfied smile lit his face as he handed the sleeping boy into the father's arms and told him to bring him every other day to change the dressing.

Late in the afternoon, certain that there would be no more patients that day, Agustín gave me a tour of his yard. His medicinal plants grew in neat rows and square patches, arranged as carefully as the jars and bottles were on the table and shelves in his working room. At the far end of the yard, leaning against a tool shed, stood an old kerosene refrigerator.

"Don't open it!" Agustín cried out, holding my arm in a firm grip.

"How could I?" I protested. "It's padlocked. What secrets do you keep in there?"

"My witchcraft," he whispered. "You do know that I practice witchcraft, don't you?" His tone was mocking, but his face was somber when he added, "I'm a specialist in healing children and bewitching adults."

"Do you really practice witchcraft?" I asked incredulously.

"Don't be obtuse, Musiúa," Agustín chided. He paused for a moment, then in an emphatic tone, added, "Doña Mercedes must have told you that the other side of healing is bewitching. They go together because one is useless without the other. I heal children. I bewitch adults," he repeated, knocking on the top of the refrigerator. "I'm very good at both. Doña Mercedes says that one day I will bewitch the same ones I healed when they were children." He smiled at my startled face. "I don't think I will. But only time will tell."

Taking advantage of his expansive mood, I finally told him what had been on my mind the whole day. That I had seen and talked to him when I was in a dreamlike state.

Agustín listened attentively, but his gaze betrayed nothing.

"I can't quite define what it was," I said, "but it wasn't a dream!" Exasperated by his unwillingness to comment or to explain, I urged him to say something.

"I like you so much that I wanted to know if you're really a medium," he said, smiling. "Now I know you are."

"I think you're humoring me," I said, even more exasperated.

Agustín's eyebrows raised in arcs of astonishment. "It must be horrible to have big feet."

"Big feet?" I stammered uncomprehendingly, looking down at my sandals. "My feet are in perfect proportion to my size."

"They should be smaller," Agustín insisted, putting

his fingers to his lips as though to suppress a smile. "Your feet are too large. That's why you live in perpetual reality. That's why you want everything explained." There was mockery in his voice, mixed with a tinge of compassion that did nothing to reassure me. "Witchcraft follows rules that cannot be empirically demonstrated or repeated, unlike other laws of nature. Witchcraft is precisely the act of persuading reason to rise above itself or, if you wish, to move below itself." He chuckled and gave me a push.

I stumbled over my feet, and he quickly grabbed my arm to keep me from falling.

"Do you see now that your feet are too big?" Agustín asked and then laughed.

I wondered if he was trying to hypnotize me, for he gazed at me without blinking. I was held captive by his eyes. Like two drops of water, they seemed to spread wider and wider, blurring everything around me. All I was aware of was his voice.

"A sorcerer chooses to be different from what he was raised to be," he continued. "He has to understand that witchcraft is a lifelong task. A sorcerer, through witchcraft, weaves patterns like webs. Patterns that transmit invoked powers to some superior mystery. Human actions have an endless, spreading network of results; he accepts and reinterprets these results in a magical way." He brought his face even closer to mine and lowered his voice to a soft whisper. "A sorcerer's hold on reality is absolute. His grip is so powerful, he can bend reality every which way in the service of his art. But he never forgets what reality is or was." Without another word he turned and walked toward the living room.

Swiftly, I followed after him. He plopped down on

the sofa and crossed his legs the way I had seen him do on my cot. Smiling up at me, he patted the place beside him. "Let's have some real witchcraft," he said, switching on the remote control of the enormous TV set.

There was no time to ask any more questions. In the next instant, we were surrounded by a group of giggling children from the neighborhood.

"Each evening they come here to watch TV with me for an hour or so," Agustín explained. "Later on, you and I will have time to talk."

After that initial meeting, I became Agustín's unbiased admirer. Attracted not only by his healing skills but by his haunting personality, I practically moved into one of the empty rooms of his house. He wove countless stories for me, including the one Mercedes Peralta wanted me to hear.

Startled by a faint moan, Agustín opened his eyes. In a shaft of light, a spider suspended on invisible thread dropped from the crumbling cane ceiling all the way to the ground where Agustín lay curled up like a cat. He reached toward the spider, crushed it between his fingers, and ate it. Sighing, he drew his knees even closer to his chest as he felt the cold of dawn seep through the cracks of the weather-beaten mud walls.

Agustín couldn't remember whether days or weeks had passed since his mother brought him to this dilapidated, abandoned hut, where bats hung from the ceiling like unlit bulbs and cockroaches swarmed around in daylight and in darkness. All he knew was that he had been hungry ever since, that the slugs, spiders, and grasshoppers he caught never stilled the gnawing pain in his swollen belly.

Agustín heard the faint moan again. It came from the shadowy corner at the far end of the room. He saw an apparition of his mother sitting on the mattress, her mouth slightly open as she rubbed her naked belly. She was riding the mattress as though she were on a donkey, her naked shadow moving up and down on the soot-stained wall.

Only a few hours before, he had seen his mother struggling with a man. He had seen her thin legs, like black snakes, wrapped tightly around the man's torso, squeezing the breath out of him. And when he heard his mother's piercing scream, followed by a silence that had lasted for the rest of the night, he knew that the man had won the struggle. He had killed her.

Agustín's tired eyes closed with pleasure at the thought that he was now an orphan. He was safe. They would take him at the mission. Half-conscious of his mother's ghostly sighs, giggles, and whispers whirling about the room, he dozed off again.

A loud groan shattered the morning stillness. Agustín opened his eyes and pressed his fist against his lips to stifle a scream as he saw the same man from the night before sit up on the mattress.

Agustín didn't know the man. Yet, he was sure he was from Ipairí. He vaguely remembered seeing him talking to his mother in the plaza. Had the women from the small hamlet in the hills sent the man to take him back? To perhaps kill him? It couldn't be. He must be having a vivid horrible dream.

The man cleared his throat and spat on the ground. His voice filled the room. "I'll take you away today. But I can't take the boy. Why didn't you leave him with the Protestants? You know that they have a place for children; even if they won't take him, they'll feed him."

When Agustín heard his mother's harsh reply he knew that he was wide awake. He knew that she was not a ghost.

"The Protestants won't take any children unless they are orphaned," his mother said. "There was nothing else I could do but bring the boy to this abandoned shack. I'm waiting for him to die."

"I know of a woman who'll take him," the man said. "She'll know what to do with him. She's a witch."

"It's too late now," his mother said. "I wish I had given Agustín to a witch when he was born. Ever since he was a baby, a witch in Ipairí wanted him. She used to feed him strange potions and hang amulets around his wrists and neck, allegedly to guard him from calamities and disease. I know she cast a spell on the boy. That witch is responsible for all my misfortune." His mother was silent for a moment; then in a strangled whisper, as though she were under attack by an unseen enemy, she added, "I'm terrified of witches. If I went to one now, she'd know that I haven't been feeding the boy. She'd kill me."

Tears rolled down Agustín's cheeks as he remembered the days in Ipairí when his mother used to cradle him in her arms. She would smother him with kisses and tell him that his eyes were like pieces of the sky. But when the women in the neighboring shacks forbade their children to play with him, his mother became a different person. She no longer touched or kissed him. Finally, she ceased speaking to him altogether.

One afternoon, a woman carrying a dead child in

her arms burst into their shack. "Blue eyes in a black face," she screamed at Agustín's mother, "that's the work of the devil. That's the devil himself. He killed my baby with the evil eye. If you don't get rid of that boy, I will."

That same night, his mother fled with him to the hills. Agustín was certain that it was that woman who had cast a spell on his mother so she would hate him.

The man's loud voice cut into Agustín's reveries.

"You don't have to take him to the witch yourself. I can leave word with her to pick the kid up tonight. We'll be gone by then. I'll take you far away from here, where no witch will ever find you," the man promised.

His mother remained silent for a long time; then she flung her head back and laughed hysterically. She rose from the mattress and wrapped the dirty blanket tightly around her body. Stepping around the broken table and the few crates scattered about, she made her way across the room.

"Look at him," she hissed, jerking her chin toward the corner where Agustín lay curled up, pretending to be asleep. "He's only six years old, yet he looks like an evil old man. His hair has fallen out. His body is covered with scabs. His stomach is swollen with parasites. Yet, he survives. He has no clothes. He sleeps without a blanket. Yet, he doesn't even catch cold." She turned toward the man on the mattress. "Can't you see that he is indeed the devil? The devil will find me wherever I go." His mother's eyes shone feverishly bright under her disheveled hair. "The thought of having suckled the devil at my own breast fills me with fear and revulsion."

She reached up to a niche in the wall where she had

hidden the corncakes the man had brought her last night. She gave one to the man, and nibbling on the other one, she lowered herself beside him on the mattress.

In a monotonous, trancelike tone she recounted that Agustín was a changeling. "One of the nurses at the hospital changed my own baby for the devil," she continued, her tone suddenly vehement. "Everyone knew that I was going to have a girl. My pregnant belly was broad instead of pointed. My hair began to fall out. Blotches and blemishes appeared on my skin. My legs swelled. Those are the symptoms of carrying a girl.

"At first, even though I knew he was a changeling, I couldn't help but love him. He was so beautiful and so clever. He never cried. He spoke before he walked, and he sang like an angel. I refused to believe any of the women in Ipairí who accused Agustín of having the evil eye. Even after my stillborn pregnancy I didn't pay any attention to the neighbors' insinuations. I just thought they were ignorant, and worst of all, envious of the boy's beautiful eyes. After all, who ever heard of a child having the evil eye?" She scraped out the white, soft center of the corncake and flung the dry crust across the room. "But when my man died in an accident at the mill, I had to agree with the women." She covered her face with her hands and quietly added, "Agustín has never been ill in his life. I should have left him to his fate in Ipairí. Then his death would not be on my conscience."

"Let me get word to the woman I've been telling you about," the man said, his voice soft, yet persuasive. "I know she'll take him."

At great length he explained about his job at the

pharmaceutical laboratory. He worked in the store-room and was on very good terms with his boss. He foresaw no difficulties in convincing the man of his need for an advance. "With the money, the two of us can go to Caracas," he said. He rose and dressed. "Wait for me at the laboratory. I'll be out by five. I'll have everything arranged by then."

Agustín reached for the dry crust on the ground. On unsteady legs, he walked toward the narrow, back doorway, which no longer had a door, and stepped out into what had once been a yard. He headed toward his favorite place, the gnarled, no-longer-blooming acacia tree overhanging the ravine. He sat on the ground, his legs extended in front of him, his naked back resting against a portion of the crumbling low wall that had once encircled the grounds.

The scrawny, sickly looking cat that had followed him all the way from Ipairí rubbed its coarse fur against his thigh. Agustín gave it a small piece of the crust, then pushed the cat away toward the lizards scuttling in and out of the crevices in the mud wall. He would not part with another crumb. He was never capable of satisfying his own relentless hunger; a hunger that filled his days and nights with dreams of food. With a sigh on his lips he dozed off.

Startled by a gust of wind, he woke up. Dead leaves swirled in a circle around him. The leaves rose high up in the air and then descended in brown rustling whirlpools into the ravine. He could hear the mur-muring stream below. When it rained the shallow water grew into a seething river, sweeping along trees and dead animals from the hamlets in the mountains.

Agustín turned his head slightly and gazed at the

silent hills around him. Thin columns of smoke drifted up into the sky, melting with the moving clouds. Could the Protestant mission be that close? he asked himself. Or perhaps the smoke was from the house of the woman who wasn't afraid to take him. He rested his cheek on his small bony hand. Flies buzzed around his open mouth. He pressed his parched lips together, spread his legs, and urinated. He was hungry. He could feel the pain inside him as he again fell asleep.

The sun was high when Agustín awoke. The cat was nearby, devouring a large lizard. He crawled toward the feline. It snarled viciously, holding the half-eaten reptile tightly under its paw. Agustín kicked the cat in the stomach, then reached for the slippery entrails and swallowed them. He looked up and found his mother watching him from the doorway.

"Holy Virgin!" she exclaimed. "He isn't human." She crossed herself. "It won't be long before he poisons himself." Again she made the sign of the cross and, folding her hands in prayer, murmured, "Holy Father. Get him out of my way. Make him die a natural death, so I won't have him on my conscience." She went inside, lifted the mattress, and pulled out her only dress. She caressed it and lovingly pressed the wrinkled dress against her body, then shook it repeatedly and laid it out on the mattress with great care.

Curiously, Agustín watched her light a fire in the cooking pit. Humming a little tune, she retrieved the coffee and the pieces of sugar loaf she kept in a crate nailed high up on the wall. He wanted a piece of that sugar. He tried to stand up, but overcome by nausea he crouched with his elbows against the ground and vomited unchewed pieces of lizard. Salty tears dribbled down his sunken cheeks. He gagged repeatedly, foam and bile spurting from his trembling lips. He wiped his mouth and chin on his shoulders. With a painful moan he tried to straighten up but slumped forward on the ground.

The sound of the murmuring ravine engulfed him like a soft veil. When the smell of coffee filtered through his nostrils and he heard his mother say that she had made him sweet coffee, he knew that he was dreaming. His dry lips grimaced. He wanted to smile when he heard her laugh; that high, abrupt, happy laughter he used to know so well. He wondered if she would put on her red dress and meet the man at the pharmaceutical laboratory.

Agustín opened his eyes. On the ground next to him stood a small tin filled with coffee. Afraid the vision would vanish, he reached out and lifted the can to his mouth. Indifferent to the burning pain on his lips and tongue, he sipped the strong, very sweet brew. It cleared his head and stopped his nausea.

Dreamily, Agustín gazed at the slanted rain lines in the distance. Within moments dark clouds, edged with gold, floated across the sky. The clouds stained the hills with purple shadows and turned the sky a smoky black. A cold wind, followed by a deafening roar, rose from the bottom of the ravine. The rainwater from the distant hills gushed down the deep gorge with outrageous force. Within moments large heavy drops burst from the sky.

Agustín rose, tilted his face skyward, and, with arms outstretched, welcomed the soothing coolness that washed him clean. Driven by an inexplicable impulse, he went into the house and picked up the dress on the mattress. Clutching it with trembling hands, he hurried outside to the very edge of the ravine and threw the garment into the wind. It flew like a kite, landing on a leafless branch of the old acacia tree overhanging the steep slope.

"You devil! You monster!" his mother screamed, rushing toward him, her hair tumbling wildly about her face, her arms extended. As if transfixed by the sound of the roaring water, she just stood there between the boy and the fluttering dress, her eyes filled with hatred, unable to say a word. Then, holding on to weeds and exposed roots, she carefully eased herself toward the overhanging branch of the acacia tree.

Agustín watched her from behind the gnarled trunk with fascinated interest. Her feet moved with unerring agility on the steep slippery ground. She will get the dress by any means, he thought. He felt anger and fear. She was only a few inches away from it. She stretched her arm as far as she could. She touched the dress with the tip of her fingers and then lost her footing and tumbled over the brink.

Her horror-stricken scream mingled with the sound of the roaring water was carried away by the wind.

Agustín moved closer to the edge. His eyes shone with a hollow depth as he saw his mother's body spin helplessly in the thick brown water on its journey to the sea. The storm died away. The rain ceased. The wind dropped; all but the turbulent water in the ravine regained its habitual murmuring calm.

Agustín walked into the house, lay down on the mattress, and covered himself with the thin, dirty blanket. He felt the coarse, wet fur of the cat seeking the warmth of his body. He pulled the blanket over his eyes and fell into a deep dreamless sleep.

It was night when he awoke. Through the open doorway he could see the moon entangled in the barren branches of the acacia tree. "We'll go now," he murmured, stroking the cat. He felt strong. It would be easy to walk across the hills, he decided. With each other as companions, he had the vague certainty that he and the cat would find the Protestant mission or the house of the woman who was not afraid to take him.

23

Mercedes Peralta came rushing into my room, sat on my bed, and shifted about until she was comfortably settled.

"Unpack your gear," she said. "You can't go to see Agustín anymore. He's left for his yearly trip to remote areas in the country."

She spoke with such certainty that I had the feeling she had just finished talking to him over the telephone. But I knew there wasn't one in the neighborhood.

Candelaria came at that moment into the room holding a tray with my favorite dessert: guava jelly and a few slices of white cheese.

"I know it's not the same as sitting spiritually with Agustín in front of a TV set," she remarked, "but I'm all you have for the moment." She placed the tray on the night table and sat down on the bed opposite from doña Mercedes.

Doña Mercedes laughed and urged me to eat my treat. She said that Agustín was known in distant, godforsaken towns and visited them yearly. At great length she talked about his gift for healing children.

"When will he be back?" I asked. The thought that I might not see him again filled me with indescribable sadness.

"There's no way to know," doña Mercedes said. "Six months, perhaps even longer. He does this because he feels he has a great debt to pay."

"Whom does he owe?"

She looked at Candelaria, then both of them looked at me as though I ought to have known.

"Witches understand debts of this kind in a most peculiar manner," doña Mercedes finally said. "Healers pray to the saints and to the Virgin and to our Lord Jesus Christ. Witches pray to power; they entice it with their incantations." She rose from the bed and paced about the room. Softly, as though she were talking to herself, she continued to say that although Agustín prayed to the saints, he owed something to a higher order, an order that was not human.

Doña Mercedes was silent for a few moments, looking at me but allowing no expression to be read on her face.

"Agustín has known about that higher order all his life, even as a child," she continued. "Did he ever tell you that the same man who was going to take his mother away found him on a pitch-black night, in the rain, already half-dead, and brought him to me?"

Doña Mercedes did not wait for my response but quickly added, "To be in harmony with that higher order has always been the secret of Agustín's success. He does it through his healing and bewitching."

Again she paused for a moment, looking up at the ceiling. "That higher order made Agustín and Candelaria a gift," she continued, lowering her gaze toward me. "It helped them from the moment they were born. Candelaria pays part of her debt by being my servant. She is the best servant there is."

Doña Mercedes moved toward the door, and before

stepping outside, she turned to face Candelaria and me, a dazzling smile on her face. "I think that in some measure you, too, owe a great deal to that higher order," she said. "So try by all means to pay back the debt you have."

Not a word was said for a long time. The two women looked at me with a sense of expectancy. It occurred to me that they were waiting for me to make the obvious connection—obvious to them. Just as Candelaria was a born witch, Agustín was a born sorcerer.

Doña Mercedes and Candelaria listened to me with beaming smiles.

"Agustín is capable of making his own links," doña Mercedes explained. "He has a direct connection to that higher order, which is the wheel of chance itself and the witch's shadow as well. Or whatever it is that makes that wheel move."

PART SEVEN

24

Sharing the faint light of the bulb above us, Candelaria and I sat across from each other at the kitchen table. She was studying the glossy pictures in the magazine I had bought for her; I was transcribing my tapes.

"Did you hear a knock at the front door?" I asked, pulling the earphone from my ear.

Totally oblivious to my words, she pointed to the picture of a blond model. "I can't decide which girl I like better," she mused. "If I cut out this one, I'll lose the one on the other side of the page, the brunette walking down the street with a tiger on a leash."

"I would save the one with the tiger," I suggested. "There will be more blond models in the magazine." I touched her arm. "Listen, someone's at the door."

It took Candelaria a moment to draw herself away from the magazine and another moment to realize that indeed there was someone knocking. "Who could it possibly be at this late hour?" she mumbled indifferently, as she shifted her attention back to the glossy pages.

"Perhaps it's a patient." I glanced at my watch. It was almost midnight.

"Oh no, my dear," Candelaria said calmly and looked up. "No one ever comes at this hour. People know

that doña Mercedes doesn't treat anyone this late unless it's an emergency."

Before I had a chance to say that it probably was
an emergency, there was another, this time more insistent, knock.

I hurried to the front of the house. For a moment I
hesitated outside the healing room, deliberating whether
I should let Mercedes Peralta know that there was
someone at the door.

For three days she had been in that room. Day and
night she had lit candles on the altar, smoked cigar
after cigar, and, with a rapturous expression on her
face, had recited unintelligible incantations until the
walls vibrated with the sound. She had never answered
any of my questions. Yet, she seemed to welcome my
interruptions when I brought her food or insisted she
rest for a few hours.

Another knock sent me hurrying to the front door,
which Candelaria always bolted as soon as it got dark.
An unnecessary precaution, for anyone wanting to come
inside could have done so through the open kitchen.

"Who is it?" I asked before unlatching the iron bolt.

"*Gente de paz*, peaceful folk," a man's voice answered.

Amazed to hear someone with a faint foreign accent
reply in the archaic convention dating from the days
of the Spanish Conquest, I automatically responded in
the required manner, "Hail the Virgin Mary," and
opened the door.

The tall, white-haired man leaning against the wall
regarded me with such a baffled expression on his
face, I burst into laughter.

"Is this Mercedes Peralta's house?" he asked in a
halting voice.

I nodded, studying his face. It was not so much that it was wrinkled but rather eroded, ravaged as though by grief or pain. His watery blue eyes were sunken in wide circles of age and weariness.

"Is Mercedes Peralta in?" he asked, looking past me into the dimly lit hallway.

"She is," I replied. "But she doesn't see people this late."

"I've been walking around town for hours, pondering whether I should come," he said. "I need to see her. I'm an old friend or an old enemy."

Shaken by the anguish and despair in the man's voice, I invited him inside. "She's in her working room," I said. "I'd better let her know that you've come to see her." I stepped ahead of him and smiled encouragingly. "What is your name?"

"Don't announce me," the man begged, gripping my arm. "Let me go in by myself. I know the way." Stiffly, he limped across the patio and down the corridor. He paused for a second in front of doña Mercedes' room, then climbed the two steps leading inside.

I followed close behind him ready to take the blame should Mercedes Peralta be annoyed by the intrusion. For an instant, I thought she had already gone to bed. But as soon as my eyes became accustomed to the shadowy darkness, I saw her sitting in her high-backed chair at the far end of the room, barely outlined by the faint light of a single candle burning on the altar.

"Federico Mueller!" she gasped, staring at him in total panic. She seemed not to trust her vision and repeatedly rubbed her eyes with her hands. "How can it be? All these years I thought you were dead."

Awkwardly, he went down on his knees, buried his face in the healer's lap, and cried with the abandonment of a despairing child. "Help me, help me," he repeated in between sobs.

Hastily, I moved toward the entrance, only to halt abruptly when I heard Federico Mueller fall on the floor with a dull thump.

I wanted to summon Candelaria, but doña Mercedes stopped me. "How extraordinary!" she exclaimed in a trembling tone. "Everything is fitting into place like a magical jigsaw puzzle. This is the person you remind me of. You brought him back to me."

I wanted to tell her that I saw no similarity between the old man and myself, but she sent me to her bedroom to fetch her basket with medicinal plants. When I returned, Federico Mueller was still lying curled up on the floor. Doña Mercedes was trying to revive him.

"Get Candelaria," she said. "I can't handle Federico Mueller by myself."

Candelaria had heard the commotion and was already standing by the entrance. She walked in. There was an expression of disbelief, of sheer horror in her eyes. "He's come back," she murmured, approaching Federico Mueller. She crossed herself, then turned to doña Mercedes and asked, "What do you want me to do?"

"His soul is detaching itself from his body," she answered. "I'm too weak to try to push it back."

Candelaria sat on her haunches and swiftly moved Federico Mueller's inert body to a sitting position. She gave him a sort of bear hug from behind. The bones of his back cracked as if they were breaking into a hundred pieces.

Candelaria propped him in a sitting position against the wall. "He's very ill," she said to me. "I think he's come back here to die." She left the room crossing herself.

Federico Mueller opened his eyes. He took in everything in one glance, then he looked at me as if he were silently begging me to leave him alone with doña Mercedes.

"Musiúa," she said in a weak voice as I was walking out of the room, "since you have brought him back to my life, you ought to stay."

I sat down awkwardly on my stool. He began to talk to no one in particular. He rambled on incoherently for hours. Mercedes Peralta listened attentively. Whatever he was saying seemed to make all the sense in the world to her.

A long silence ensued after Federico Mueller stopped talking. Slowly, doña Mercedes rose and lit a candle in front of the statue of the Virgin. Poised before the altar, she looked like an ancient wood statue, her face an expressionless mask. Only her eyes seemed alive as they filled with tears. She lit a cigar and drew each breath deep inside her, as if she were feeding a force within her chest.

The flame grew brighter as the candle shrank. It cast an eerie light on her features as she turned to face Federico Mueller. Mumbling a soft incantation, she massaged first his head and then his shoulders.

"You can do anything you want with me," he said, pressing both her palms against his temples.

"Go into the living room," doña Mercedes said, her voice a shaky whisper. "I'll be along shortly with a valerian potion. It will put you to sleep." Smiling, she patted his hair into place.

Hesitantly, he limped across the patio and down the

corridor. The sound of his steps echoed faintly through the house.

Mercedes Peralta turned once again to the altar but could not reach it. She was beginning to fall, when I jumped up and caught her. Feeling the uncontrollable tremor of her body, I realized how immense had been her stress and her poise. She had comforted Federico Mueller for hours. I had seen only his turmoil; she had revealed nothing about her own.

"Musiúa, tell Candelaria to get ready," doña Mercedes said, stepping into the kitchen where I was writing. "You're taking us in your jeep."

Certain that she was already asleep, I went immediately to look for Candelaria in her room. She was not there. The door of her wardrobe stood wide open, exposing the bevel-edged mirror on its door and all her clothes. They were arranged not only by color but also by the length of the hems. Her narrow bed—a frame of laths and a horsehair mattress—stood between two bookcases filled with romance novels and photo albums containing cutout magazine pictures. Everything was in immaculate order, nothing was rumpled.

"I'm ready," Candelaria said behind me.

Startled, I turned around. "Doña Mercedes wants you to—" She did not let me finish, but propelled me toward my room down the corridor.

"I've taken care of everything," she assured me. "Hurry up and change. We don't have much time."

On my way out I peeked into the living room. Federico Mueller was sleeping peacefully on the couch. Doña Mercedes and Candelaria were already waiting for me in my jeep. There was no moon or a single star in the sky, yet it was a lovely night, soft and black with a cool wind blowing from the hills.

Following Candelaria's directions, I drove the two women to the homes of the people who regularly attended the spiritualists' meeting. As was customary, I waited outside. Except for Leon Chirino, I had never met any of them, yet I knew where each one of them lived. I wondered if the two women were setting a date for a séance, for they did not stay long at any of the houses.

"And now to Leon Chirino's house," Candelaria said, helping doña Mercedes settle in the backseat.

Candelaria seemed angry. Nonstop she rambled on about Federico Mueller. Although I was bursting with curiosity, I could not pay attention to her seemingly incoherent statements. I was too preoccupied watching the distraught look on doña Mercedes' face in the rearview mirror. She opened her mouth several times to speak, but instead she shook her head and looked out the window, seeking aid and comfort from the night.

Leon Chirino took a long time coming to the door. He must have been sound asleep and unable to hear Candelaria's impatient, loud banging. He opened the door with his arms crossed, protecting his chest from the cold, humid breeze spreading the dawn across the hills. There was a look of foreboding in his eyes.

"Federico Mueller is at my house," doña Mercedes said before he had time to even greet her.

Leon Chirino did not say a word. Yet, it was evident that he had been thrown into a state of profound agitation, of great indecision. His lips trembled, and his eyes alternately shone with rage or filled with tears under his white, bushy brows.

He motioned us to follow him to the kitchen. He made sure doña Mercedes was comfortably settled in a hammock hanging near the stove, then he made a fresh pot of coffee, while we sat in complete silence.

As soon as he had served Candelaria and me a cup, he helped doña Mercedes into a sitting position and, standing behind her, proceeded to massage the back of her head. He moved down to her neck, then to her shoulders and arms, all the way to her feet. The sound of his melodious incantation floated over the room, clear like the dawn, peaceful and infinitely lonely.

"Only you know what to do," Leon Chirino said to her, helping her up. "Do you want me to come with you?"

Nodding, she embraced him and thanked him for lending her his strength. A mysterious smile curved her lips as she turned to the table and leisurely sipped her cup of coffee.

"Now we have to see my *compadre*," she said, taking my arm. "Please take us to *El Mocho*'s house."

"Lucas Nuñez?" I asked, looking from one to the other. All three nodded, but no one said a word. I had remembered Candelaria's comment about the godfather of doña Mercedes' adopted son. Candelaria had told me that the man blamed himself for Elio's death.

The sun had already risen above the mountains when we reached the small town along the coast where Lucas Nuñez lived. The place was hot and salty from the sea and musky with flowering mimosa trees. The town's main street lined with brightly painted colonial houses, a small church, and a plaza ended at the edge of a coconut plantation. Beyond was the sea. It could not be seen, but the wind carried the sound of waves breaking on the shore.

Lucas Nuñez's house stood on one of the town's side streets, which were not really streets but wide paths covered with stones. Doña Mercedes rapped lightly on the door and, without waiting for an answer, pushed it open and stepped inside a dark, damp room.

Still blinded by the brightness outside, I could at first barely make out the silhouette of a man reading at a wooden table in a small back patio. He gazed at us with such a desolate expression on his face I wanted to flee. Haltingly, he stood up and silently embraced doña Mercedes, Leon Chirino, and Candelaria. The man was tall and bony; his white hair was cropped so close to his head that the darkness of his scalp shone through.

I felt a strange anguish upon noticing his hands and realized why he was nicknamed *El Mocho,* the maimed one. The first joint of each finger was missing.

"Federico Mueller is at my house," doña Mercedes said softly. "The musiúa here brought him to my door."

Slowly, Lucas Nuñez turned toward me. There was something so intense about the man's narrow face, about his shiny eyes, that I shrank back.

"Is she related to him?" he asked in a harsh voice, no longer seeming to see me.

"The musiúa has never seen Federico Mueller in her life," doña Mercedes remarked. "But she brought him to my door."

Lucas Nuñez leaned against the wall. "If he is in your house, then I will kill him," he declared in a strangled whisper.

Doña Mercedes and Leon Chirino each took him by an arm and led him into one of the rooms.

"Who is this Federico Mueller?" I asked Candelaria. "What did he do?"

"But, Musiúa," she said impatiently. "I've been telling you during the whole trip about the horrible things Federico Mueller did." She looked at me baffled, shaking her head in disbelief. Despite my insistence that she repeat them, she would not say another word about Federico Mueller.

Instead of going to rest in her hammock upon returning to her house, Mercedes Peralta asked Candelaria and me to join her in her working room. She lit seven candles on the altar and, reaching behind the folds of the Virgin's blue mantle, pulled out a revolver.

Horrified and fascinated, I watched her caress the gun. She smiled at me and pressed the revolver into my hands. "It's unloaded," she said. "I unloaded it the day you arrived. I knew then that I wasn't going to need it, but I didn't know that you were going to bring him back to me." She went over to her chair and, heaving a deep sigh, sat down. "I've had that gun for almost thirty years," she went on. "I was going to kill Federico Mueller with it."

"And you should do it now!" Candelaria hissed through clenched teeth.

"I know what I'm going to do," doña Mercedes went on, ignoring the interruption. "I'm going to take care of Federico Mueller for as long as he lives."

"Dear God!" Candelaria exclaimed. "Have you lost your mind?"

A childlike look of innocent hope, a wave of

affection, shone in doña Mercedes' eyes as she regarded us intently. She held up her hand, pleading us to silence. "You brought Federico Mueller to my door," she said to me. "And now I know that there is nothing to forgive. Nothing to understand. And he came back to make me realize just that. This is why I'll never mention what he did. He was dead, but he's not now."

25

There were several empty rooms in the house, but Federico Mueller chose to sleep in the narrow alcove back of the kitchen. It was just large enough for a cot and a night table.

Quite vehemently, he declined my offer to drive him to Caracas and get his belongings. He said that nothing of what he had there would be of any value to him now. Yet, he was grateful, when at doña Mercedes' prompting, I bought him several shirts and a pair of khaki pants and toiletries.

And thus, Federico Mueller became part of the household. Doña Mercedes pampered him. She indulged him. Every morning and again every afternoon she treated him in her working room. And each night she made him drink a valerian potion laced with rum.

Federico Mueller never left the house. He spent all his time either in a hammock in the yard or talking to doña Mercedes. Candelaria ignored his existence; he did likewise not only with her but also with me.

One day, however, Federico Mueller began to speak to me in German, haltingly at first; it cost him a tremendous effort to form the words. But soon he gained a total command of the language, and never again did he speak a word of Spanish with me. That changed him radically. It was as though his problems, whatever they may have been, were encased in the sound of Spanish words.

Candelaria was, at first, mildly curious about the foreign language. She began asking Federico Mueller questions and ended up succumbing to his innate charm. He taught her German nursery rhymes, which Candelaria sang the whole day long with faultless pronunciation. And he repeated to me again and again in a perfectly coherent way what he had said to doña Mercedes the night he arrived.

As happened every night, Federico Mueller woke up screaming. He sat up in bed, his back pushed against the headboard in an effort to escape that one particular face; it always came so close to him he could see the cruel mocking glint in the man's eyes and his gold-rimmed teeth as he laughed in great guffaws. Beyond him were all the other faces of the people who always populated his nightmares: faces distorted by pain and fear. They always screamed in agony, begged for mercy. All of them except her. She never screamed. She never broke her stare. It was a look he could not bear.

Moaning, Federico Mueller pressed his fists against his eyes, as if with that gesture he could keep his past at bay. For thirty years he had been tormented by those nightmares and by the memories and visions that would follow in a wave of dreadful lucidity.

Exhausted, he slid back under the covers. Something palpable, yet unseen, lingered in the room. It prevented him from falling asleep. He pushed the blanket aside and, reluctant to turn on the light, limped across to the window and pulled back the curtain.

Spellbound, he gazed at the white mist of dawn filtering into the room. He strained his eyes wide open to reassure himself that he was not dreaming. As it had so often happened, she materialized out of that formless haze and sat by his working table amid the stuffed birds that stared at him impassively from their dead, empty glass eyes. Carefully, he approached the figure. Swiftly she vanished, like a shadow that leaves no trace.

The bells of the nearby church and the hurried steps of old women on their way to early mass echoed through the silent streets. The familiar sounds reassured him that today was going to be like any other day. He washed and shaved, then prepared his morning coffee and ate standing at the stove. Feeling decidedly better, he settled down to work on his birds. A vague restlessness, some undefined dread, prevented him from finishing his work on the owl he had promised a client for that afternoon. He put on his good suit and went outside for a walk.

The city still had an air of restful clarity at that early hour. Slowly, he limped down the narrow street. The section of Caracas where he lived had been bypassed by the frenzy of modernization that had swept through the rest of the city. Except for a casual greeting, he never stopped to talk to anyone. Yet, he felt oddly protected by these old streets with their one-story colonial houses, alive with the laughter of children and the voices of women gossiping in front of their doors.

At first, people had talked a great deal about him, but he never gave in to the need to explain his presence. He was aware that because of his aloofness, his neighbors speculated and were suspicious of him.

Over the years, as was to be expected, people's

interest in him finally waned. Nowadays, they merely thought of him as an eccentric old man who stuffed birds for a living and wanted to be left alone.

Federico Mueller caught a glimpse of himself in a mirror outside a shop. As always when he saw his reflection, he couldn't help but be startled to discover that he looked so much older than his years could possibly warrant. Not a vestige remained of the tall, handsome man with blond curls and a deep tan. Although he had been only thirty when he first came to live in this section of Caracas, he already looked the way he did now at sixty: old before his time, with a useless leg, white hair, deeply etched wrinkles, and a deathlike pallor that wouldn't disappear regardless of how long he stayed outdoors.

Shaking his head, he resumed his walk toward the plaza and rested on a bench. A few old men were already about, sitting with their hands between their knees, each one lost in his own memories. He found something oddly disturbing in their unshared solitude. He rose and walked on, limping through block after block of crowded streets.

The sun was hot. The contours of buildings had lost their early-morning preciseness, and the noise in the streets intensified the dizzying shimmer of the haze hanging over the city. And again, as he had done so many times before, he found himself standing in front of the same bus depot. His eyes caught a dark face in the crowd.

"Mercedes," he whispered, knowing that it couldn't possibly be her. He wondered if the woman had heard him, for suddenly she looked into his eyes. It was a rapid, yet deliberate glance that filled him with apprehension and hope. Then the woman vanished in the crowd.

"Have you seen a dark, tall woman pass by?" he asked one of the hawkers roaming around the bus depot, his tray of candies and cigarettes strapped in front of him.

"I've seen hundreds of women," the man said, making a wide circle with his hand. "There are lots of women around here." He grabbed Federico Mueller's arm and turned him slightly to the left. "See those buses over there? They are filled with women. Old ones, dark ones, tall ones. Anyway you like them. They are all going to the coastal towns." Laughing, the man continued weaving in and out of the waiting buses, advertising his wares.

Possessed by an irrational certainty that he would find that face, Federico Mueller got on a bus and walked down the aisle gazing intently at each passenger. They stared back at him in silence. For an instant, he thought that all the faces resembled hers. He had to rest for a moment, he thought, and sat on one of the empty seats at the back of the bus.

A faint, faraway voice demanding his ticket roused him from his slumber. The words vibrated in his head. A drowsiness pressed heavily on his brow, and he had difficulty opening his eyes. He gazed out the window. The city was far behind. Puzzled and embarrassed, he looked up at the ticket collector. "I didn't intend to go anyplace," he stammered apologetically. "I only came looking for someone." He paused for a moment, then mumbled to himself. "Someone I hoped and dreaded to find on this bus."

"That happens," the man remarked sympathetically. "Since you have to pay the full fare, you might as well take advantage of the ride and go all the way to Curmina." He smiled and patted him on the shoulder. "There you can get a bus that will take you back to the capital."

Federico Mueller handed him some money. "When does the bus come back to Caracas?" he asked.

"Around midnight," the man said vaguely. "Or whenever there are enough people to make the trip worthwhile." He gave him back his change, then continued down the aisle, and collected the rest of the tickets from the passengers.

It was fate that I had to catch this bus without having planned to do so, Federico Mueller thought. A half smile flittered across his face. His worn eyelids closed with a feeling of hope, quiet and deep. Fate was finally forcing him to surrender to his past. An unknown peacefulness filled him as he recalled that past.

It all began at a party in Caracas, where he was approached by a high-ranking general in the government, who asked him point-blank to join the secret police. Believing him to be drunk, Federico did not take the man's words seriously. It came as a surprise when a few days later an army officer knocked on his door.

"I'm Captain Sergio Medina," he introduced himself. There had been nothing sinister about the short, powerfully built man with the copperish skin and the gold-rimmed teeth that flashed in a strong open smile. Convincingly, he talked about the excitement involved in the job they had in mind for him, the good pay, the fast promotions. Flattered and intrigued, Federico accompanied Medina to the general's house.

Patting him affectionately on his back, like an old

friend, the general took him to his study. "This job will earn you the respect and gratitude of this country," the general said. "A country that, after all, is your own and yet isn't. This will be your chance to truly become one of us."

Nodding, Federico could not help but agree with the general. He had been sixteen years old when his parents had immigrated to Venezuela. Under the auspices of a government program, they had settled in the interior to farm the vast acreages of land allotted to them, which they had hoped to own one day. After an accident that killed both of his parents, Federico, not in the least interested in farming, apprenticed himself to a German zoologist, an expert in taxidermy who taught him all he knew.

"I can't think how I could be of use to you," Federico said to the general. "All I know is how to trap and stuff birds."

The general laughed uproariously. "My dear Federico," he emphasized, "your experience as a taxidermist is the ideal cover for the job we have in mind for you." He smiled confidentially and, leaning closer, added, "We have accurate reports of a subversive group operating in the Curmina area. We want you to find out about them." He laughed again, gleefully, like a child. "So far, we have been unsuccessful with the men we have sent into the area. But you, my friend, a musiú trapping birds, will not arouse any suspicion."

Federico was never given the opportunity to refuse the job. Within days, a brand-new jeep equipped with the latest instruments and chemicals of a quality he had never been able to afford were put at his disposal.

* * *

Federico was always careful when in the hills. One morning, however, upon seeing a rare toucan in one of his traps, he leapt out of his hammock without first putting on his boots. He felt a sting between his toes. He swore and thought he had stepped on a thorn. But when a sharp pain radiated from the small punctures— where two little drops of blood had formed—and quickly spread through his whole foot and up his leg, he knew he had been bitten by a snake. A snake he had neither seen nor heard.

He rushed to his jeep parked nearby and rummaged through his gear until he found his first-aid kit. He tied a handkerchief halfway up the calf of his leg, then expertly cut across the two punctures and bled the wound. But too much poison had already gone into the bloodstream. Flashing pains shot all the way to his buttocks, and his foot swelled to twice its size. He would never make it to Caracas, he thought, easing himself behind the steering wheel. He would have to take his chances in the nearest town.

The nurse at the dispensary near the plaza calmly informed him that they were out of antivenin serum.

"What am I supposed to do? Die?" Federico shouted, his face contorted with anger and pain.

"I hope not," the nurse remarked calmly. "I'm sure you've already discarded the chances of reaching Caracas in time." She studied him, carefully considering her next words. "I know of a healer here. She has the best *contras*, the secret potions to counteract a snake's poison." The nurse smiled apologetically. "That's why we hardly ever stock up on serum. Most victims prefer to go to her." She examined the swollen foot once more. "I don't know what kind of snake bit you, but it looks bad to me. Your only chance is the healer. You'd better take it."

Federico had never been to a witch doctor in his life, but at that moment he was willing to try anything. He didn't want to die. He was beyond caring who helped him.

The nurse, assisted by two customers from the bar across the street, carried Federico to the witch doctor's house in the outskirts of town. He was put on a cot in a smoke-filled room that smelled of ammonia.

At the rasping sound of a match, Federico opened his eyes. Through the haze of smoke, he saw a tall woman lighting a candle on an altar. In the flickering light her face was like a mask, very still with high-molded bones over which her tautly stretched skin, dark and smooth, shone like polished wood. Her eyes, hooded by heavy lids, revealed absolutely nothing as they looked into his.

"A *macagua* bite for sure," she diagnosed, shifting her gaze to his foot. "That snake gave you all she had. You were lucky the nurse brought you here. There is no serum for this kind of poison." She pulled up a chair beside him, then examined his foot with great attention, her long fingers soft and gentle as she probed the skin around the wound. "You don't have to worry," she stated with absolute conviction. "You're young. You'll survive the poison and my treatment."

Turning toward the table behind her, she reached for two large decanters filled with a syruplike greenish brown liquid in which roots, leaves, and snake entrails floated around. From one jar, she poured a certain amount in a metal plate; from the other one, she half filled a small tin mug.

She lit a cigar. Inhaling deeply, she closed her eyes

and swayed her head. Abruptly, she bent over his foot and blew what seemed to be the accumulated smoke of the entire cigar into the cut he had made with his knife. She sucked the blood, then quickly spit it out and rinsed her mouth with a clear, strong-smelling liquid. Seven times she repeated this procedure.

Thoroughly exhausted, she rested her head against the back of her chair. A few moments later she began to mumble an incantation. She unbuttoned his shirt, and with her middle finger which she had dipped into the cigar's ashes, she drew a straight line from the base of his throat down to his genitals. With remarkable ease, she turned him around, pulled off his shirt, and painted a similar line down his back.

"I've halved you now," she informed him. "The poison can't go over to the other side." She then retraced the back and front lines with a dab of fresh ashes.

In spite of his pain, Federico laughed. "I'm sure the poison spread all over my body a long time ago," he said.

She held his face between her hands, forcing him to look into her eyes. "Musiú, if you don't trust me, you'll die," she warned him, then proceeded to wash his foot with the liquid she had poured into the metal plate. That done, she reached for the tin mug. "Drink it all," she commanded, holding it to his lips. "If you throw up, you're done for."

Uncontrollable waves of nausea threatened to bring the foul-tasting potion up.

"Force yourself to keep it down," she urged him, placing a small rectangular pillow filled with dried maize kernels under his neck. She watched him attentively as she soaked a handkerchief in a mixture of

253

rose water and ammonia. "Now breathe!" she ordered, holding the handkerchief over his nose. "Breathe slowly and deeply."

For a moment he struggled under the suffocating pressure of her hand, then gradually relaxed as she began to massage his face. "Don't get close to pregnant women. They'll neutralize the effect of the *contra*," she admonished.

He looked at her uncomprehendingly, then mumbled that he did not know any pregnant women.

Seemingly satisfied with his statements, Mercedes Peralta turned to the altar, lined up seven candles around the statue of Saint John, and lit them. Silently, she gazed at the flickering flames, then with a sudden jerk, she threw back her head and recited an oddly dissonant litany. The words turned into a cry, which rose and fell with the regularity of her breathing. It was an inhuman-sounding lament that caused the walls to vibrate and the candle flames to waver. The sound filled the room, the house, and went far beyond, as if it were meant to reach some distant force.

Federico was vaguely aware of being moved into another room. The days and nights blurred into each other as he lay half-conscious on the cot, hounded by fevers and chills. Whenever he opened his eyes, he saw the healer's face in the darkness, the red stones in her earrings shining like an extra pair of eyes. In a soft melodious voice, she sent the shadows, the terrible phantoms of his fever, scurrying to their corners. Or, as if she were part of his hallucinations, she identified those unknown forces and commanded him to wrestle with them.

Afterward, she bathed his sweat-covered body and massaged him until his skin was cool again. There

were times when Federico felt someone else's presence
in the room. Different hands, larger and stronger, yet
as gentle as the healer's, cradled his head while she
urged him in a harsh tone to drink the foul-tasting
potions she held to his lips.

The morning she brought him his first meal of rice
and vegetables, a young man holding a guitar followed
her into the room.

"I'm Elio," he introduced himself. Then strumming
his guitar, he began to sing a funny little ditty that
related the events of Federico's bout with the poison.
Elio also told him that the day the nurse at the dispensary brought him to his mother's house, he set out
for the hills and, with his machete, slayed the *macagua*
that had bitten him. Had the snake survived, the potions and incantations would have been useless.

One morning, upon noticing that the purple swollen
flesh had returned to normal, Federico reached for his
laundered clothes hanging over the bedstead. Eager to
test his strength, he walked out into the yard, where
he found the healer bent over a tub filled with rosemary
water. Silently, he watched her dip her hands into the
purple liquid.

Smiling, she looked up at him. "It keeps my hair
from turning white," she explained, combing her fingers repeatedly through her curls.

Bewildered by the surge of desire welling up inside
him, he moved closer. He longed to kiss the drops of
rosemary water trickling down her face, her neck, into
the bodice of her dress. He didn't care that she might
be old enough to be his mother. To him she was ageless
and mysteriously seductive.

"You saved my life," he murmured, touching her

face. His fingers lingered on her cheeks, her full lips, her warm smooth neck. "You must have added a love potion to that foul-tasting brew you forced me to drink every day."

She looked straight into his eyes but did not answer.

Afraid she had taken offense, he mumbled an apology.

She shook her head, her raspy laughter starting low in her throat. He had never heard such a sound. She laughed with her whole soul, as if nothing else in the world mattered. "You can stay here until you're stronger," she said, tousling his blond curls. In her veiled eyes, there was a hint of mockery but also of passion.

Months passed swiftly. The healer accepted him as her lover. Yet, she would never let him stay a full night in her room.

"Just a little longer," he pleaded each time, caressing the silken texture of her skin, fervently wishing that for once she would give in to his demand. But she always pushed him out into the darkness and, laughing, would close the door behind him.

"Perhaps if we stay lovers for three years," she used to tell him every time.

The rainy season had almost come to an end before Federico resumed his trips into the hills. Elio accompanied him, at first to protect him, but soon he, too, was caught up with trapping and stuffing birds. Never before had Federico taken someone with him. Despite the ten-year age difference, they became the best of friends.

Federico was surprised at how readily Elio endured the long hours of silence as they waited for a bird to fall into a trap; and how much he enjoyed their leisurely walks along the cool, hazy summits, where one was easily overtaken by fog and wind. He was often tempted to tell Elio about Captain Medina, but somehow he never dared to break that intimate, fragile stillness.

Federico felt a vague guilt about the easy days in the hills and the secret nights with the healer. Not only had he convinced Elio and the healer, but he himself had begun to believe that Captain Medina was merely the middleman from Caracas who sold his stuffed birds to schools, museums, and curio shops.

"You've got to do better than catch those damn birds," Medina said to him one afternoon as they were having a beer at a local bar. "Mingle more with the healer's patients. Through gossip, one learns the most astounding things. At any rate, you must finish your brilliant maneuver."

Federico had been surprised and, in turn, upset when Medina had congratulated him on his clever scheme. The captain actually believed that Federico had let the snake bite him on purpose.

"It's the intellectuals, the educated people, who plan and plot against a dictatorship," Federico said. "Not poor farmers and fishermen. They are too busy making a living to notice what kind of government they have."

"Musiú, you aren't paid to give me your opinions," Medina cut him short. "Just do what you're supposed to do." He turned the empty beer glass in his hands, then looked up at Federico and added in a whisper, "Not too long ago the leader of a small, but fanatic, revolutionary group escaped from jail. We have reason to believe that he's hiding in the area." Laughing, Medina placed his right hand on the table. "He left in jail the first joint of each of his fingers. For that, he's now called *El Mocho*."

The rain had kept on falling since early afternoon; the sound of the defective gutter by his window prevented Federico from falling asleep. He went out into the corridor and was about to light a cigarette when he heard a soft murmur coming from the healer's working room.

He knew it was not the healer. That morning he had driven her to a neighboring town where she was to attend a séance. Federico tiptoed down the corridor. Among the different voices, he distinctly recognized Elio's excited voice. At first, he could not make much sense of their conversation, but when the words "dynamite," "the proposed dam in the hills," and "the dictator's unofficial visit to it" cropped up several times, he realized with disturbing clarity that he had unwittingly stumbled on a plot to assassinate the head of the military government. Federico leaned against the wall, his heart beating violently, then resolutely walked up the two steps into the dark room.

"Elio! Is that you?" Federico said. "I heard voices and got worried."

There were several men in the room; they recoiled instantly into the shadows. Elio was not in the least perturbed. He took Federico by the arm and introduced him to the man sitting on the chair by the altar.

"Godfather, this is the musiú I've been telling you about," he said. "He's a friend of the family. He's to be trusted."

Slowly, the man rose. There was something saintly about his bony face, with the wide cheekbones standing out sharply under his dark skin and eyes that shone with a chilling fierceness. "A pleasure to meet you," he said. "I'm Lucas Nuñez."

For a moment Federico stared at the proffered hand, then shook it. The first joint of each finger was missing.

"I feel that you can be trusted," he said to Federico. "Elio says that you may be willing to help us."

Nodding, Federico closed his eyes, afraid his voice and gaze would betray his turmoil.

Lucas Nuñez introduced him to the group of men. One by one they shook his hand, then sat back on the floor, forming a half-circle. The faint flicker of the candles on the altar barely outlined their faces.

Federico listened attentively to Lucas Nuñez's precise, calm arguments as he discussed the past and present political situation in Venezuela.

"And how can I help you?" Federico asked him at the end of his explanation.

Lucas Nuñez's eyes revealed a sad, reflective mood; his face clouded over, struck with unwelcome memories. But then, he smiled and said, "If the others agree, you could drive some explosives into the hills for us."

They all agreed instantly. Federico sensed that they had accepted him so fully and so quickly because they knew he was Mercedes Peralta's lover.

It was after midnight when their conversation ceased, bit by bit, like the flapping wings of an injured bird. The men looked pale, haggard. Federico felt a chill as they embraced him. Without a sound, they left the room and disappeared into the darkness of the hall.

He was stunned by the devilish irony of his situation. Lucas Nuñez's last words rang in his ears. "You're the perfect man for the job. No one will suspect a musiú trapping birds in the hills."

Federico pulled the jeep over to a small clearing beside the road. A light drizzle swathed the hills as with gauze, and the half-moon filtering through the misty clouds gave a spectral radiance to the landscape.

Silently, he and Elio unloaded the well-padded box packed tightly with dynamite sticks.

"I'll carry the stuff down to the shack," Elio said, smiling reassuringly. "Don't look so worried, Federico. They'll have the bridge mined by dawn."

Federico watched him descend the steep overgrown trail into the shadows below. Often he had come with him to this spot, looking for wild *pomarrosas,* a peculiarly fragrant fruit that smells like rose petals. It was the healer's favorite fruit.

Federico sat on a fallen tree trunk and buried his face in his hands. Except for the vague guilt he had felt, at times, for accepting the generous pay—which far exceeded the worth of even the rarest of birds he had delivered to Medina—he had dismissed all thought regarding the implications of what he was doing. Until now, it had all seemed to him like a make-believe adventure in a movie or in some exotic novel. It had nothing to do with having to betray people he knew and loved, people who trusted him.

He wished Elio would hurry. He had seen Medina's jeep parked in a secluded place on the outskirts of town, secretly following him. He had told Medina everything, and now it was too late to regret it.

Federico leapt to his feet as a dazzling flash of lightning illuminated the sky. Thunder broke in a deafening roar, echoing in the depths of the ravine. Rain came in a solid sheet, so dense it blurred everything around him.

"What a fool I am!" he cried out loud, running down the steep trail. With absolute certainty, Federico knew that Medina had no intention of honoring his promise to spare the healer and her son, that he had only given it as a means to get Federico to divulge everything he knew.

"Elio!!" Federico screamed, but his shout was drowned by the resounding volley of a machine gun and the startled cries of hundreds of birds rising up into the dark sky.

In the few minutes that it took him to reach the shack, his mind raced through a nightmare. With devastating clarity he saw how his life, in one instant, had taken a fatal turn. Almost mechanically, he went through the motions of sobbing over Elio's lifeless, torn body. He neither heard nor saw Medina and the two soldiers entering the shack.

Medina was shouting at one of his men, but his voice was only a distant murmur. "You goddamn fool! I told you not to shoot! You could have had us all blown to pieces with that dynamite."

"I heard someone running in the dark," the soldier defended himself. "It could have been an ambush. I don't trust this musiú!"

Medina turned away from the man and pointed his flashlight into Federico's face. "You're dumber than I thought," he spit. "What did you think this was going to be? Make believe?" He ordered the soldiers to take the box with the explosives up the ravine.

Federico brought the jeep to such a violent halt in front of the healer's house that he pitched forward, hitting his head on the windshield. For a moment he sat dazed looking uncomprehendingly at the closed door, at the closed shutters. No light shone through the cracks of the wooden panels, yet the blaring sound of a radio playing a popular tune could be heard for miles.

Federico went around to the yard, where he saw the army jeep parked on the side street. "Medina!" he screamed, running across the patio through the kitchen to the healer's working room.

Defeated, utterly worn-out, he fell to the ground, not far from where the healer lay moaning in the corner by the altar.

"She doesn't know anything," Federico shouted. "She's not involved in this."

Medina threw his head back and laughed uproariously; his gold-rimmed teeth caught the light of the candles burning on the altar. "To be a double-crossing spy, you have to be infinitely more clever than I," he said. "I have practice. Being cunning and suspicious is my livelihood." He kicked Federico in the groin. "If you wanted to warn her, you should have come here first and not wasted time crying over the boy you killed."

The two soldiers grabbed the healer by the arms, forcing her to stand up. Her half-closed eyes were bruised and swollen. Her lips and nose were bleeding. Shaking herself loose, she glanced around the room until her eyes found Federico.

"Where is Elio?" she asked.

"Tell her, Federico." Medina laughed, his eyes shining with malice. "Tell her how you killed him."

Like an enraged animal unleashing its last strength, she pushed Medina against the altar, then turned to one of the soldiers and reached for his gun.

The soldier fired a shot.

The healer stood still, her hands pressed on her

chest, trying to stop the blood from seeping through the bodice of her dress. "I curse you to the end of your days, Federico." Her voice dropped; the words were unclear. She seemed to be reciting an almost inaudible incantation. Softly, like a rag doll, she collapsed on the ground.

With a last surge of lucidity, Federico made a final decision: in death, he would join the people he had betrayed. His thoughts ran ahead of him. He would atone by killing the men responsible for everything: himself, and his accomplice—Medina.

Federico unsheathed his hunting knife and plunged it into Medina's heart. He expected to be killed instantly, but one of the soldiers only shot him in the leg.

Hand-cuffed, blindfolded, and gagged, Federico was carried outside into a car. He wondered if it was already daylight, for he heard the mocking babble of a flock of parrots crossing the sky.

He was certain they had arrived in Caracas when the car stopped hours later. He was put into a cell. He confessed to anything his torturers hinted at; everything he said was immaterial to him. His life had already ended.

Federico had no idea how long he remained in jail. Unlike the other prisoners, he did not count the weeks, months, and years. All the days were the same to him.

One day he was set free. It was a morning of great agitation. People were screaming, crying, and laughing in the streets. The dictatorship had come to an end. Federico moved to an old section of the city and he began to stuff birds again. He no longer went into the hills to trap them, however.

26

"Human nature is most strange," doña Mercedes said. "I knew that you were going to do something for me. I knew it from the first moment I laid eyes on you. And yet, when you did what you were here to do, I couldn't believe my eyes. You have actually moved the wheel of chance for me. I can say that you enticed Federico Mueller to return to the realm of the living. You brought him back to me by the force of your witch's shadow."

My retort was cut off before I had time to open my mouth. "During all these months you've been at my house," she said, "you have been under my shadow, in a minimal way, of course; yet the usual would've been for me to make a link for you, and not the other way around."

I wanted to clarify matters. I insisted that I had not done anything. But she would not hear of it. For the sake of understanding, I proposed a line of thought: She had made the link herself with her conviction that I was the one who would bring her something.

"No," she said, puckering her face. "Your reasoning is wrong. It makes me very sad that you seek explanations that only impoverish us."

She rose and embraced me. "I feel sorry for you,"

she whispered in my ear. Suddenly, she laughed, a joyful sound that dispelled her sadness. "There is no way to explain how you've done this," she said. "I'm not talking about human arrangements or about the shadowy nature of witchcraft but about something as elusive as timelessness itself." She almost stammered, searching for words. "All I know and feel is that you made a link for me. How extraordinary! I was trying to show you how witches move the wheel of chance, and then you moved it for me yourself."

"I told you I can't take credit for that," I insisted and meant it. Her fervor embarrassed me.

"Don't be so thick, Musiúa," she retorted in an annoyed tone that reminded me of Agustín. "Something is helping you to create a transition for me. You can say, and be thoroughly accurate in saying it, that you have used your witch's shadow without even knowing it."

PART
EIGHT

27

The rainy season was almost over. Yet it still rained every afternoon, a torrential downpour accompanied by thunder and lightning.

Usually, I spent these rainy afternoons with doña Mercedes in her room, where she lay in her hammock, either bemused with or indifferent to my presence. If I asked her a question, she would answer me; if I said nothing, she would remain silent.

"No patient ever comes after the rain," I said, watching the downpour from her bedroom window.

The storm was soon over, and it left the street flooded. Three buzzards landed on a nearby roof. With wings outstretched they leapt about, then lined up at the very ridge and faced the sun bursting through the clouds. Half-naked children came out of their houses. They booed the buzzards away, then chased one another across the muddy puddles.

"No one ever comes after the rain," I repeated and turned to doña Mercedes, who was sitting silently in her hammock, one leg crossed over the other, staring at her cutoff shoe. "I think I'll go and visit Leon Chirino," I said and got up from my chair.

"I wouldn't do that," she mumbled, her gaze still on her toes. She looked up. There was a heavy brooding look in her eyes. She hesitated, frowning and biting her lips, as if she wanted to say something else. Instead, she rose and, taking my arm, led me to her working room.

Once inside, she moved with great speed, her skirt swishing noisily as she went from one corner to another, looking over and over again in the same places, turning everything upside down on the table, on the altar, and inside the glass cabinet. "I can't find it," she finally said.

"What did you lose?" I asked. "Perhaps I know where it is."

She opened her mouth to speak, but instead she turned to the altar. She lit a candle, then a cigar, which she puffed on nonstop until it was just a stub, her eyes fixed on the ashes falling on the metal plate in front of her. She turned abruptly, stared at me still standing by the table, and went down on her haunches. She crawled underneath the table and, reaching behind the bottles, dragged out a long gold chain on which a clump of medals was attached.

"What are you—" I stopped in midsentence as I remembered the night she threw the chain high up in the sky. "When you see the medals again, you'll return to Caracas," she had said. I never found out if some kind of trick had been involved or if I had merely been too tired to witness their fall. I had totally forgotten about the medals, for I had not seen them since.

Mercedes Peralta was grinning as she stood up. She hung the medals around my neck and said, "Feel how heavy they are. Pure gold!"

"They really are heavy!" I exclaimed, bouncing the clump in my hand. Smooth and shiny, the medals had a luxuriant orange tinge to them, characteristic of Venezuelan gold. They ranged in size from a dime to a silver dollar. Not all of them were religious medals. Some bore the likeness of Indian chieftains from the time of the Spanish Conquest. "What are they for?"

"To diagnose," doña Mercedes said. "To heal. They're good for anything I choose to do with them." Sighing loudly, she sat on her chair by the table.

With the chain still around my neck, I stood in front of her. I wanted to ask her where I should put the medals, but a feeling of utter desolation rendered me speechless. As I gazed into her eyes, I saw boundless melancholy and longing reflected in them.

"You're an experienced medium now," she murmured. "But your time here has ended."

She had tried for a week to help me summon the spirit of her ancestor. It seemed that my incantations had no more power. We had failed to lure the spirit as I alone had done every night for months.

Doña Mercedes laughed a little tinkling laughter that sounded oddly ominous. "The spirit is telling us that it's time for you to move on. You have fulfilled what you came to do. You came to move the wheel of chance for me. I moved it for you the night I saw you at the plaza from Leon Chirino's car. It was at that precise instant that I wished you to come here. Had I not done so, you would never have found me regardless of who sent you to my door. You see, I, too, used my witch's shadow to make a link for you."

She gathered the boxes, candles, jars, and scraps of material from the table, piled them in her arms, then carefully eased herself out of her chair. "Help me," she said, pointing with her chin to the glass cabinet.

After placing each item neatly on the shelves, I turned to the altar and lined up the knocked-over saints.

"A part of me will always be with you," doña Mercedes said softly. "Wherever you go, whatever you do, my invisible spirit will always be there. Fate has woven its invisible threads and tied us together."

The thought that she was saying good-bye brought tears to my eyes. It struck me like a revelation that I had taken her for granted, loved her carelessly and easily the way one loves the old. I had no time to express my feelings, for at that moment an old woman burst into the room.

"Doña Mercedes!" she cried out, clutching her folded hands against her shriveled bosom. "You have to help Clara. She's had one of her attacks, and there is no way I can bring her here. She's just lying on her bed as if she were dead." The woman spoke rapidly out of the side of her mouth, her voice rising sharply as she moved toward the healer. "I don't know what to do. There is no use calling the doctor, for I know that she's having one of her attacks." She paused and crossed herself, and as she looked about the room, she discovered me. "I didn't realize you were with a patient," she mumbled contritely.

Offering the woman a chair, doña Mercedes put her at ease. "Don't worry, Emilia. The musiúa is no patient. She's my helper," she explained. Then she sent me to fetch her basket from the kitchen.

As I stepped outside I heard doña Mercedes ask Emilia if the aunts had been to visit Clara. I took my time closing the curtain behind me so that I could hear the woman's answer.

"They finally left this morning," she said. "They have been here for almost a week. They want to move back here. Luisito came, too. As usual he was anxious to take Clara back with him to Caracas."

Although I had no way of assessing what the information meant to doña Mercedes, I knew that she deemed it necessary to include the house in her treatment, for she sent Emilia to the drugstore to purchase a bottle of *lluvia de oro,* golden rain; a bottle of *lluvia de plata,* silver rain; and a bottle of *la mano poderosa,* the powerful hand. These flower extracts, mixed with water, are used to wash the bewitched as well as their houses. It is a task the bewitched themselves have to perform.

The valley and the gentle slopes south of town, where sugarcane fields used to be, had been claimed by industrial centers and unattractive rows of boxlike houses. Amid them, like some relic of the past, stood what remained of the hacienda *El Rincón:* a large pink house and an orchard.

For a long time doña Mercedes and I stood gazing at the house, the peeling paint, the closed doors, and shutters. Not a sound came from inside. Not a leaf stirred in the trees.

We walked through the front gate. The traffic noise from the wide streets around us was muted by the crumbling high wall enclosing the property and by the tall casuarina trees, which also shut out the direct sun.

"Do you think Emilia has returned?" I whispered, intimidated by that eerie silence, by the afternoon shadows falling across the wide walkway.

Without answering, doña Mercedes pushed open

the front door. A gust of wind redolent of decay scattered dead leaves at our feet. We walked along the wide corridor bordering the inside patio full of shade and humidity. Water trickled from a flat dish held perfectly balanced on the raised hands of a chubby angel.

We turned a corner and continued along another corridor past endless rooms. Half-opened doors allowed glimpses of unmatching odds and ends of furniture thrown together in the most haphazard fashion. I could see sheets draped over couches and armchairs, rolled-up carpets, and statues. Beveled mirrors, portraits, and paintings were propped against the walls, as if waiting to be rehung. Doña Mercedes, not in the least perturbed by the chaotic atmosphere of the house, only shrugged her shoulders when I commented on it.

With the confidence of someone familiar with her surroundings, she stepped into a large, dimly lit bedroom. At the very center stood a wide mahogany bed draped with mosquito nets as delicate as mist. Dark, heavy curtains covered the windows, and a black cloth was flung over the mirror on the dresser. The smell of burning tallow, incense, and holy water made me think of a church. Books lay everywhere, piled carelessly on the floor, on the bed, on the two armchairs, on the night table, on the dresser, and even on an upside-down chamber pot.

Mercedes Peralta turned on the lamp by the night table. "Clara," she called softly, pushing the netting aside.

Expecting to see a child, I stood gaping at a young woman, perhaps in her late twenties, propped against the raised headboard with her limbs all awry like a rag doll that had been carelessly tossed on the bed. A red Chinese silk robe embroidered with dragons barely covered her voluptuous figure. In spite of her disheveled appearance, she was stunningly beautiful, with high slanted cheekbones, a sensual full mouth, and dark skin burnished to a fine gloss.

"*Negrita, Clarita,*" doña Mercedes called, shaking her gently by the shoulder.

The young woman opened her eyes with a start—like someone awakening from a nightmare—then shrank back, her pupils enormously dilated. Tears flowed down her cheeks, but no expression crossed her face.

Pushing the books onto the floor, doña Mercedes placed her basket at the foot of the bed, retrieved a handkerchief, sprinkled it with perfumed water and ammonia, her favorite remedy, and held it under the woman's nose.

The spiritual injection, as doña Mercedes called it, did not seem to affect the young woman, for she only stirred slightly. "Why can't I die in peace?" she asked, her voice querulous with fatigue.

"Don't talk nonsense, Clara," doña Mercedes said, rummaging through her basket. "When a person is ready to die, I'll gladly help them prepare for their eternal sleep. There are sicknesses that bring a body's death, but your time to die hasn't come yet." As soon as she had found what she was after, she rose and motioned me to come closer. "Stay with her. I'll be back shortly," she whispered in my ear.

Uneasily, I watched her leave the room, then shifted my attention to the bed, and caught sight of the death-like stillness in the woman's face. She did not even appear to be breathing, but she seemed aware of my intense scrutiny: her lids slowly opened, flickering lazily, hurt by the dim light. She reached for the brush on the night table. "Would you braid my hair for me?" she asked.

Smiling, I nodded and took the brush. "One or two braids?" I asked, running the brush through her long curly hair over and over to get out the tangles. Like doña Mercedes' and Candelaria's, her hair smelled of rosemary. "How about one nice thick braid?"

Clara did not answer. With a fixed, but absent, gaze she stared at the farthest wall in the room, where oval-framed photographs hung surrounded by palm fronds braided in the form of a cross.

With her face contorted by pain she turned toward me. Her limbs began to shake violently. Her face darkened as she gasped for air and tried to push herself up the headboard.

I ran to the door, but afraid to leave her all by herself, I did not dare go out of the room. Repeatedly, I called for doña Mercedes; there was no answer. Certain that some fresh air would do Clara good, I stepped over to the window and pulled open the curtain. A faint glimmer of daylight still lingered outside. It made the leaves of the fruit trees vibrate with color and chased the shadows out of the room. But the warm breeze drifting through the window made Clara only worse. Her body shook convulsively; heaving and gasping, she collapsed on the bed.

Afraid that she might be suffering from an epileptic seizure and might bite off her tongue, I tried to get the hairbrush between her chattering teeth. That filled her with terror. Her eyes dilated further. Her finger-nails turned purple, and her wildly racing heartbeat throbbed in the swelling veins of her neck.

At a total loss as to what to do, I clutched the gold medals, which were still around my neck, and swung them back and forth in front of her eyes. I was not guided by any definite thought or idea; it was a purely automatic response. *"Negrita, Clarita,"* I murmured the way I had heard doña Mercedes call her earlier.

With a feeble effort, Clara tried to lift her hand. I lowered the chain within her reach. Moaning softly, she clasped the medals and held them against her breasts. She seemed to be drawing strength from some magic force, for the swollen veins in her neck receded. Her breathing became easier. Her pupils went back to normal, and I noticed that her eyes were not dark but a light brown, like amber. A faint smile formed on her lips, which stuck dryly to her teeth. Closing her eyes, she let go of the medals and slipped sideways on the bed.

Doña Mercedes walked in so swiftly that she seemed to materialize at the foot of the bed, as if conjured up by the shadows invading the room. In her hands, she held a large aluminum mug filled with a strong-smelling potion. Tightly clasped under her arm was a pile of newspapers. Pressing her lips firmly together, she gestured me to remain silent, then placed the mug on the night table and the newspapers on the floor. She picked up the gold chain from the bed and, smiling, hung the medals around her neck.

Mumbling a prayer, she lit a candle and again rummaged through her basket until she found a tiny black clump of dough wrapped in leaves. She rolled the dough between her palms into a ball and dropped it into the mug. It dissolved instantly with a fizzling sound. She stirred the potion with her finger and, after tasting it, brought the mug to Clara's lips.

"Drink it all," she ordered. Silently, with an oddly detached expression on her face, she watched Clara gulp the liquid down.

An almost imperceptible smile appeared on Clara's face. It quickly turned into a harsh laughter and ended in a terrified chatter, of which I did not catch a single word. Moments later, she lay flat on the bed, whispering broken excuses and asking forgiveness.

Totally unperturbed by her outburst, doña Mercedes bent over Clara and massaged around her eyes, her fingers describing identical circles. She moved to her temples, then with downward strokes, massaged the rest of her face, as if she were pulling off a mask. Expertly, she rolled Clara toward the edge of the bed. Then, making sure her head was hanging directly over the newspapers on the floor, she pressed hard on Clara's back until she vomited.

Nodding with approval, doña Mercedes examined the dark clump on the floor, wrapped it in the papers, and tied the bundle with a string. "Now we'll have to bury this mess outside," she said, and in one swift motion she lifted Clara off the bed. Gently, she wiped her face clean and tightened the belt on her robe.

"Musiúa," doña Mercedes called, turning toward me, "hold Clara's other arm."

With the young woman in between us, we slowly shuffled down the corridor out into the yard and down the wide cement steps that led to the terraced slope where fruit trees grew. There doña Mercedes buried the bundle in a deep hole she made me dig. Clara sat on the stone steps and watched us indifferently.

* * *

For six consecutive days Clara fasted. Every afternoon at precisely six o'clock, I drove doña Mercedes to *El Rincón*. She treated Clara in exactly the same manner. Each session ended under a fruit tree, where the newspaper bundle, smaller each day, was buried.

On the sixth and last day, hard as she tried, Clara did not vomit. Nevertheless, doña Mercedes made her bury the empty, bundled-up paper.

"Will she be all right now?" I asked on the way home. "Are the sessions over?"

"Not quite, to both questions," she said. "Starting tomorrow, you're going to see Clara every day by yourself as part of her treatment." She patted my arm affectionately. "Get her to talk to you. It'll do her a lot of good. And," she added as an afterthought, "it'll do you a lot of good too."

Clothes and shoebox in hand, Clara hurried down the corridor into the bathroom. She dropped everything on the floor, then took off her nightgown and admired herself in the mirrored walls. She moved closer to see if her budding breasts had grown a bit more overnight. A satisfied smile spread over her face as she bent her head and counted her few pubic hairs. Humming a little tune, she turned on the hot- and cold-water faucets in the enormous shell-shaped bathtub, then went over to the dressing table and carefully examined the various bottles arranged on the marble top. Unable to decide which of the bath gels or salts to use, she poured a small amount of each into the water.

For a moment she stood staring at the foaming bubbles. How different it had been in Piritú. Water had to be drawn from the river or from the newly installed municipal faucet by the road and had to be carried up the hill in tin cans.

Only a year had passed since her arrival at *El Rincón,* yet it seemed she had been living in this large old house forever. She had made no conscious effort to forget her life in Piritú. Her memories, however, had begun to fade like visions in a dream. All that remained was her grandmother's face, with the sound of her rocking chair creaking on the dirt-packed floor on that last day in the shack.

"You're almost grown up, *Negra,*" her grandmother had said, her face looking older, more tired than it ever had before. The child knew at that instant that the only person she had in the world was going to die.

"That's what old age does," her grandmother had said, aware of the child's realization. "When a body is ready to die, there is nothing one can do but lie down and close one's eyes. I've already traded my rocking chair for a coffin, and this shack for a Christian burial."

"But grandmother—"

"Hush, child," the old woman stopped her in mid-sentence. She pulled out a handkerchief from her skirt pocket, untied the knot in one corner, and counted the few coins she kept there for an emergency. "It's enough to get you to *El Rincón.*"

She ran her fingers over the child's face, then braided her long curly hair. "No one knows who your father is, but your mother, my daughter, is don Luis's illegitimate child. She left for Caracas right after you were born. She went to seek her fortune, but fortune doesn't need to be sought." Her voice trailed off; she had lost her train of thought. After a long silence she added, "I'm sure don Luis will recognize you as his granddaughter. He's the owner of *El Rincón*. He's old and lonely." She took the child's hands in hers, pressed them against her wrinkled cheeks, and kissed the leaf-shaped mole in her right palm. "Show this to him."

The candle burning before the figure of a black Christ blurred before the child's eyes. She let her gaze wander to the cot in the corner, to the basket stuffed with starched, unironed clothing, to the wheelbarrow leaning against the wall in which she pushed her grandmother around. For one last time her eyes rested on the old woman. Settled back in her rocking chair, she stared with empty eyes into the distance, her face already shrunken with death.

It was dusk when the bus driver let her off right in front of the recessed arched doorway built into the wall surrounding *El Rincón*. She walked up the terraced hillside, where fruit trees grew all evenly spaced from one another. Halfway up she stopped short and remained utterly still, her whole being taken over by the sight of a small tree covered with white blossoms.

"That's an apple tree," a voice said. "And who are you? Where have you come from?"

For an instant, she believed it was the tree that had spoken, then she became aware of an old man standing beside her. "I fell out of the apple tree," she said, holding out her hand in greeting.

Surprised by her formal gesture, he stared at her hand. Instead of shaking it, he just held it in his, her palm turned up. "Strange," he murmured, his thumb moving over the leaf-shaped mole. "Who are you?" he asked again.

"I think I'm your granddaughter," she said hopefully. She had taken an instant liking to him. He was frail-looking, with silver-white hair that contrasted sharply with his tanned face. From his nose to the corners of his mouth ran two deep lines. She wondered if they had been drawn by worry and hard work or by smiling a lot.

"Who sent you here?" the old man asked, his thumb still rubbing over the leaf-shaped mole.

"My grandmother, Eliza Gomez, of Piritú. She used to work here. She died yesterday morning."

"And what's your name?" he asked, studying her upturned face with the wide, amber-colored eyes, the fine nose, the full mouth, and the determined angle of her chin.

"They call me *La Negra* . . . ," she faltered under his intense scrutiny.

"*La Negra Clara,*" he said. "That was my grandmother's name. She was as dark as you." To make light of his words, he led her around the apple tree. "It was the size of a parsley sprig when I brought it back with me from a trip to Europe. People laughed at me, saying that the tree would never grow in the tropics. It's old now. It hasn't grown very tall, nor has it ever borne any fruit. But once in a while it dresses itself all in white." Wistfully, he looked at the delicate blossoms; then his glance came to rest on the child's eager face, and he said, "It's just as well that you fell out of the apple tree. This way I'll never take such a gift for granted."

* * *

Emilia's voice roused Clara from her reveries. *"Negraaaaa,"* she called, sticking her head through the door. "Hurry up, child. I heard the car down the road."

Hastily, Clara stepped out of the tub, dried herself, and still half-wet, slipped into her favorite dress. It was yellow with embroidered daisies around the collar, the sleeves, and the waistband. Looking at herself in the mirror, she giggled. The dress made her look even darker, but she liked it. She had no doubt that her cousin Luisito would like it, too. He was to spend the whole summer at *El Rincón*. She had never met him. Last summer his parents had taken him to Europe.

Upon hearing the sound of an engine, Clara rushed along the corridor to the living room just in time to see from the open window a shiny black limousine pull up the driveway. Amazed, she watched the uniformed chauffeur and a corpulent woman dressed in a white smock alight from the car.

Somber faced, they unloaded an endless number of suitcases, boxes, baskets, and bird cages. Silently, they carried everything inside, disdaining Emilia's help when she ran out to give them a hand. Before they were quite done, a loud, uninterrupted honking echoed down the road. Within moments a second car, just as large, black, and shiny as the first one, pulled up.

A short fat man, dressed in a beige *guayabera*, a Panama hat, and dark pants stuffed into boots that creaked with newness, moved out from behind the steering wheel. Clara knew it was Raul, a very important man in the government and her grandfather's son-in-law.

"Don Luis!" Raul shouted. "I've brought your daughters, the Three Graces!" He bowed low, almost sweeping the ground with his hat, then opened the back door of the limousine and held out his hand to help three women out of the car: the twins, Maria del Rosario and Maria del Carmen, and the youngest sister, Maria Magdalena, Raul's wife.

"Luisito," Raul called, opening the car's front door. "Let me help you with those . . ."

Clara, not waiting to hear the rest of his words, rushed outside. "Luisito! I've been looking forward—" She came to a dead halt. Bewildered, she stared at the little boy holding on to a pair of crutches. "I didn't know you had an accident."

Glowering, Luisito looked into her dark face. "I didn't have an accident," he said matter-of-factly. For being so slight and frail, he had a booming voice. "I had poliomyelitis," he explained and noticing her uncomprehending expression, he added, "I'm a cripple."

"A cripple?" she repeated with a quizzical, yet calm, acceptance. "No one told me." His little white hands and dark curls framing his pale, delicately featured face made her think of something unworldly. He reminded her of the blossoms on the apple tree. She knew him to be thirteen, a year older than she, but to look at him one would think he was seven or eight.

His lips turned up at the corners, twitching, as if he had guessed her thoughts and was suppressing his laughter.

"Oh, Luisito." She sighed with relief and bent to kiss his cheek. "You look like an angel."

"Who is she?" one of the twins asked, turning to

Emilia. "Did you find someone to help you in the kitchen? Is she a relative of yours?"

"I'm Clara!" the child retorted, planting herself between the housekeeper and the aunt. *"La Negra Clara,* your niece!"

"My what?" the woman shrieked, grabbing Clara by the arm and shaking her.

"Negrita, Clarita," the boy cried excitedly. With the aid of only one crutch he limped toward her. "Didn't you hear, Aunt Maria del Rosario? She's my cousin!" Taking Clara's hand, he pulled her away from his startled parents and his aunts. "Let's see what's keeping Grandfather."

Before Clara could explain that Grandfather was in town, Luisito had turned to the wide gravel path that led to the orchard behind the house. He maneuvered his crutches so swiftly and skillfully, he made her think of a monkey rather than a cripple.

"Luisito!" Maria del Rosario called after him. "You have to rest after the long, tiring drive. It's too hot to be outdoors."

"Leave him alone," Raul said, ushering the three women inside. "The fresh air will do him good."

"Where is Grandfather?" Luisito asked, easing himself to the ground under the shade of the mango tree growing by the wall.

"In town," Clara said, sitting beside him. She was glad she had not accompanied her grandfather on his rounds as usual. She liked going with him to the barber shop, to the pharmacy, where he bought the latest medicines which he never took, and to the bar, where he had a glass of brandy and played a game of dominoes. But today, she wouldn't have missed Luisito's arrival for anything in the world.

"Let's surprise Grandfather. He didn't expect you until late in the afternoon," Clara suggested. "Let's go into town without telling anybody."

"I can't walk that far." Luisito lowered his head and slowly pushed his crutches away.

Clara sucked in her lower lip. "We'll make it," she declared with fierce determination. "I'll push you in the wheelbarrow. I'm good at that." She held her hand over his lips to stop him from interrupting her. "All you have to do is slide into the wheelbarrow and sit." She pointed to the narrow arched doorway in the wall. "I'll meet you there." She gave him no time to voice any objections but rose and ran to the tool shed halfway down the slope.

"You see how easy it was." Clara laughed and helped him into the wheelbarrow. "No one will know where we are." She placed the crutches on his lap, then pushed him along the wide, newly paved road, past factories and still-empty stretches of land.

Sighing heavily, she brought the wheelbarrow to an abrupt halt. The heat made the landscape waver in the distance. The shimmering light hurt her eyes. Her grandmother, although tiny and skinny, had certainly weighed more than Luisito, Clara thought. Yet she didn't recall having had such a hard time pushing her about as she did now with her cousin.

"It'll take forever to get into town on this road," she declared, wiping the dust and perspiration off her face with the back of her hand. "Hold on tight, Luisito!" she cried out, steering the wheelbarrow down an empty field, green with weeds from the recent rains.

"You're a genius," the boy said laughing. "This is better than anything! You make me feel very happy.

And happiness is what makes people healthy. I know it because I'm a cripple."

Excitedly, he pointed one of his crutches skyward. "Look, Clara. Look at those vultures above us. They are so powerful, so free." He grabbed her arm. "Look at them! Look at their open black wings, how their legs stretch out beneath their tails. Look at their fierce beaks dripping blood. I'll bet you they're happy, too."

"The slaughterhouse is nearby," Clara explained.

"Push me to that pack of vultures on the ground," he begged, pointing to a place where the birds had settled like black shadows at the other side of the slaughterhouse.

"Faster, Clara!" he yelled. "Faster!"

The vultures hopped aside, then lifted lazily into the air and flew low in ever tightening circles before descending again a bit farther away.

Watching his flushed face, his eyes shiny with excitement, Clara knew that she was making him happy. For a moment, her attention strayed from the uneven terrain, and she failed to maneuver the wheelbarrow around a large stone. Luisito fell forward amid a clump of tall grass. He lay so still he looked dead.

"Luisito," Clara called anxiously, kneeling beside him. He didn't respond. Carefully, she turned him around. Blood trickled from a cut on his forehead, and the weeds had scratched his cheeks.

His lids fluttered open. His eyes, round and puzzled, looked up into hers.

"You're wounded," she said. Taking his hand, she pressed it against his forehead, then showed him his bloodstained fingers. He looked so happy, so pleased with himself that she laughed.

"Let's see if you're injured anyplace else," she said. "What about your leg?"

He sat up, then lifted his pant leg and said, "The braces are fine. If the braces ever get twisted, my father knows how to adjust them."

"But what about your leg?" she insisted. "Is it all right?"

Luisito shook his head sadly. "It will never be all right," he declared and swiftly pushed down his pants. He explained to her what poliomyelitis was. "I've been to many doctors," he continued. "Father has taken me to the United States and to Europe, but I will always be a cripple." He shouted the word so many times he became exhausted by his effort and broke into a fit of coughing. He looked at her sheepishly. "I'll go with you anywhere you want me to," he said, pressing his head against her shoulder. "Clara, are you really my cousin?"

"Do you think I'm too dark to be your cousin?" she retorted.

"No," he replied thoughtfully. "You're too nice to be my cousin. You're the only one who doesn't make fun of me or look at me with pity and disdain." He pulled out a white handkerchief from his pocket, folded it into a triangle, then rolled it and fastened it around his forehead. "This will be the best summer I've ever had," he said happily. "Come on, cousin, let's find Grandfather."

Before opening the dining room door, Clara brushed a few loose strands of hair behind her ears. Since the aunts' arrival from Caracas, her grandfather and she no longer had breakfast in the kitchen.

Maria del Rosario sat at the far end of the table,

arranging flowers in a vase, tweaking them here and there with impatient gestures. Maria del Carmen, with her head buried in her missal, sat silently beside her sister. Luisito's parents, who had only stayed for a few days at *El Rincón,* had left for Europe.

"Good morning," Clara mumbled, taking her seat at the long mahogany table next to Luisito.

Don Luis looked up from his plate and winked at her impishly. He was trying to provoke the twins; he went on dunking his roll in his coffee, slurping noisily. They never ate before going to mass.

From over the rim of her hot-chocolate cup, Clara stole a glance at the disapproving faces of the twins. They no longer bore any resemblance to the oil paintings of the young beautiful girls hanging in the living room. With their sallow complexions, their sunken cheeks, and their dark hair pulled back in a small bun, they reminded her of the embittered nuns that taught catechism at school.

Of the two, Maria del Rosario was the most difficult. Clara felt anxious and uneasy in her presence. Maria del Rosario had the nervous eyes of a person who does not sleep. Eyes of impatience and alarm. Eyes that were always watching and judging. She was only agreeable when she had her own way.

One hardly noticed Maria del Carmen, on the other hand. Her heavy-lidded eyes seemed to be weighed down by some ancestral tiredness. She walked with noiseless steps and spoke in a voice so soft it seemed as though she was only moving her lips.

Maria del Rosario's sharp voice intruded on Clara's musings.

"Won't you convince Luisito that you two should go with us to mass this Sunday, Clara?" she addressed the child as if speaking to her was against her better judgment.

"No. She won't," Luisito answered for her. "We'll go in the evening, with Emilia."

Clara stuffed a fritter into her mouth to hide her smile. She knew Maria del Rosario would not insist. She hated scenes on Sunday, and there was no one like Luisito to get his way. Aside from his grandfather, he never heeded anyone's advice. He used and abused the terror he inspired by his rages whenever his aunts tried to oppose his wishes. Rages expressed in such frantic banging of his crutches against any object in front of him, obscene gestures, and foul language, it put the women on the verge of fainting.

"Clara, finish your breakfast," Maria del Rosario ordered. "The maid wants to clear everything away before we leave. She, too, wants to go to church."

Clara gulped down the rest of her hot chocolate and handed the cup to the tall, grave-looking woman the twins had brought with them from Caracas. She was from the Canary Islands and had taken over the running of the house. Emilia was not in the least upset, for all she had to do now was to prepare don Luis' food. He absolutely refused to eat the vegetarian dishes the aunts were so partial to. "Not even dogs would eat this food," he would say each time they all sat down for a meal.

Clara wasn't particularly fond of vegetarian dishes either, but she thought it the height of elegance when Maria del Rosario had the chauffeur drive her each morning to the fields of the Portuguese farmers, so that she could pick the vegetables for that day's meal and pay twice as much as Emilia would at the open market on Saturdays.

* * *

The instant Clara heard the light tap of Luisito's crutches coming down the corridor, she climbed out the window and ran halfway down the terraced slope to the mango tree growing by the wall.

Unconcerned about her yellow dress getting dirty, she stretched full length on the ground and kicked off her shoes. Unable to find a comfortable position she turned this way and that. She felt her blood hammering in her temples, in her breasts, in her thighs. It filled her with a strange desire she didn't understand. She sat up abruptly upon hearing Luisito approach.

"Why didn't you answer?" he asked, easing himself down beside her. He placed the crutches within reach and added, "They have all gone to mass, including Grandfather."

Smiling, she searched his face with tender admiration. He had a dreamy, soft-edged look, sweet, yet daring. She wanted to tell him so many things, but she could not express any of them. "Kiss me the way they do in the movies," she demanded.

"Yes," he whispered, and that one word answered all her turmoil, that strange desire she didn't understand. "Oh, *Negrita*," he mumbled, burying his face in her neck. She smelled of the earth and the sun.

Her lips moved, but there was no sound. Wide-eyed, she watched him open his pants. She couldn't shift her gaze away.

His face shone down on her with glowing animation; his eyes seemed to melt between his long lashes. Carefully, so his steel braces would not hurt her, he eased himself on top of her.

* * *

"We'll stay together forever," Luisito said. "I've convinced my parents that I'll be happier at *El Rincón*. They are going to send a tutor out here."

Clara closed her eyes. In the last three months her love for Luisito had taken on monumental proportions. Daily they lay together in the shade of the mango tree. "Yes," she whispered. "We'll stay together forever." She wrapped her arms around him.

She didn't know what she heard first: Luisito's muffled sigh or Maria del Rosario's horrified scream. The aunt shrieked. She moved closer and, lowering her voice, said, "Luisito, you are a disgrace to the family. What you have done is unspeakable." Her hard, implacable eyes never wavered for an instant from the red and white blossoms hanging over the wall. "And as for you, Clara," she went on, "your behavior comes as no surprise. No doubt you'll end up in the gutter, where you belong." She hurried up the steps. At the top, she halted. "We'll be returning to Caracas this very day, Luis. And don't pull any of your tantrums. It won't work this time. No obscene gesture, no foul language, could be worse than what you have done."

Luisito began to cry. Clara took his pale face in her hands and wiped the tears from his lashes with her fingers. "We'll love each other forever. We'll always be together," she said, and then she let him go.

Clara watched the evening shadows darken everything around her. Through a veil of tears she gazed up at the tree above her. The leaves, outlined against the starlit sky, took on unexpected forms, shapes she did not quite recognize. A swift breeze erased the patterns. All that remained was the sound of the wind, a desolate cry, bringing an end to the summer.

"Clara!" her grandfather called.

Torn between remorse and anxiety, she didn't answer. The light shimmering among the fruit trees didn't waver. The certainty that her grandfather would wait for her, even if it took her the whole night to answer, filled her with gratitude.

Slowly, she rose and brushed the leaves and the dampness from her dress. "Grandfather," she called softly, climbing the steps toward the light—and the love and understanding—that awaited her.

"Let's look at the apple tree," don Luis said. "Perhaps it'll bloom again next summer."

28

Two weeks later, on a Sunday afternoon, doña Mercedes announced that she had to go to *El Rincón*.

"Has Clara taken ill again?" I asked, alarmed.

"No," doña Mercedes said, rising from the hammock in her bedroom. "I want to make sure she follows my instructions. She's a willful patient."

Doña Mercedes rested her hands on my shoulders. "Today, you and I will help Clara. Together we'll move the wheel of chance for her." She turned to the blue- and pink-painted wardrobe that blocked the door facing the street and fumbled with the key, and before unlocking it, she looked back at me and said, "Gather all your clothes and put them in your jeep. Seeing that you're packed, Clara will think you are also leaving for Caracas. She may decide to take advantage of the ride. In the depths of her, she knows that she will be well only if she leaves *El Rincón*."

I was really surprised at the scarcity of my belongings. I had brought much more, but then I remembered that I had given away most of what I had to some of Agustín's young patients.

"Clara's story is a sort of bonus to you," doña

Mercedes said as she helped me put my bag in the jeep. "At least I didn't expect it. It came out of nowhere, but it's very appropriate. I encouraged you to talk to Clara and to spend time with her. Under her shadow, I'm sure you have felt the turns of the wheel of chance in her life. She's another person with a natural gift, a natural control over the witch's shadow."

Definitely, Clara was a very strong person. I felt that her emotional conflicts made her rather somber; she seemed, at least to me, always preoccupied, reflecting on something unsaid.

Doña Mercedes agreed with my assessment of Clara and added that Clara needed our combined help.

"Let me put it this way," she went on, "Clara is so strong that she has now engaged your witch's shadow and mine to move the wheel of chance for her."

"What is the meaning of that, doña Mercedes?"

"It means that you and I are going to help her leave, not so much because we're good samaritans, but because she is forcing us to do it."

There was a strong compulsion in me to disagree with her or, rather, to set the record straight.

"Nobody is forcing me to do anything," I said.

Doña Mercedes peered at me quizzically, her glance half-pitying, half-mocking, then she lifted my bag and gently placed it on the backseat.

"You mean to say you wouldn't move a finger to help her?" she asked in a whisper.

"No. I didn't say that. I merely said that Clara is not forcing me at all. I'd gladly do it all by myself without her asking me."

"Ah, there is the link. Clara forces us without

saying a word. Neither you nor I could remain impassive. In one way or another, we have been under her shadow too long."

Through the rearview mirror I could still see Candelaria, a hazy lonely figure waving farewell. She had fastened a yellow, blue, and red plastic pinwheel to the jeep's antenna. It whirled noisily in the wind.

"Do you think Candelaria wanted to come with us to Caracas?" I asked doña Mercedes.

"No," she mumbled. She had already settled in her seat to doze. "Candelaria hates Caracas; she always gets a headache the moment she reaches the outskirts of the capital."

As soon as I brought the jeep to a full stop in front of *El Rincón*, doña Mercedes, not waiting for me to help her out, alighted from the car and dashed into the house. Swiftly, I caught up with her and followed her toward the swishing sound of a broom.

It was Clara cleaning the patio. She looked up. She smiled but did not speak to us. She seemed to be sweeping the silence and the shadows, for there wasn't a single leaf on the ground.

Doña Mercedes lit two candles on the stone ledge circling the fountain. She closed her eyes and waited for Clara to finish.

"I did all you told me to do," Clara said, sitting between the two lit candles.

Doña Mercedes did not look at her but began to sniff the air, trying to identify some elusive scent. "Listen carefully, Clara," she said shortly. "The only thing that will keep you well is to leave this house."

"Why should I leave it?" Clara asked, alarmed.

"Grandfather left it to me. He wanted me to stay here."

"He wanted you to have the house," doña Mercedes corrected her. "He did not want you to stay here. Don't you remember he said that to you before he died?"

Seemingly indifferent to Clara's mounting agitation, doña Mercedes lit a cigar. She smoked with slow, even puffs and began to massage Clara's head and shoulders. She blew the smoke around her, as if she were outlining her form against the air.

"This house is inhabited by ghosts and memories that don't belong to you, Clara," she went on. "You were only a guest in this house. You ruled this place from the moment you arrived because you had luck and strength. These two forces were disguised in you as affection and a great ease with people. But there's no one here anymore. It's time to leave. Only ghosts remain here. Ghosts and shadows that don't belong to you."

"But what can I do?" Clara asked tearfully.

"Go to Caracas!" doña Mercedes exclaimed. "Go and live with Luisito!"

"Really, doña Mercedes!" Clara retorted indignantly. "How can you suggest such a thing. It's downright indecent."

"You sound like your aunts." Doña Mercedes regarded her cheerfully, then flung her head back and laughed. "Don't be an ass, Clara. What's indecent is to pretend to be prudish. Have you forgotten what you and Luisito have been doing since you were twelve years old?"

Clara remained silent, seemingly lost in thought. "I can't be rushed into a decision." She smiled, tracing the cement cracks on the ground with her toes. "I can't just leave all this."

"You can if you have guts," doña Mercedes said. "The musiúa here is also leaving today. We will take you to Luisito."

"And what about Emilia?" Clara asked.

"Emilia will be happy with your aunts. They have been wanting to come back to *El Rincón* for a long time," doña Mercedes remarked. "This place holds all their memories, all their feelings. Here, the three women can set back the clock to an ideal time that never was. The shadows of the past will dim the present and erase their frustrations."

Doña Mercedes was silent for an instant, then she took Clara's hands in hers, perhaps to communicate the urgency of her words. "Put on your yellow dress. Yellow suits you. It'll give you strength. Change quickly. You need nothing else. When you came to *El Rincón* you had only one dress; you should leave the same way." Seeing Clara's hesitation, she pressed her point. "This is your last chance, girl. I've already told the musiúa that the only way for you to keep well is to love Luisito with abandon and completeness, as you did when you were a child."

Clara's large eyes, bright with tears, closed in a hurt blink. "But I love him," she murmured. "You know that I have never loved anyone but him."

Doña Mercedes regarded her thoughtfully. "True," she admitted and, turning toward me, added, "She had dozens of rich suitors. She still does, and she still gets a malicious pleasure disappointing them. She's escaped from more sure engagements than I care to remember."

Clara's laughter rang out loud. She put her arm

around doña Mercedes' shoulders and brushed her lips across her cheek. "You always exaggerate everything," she said, her tone betraying how delighted she was. "But in spite of all my admirers, I never loved anyone but Luisito."

Doña Mercedes took her arm and guided her toward her room. "You have to love Luisito in the world the way you love him within the crumbling walls of *El Rincón*." She pushed her inside. "Go on and put on your yellow dress. We'll be waiting for you in the jeep."

Clara's description of Luisito had not prepared me for the astonishingly handsome man who greeted us at his apartment door in Caracas.

I knew that he was in his late twenties, but he looked like a teenager, with black curly hair, green-yellow eyes, and smooth white skin. When he smiled, his cheeks dimpled. In spite of his pronounced limp, there was nothing awkward about his movements. His engaging personality and his self-sufficient manner did not allow for pity.

Luisito was not in the least surprised to see us. And when he served us a sumptuous meal, I knew that doña Mercedes had arranged things beforehand.

We stayed until late. It was an unforgettable night. I had never seen doña Mercedes in such an expansive mood. Her flawless mimicry of the people we all knew in Curmina, her knack for recalling the most absurd situations, her talent for dramatizing them, and her shameless exaggerations turned her anecdotes into memorable tales.

It was shortly before midnight when, declining Luisito's invitation to stay for the night, Mercedes

Peralta rose and embraced both Clara and Luisito at the same time. With her arms wide open she approached me with an exuberant gesture of affection.

"Don't embrace me like that. You're not saying good-bye to me, too. I'm going back with you." I laughed and returned her embrace.

I reached for the ignition. Wrapped around my keys was a chain. With trembling fingers I untangled it. It was a long gold chain with a huge medal hanging from it.

"You better wear it," doña Mercedes said, looking at me. "It's Saint Christopher, the remarkable patron saint of travelers." A sigh of contentment escaped her lips as she settled back in her seat. "You'll be well protected. After all, you're a traveler who has stopped only for a moment."

Instead of heading for Curmina, doña Mercedes directed me along specific streets, clear across town. I had the feeling we had been driving in circles, when she finally made me stop in front of an old, green colonial house.

"Who lives here?" I asked.

"My ancestors lived here," she replied. "It's their house. And I am just a leaf of an enormous tree." She looked at me so intently she seemed to be imprinting my face in the depths of her eyes. Leaning closer, she whispered in my ear. "A witch has to have luck and strength to move the wheel of chance. Strength can be groomed, but luck cannot be beckoned. It cannot be enticed. Luck, independent of witchcraft or human arrangements, makes its own choice." She ran her fingers through my hair and over my face, feeling rather than seeing me, then added, "That's why witches are so attracted to it."

I was filled with an odd premonition. I looked at her questioningly, but she reached for her basket and pulled out a reddish brown leaf shaped like a butterfly.

"Look at it carefully," she said, handing me the leaf. "The spirits of my ancestors told me to always carry a dry leaf. I am this leaf, and I want you to throw it through that window." She pointed to the house in front of us. "As you throw it, recite an incantation. I want to know how powerful your incantations are."

Willing to humor her, I examined the leaf from every angle, turning it over and over. I surveyed its surface and searched its depths. "It's beautiful," I said.

"Throw it through the window," she repeated.

I climbed up the wrought-iron grill, pushed the heavy curtain aside, and threw the leaf inside as an incantation flowed out of me. Instead of falling to the ground, the leaf fluttered upward toward the corner by the ceiling like a moth. Alarmed, I jumped down.

Mercedes Peralta was no longer in the jeep. Certain that she had gone into the house, I knocked softly on the door. It was open. "Doña Mercedes," I whispered and stepped inside.

The house, built around a patio and shadowy corridors, was like a silent dark cloister. Long rain gutters dropped from the dark roof, and metal rings dangled from the ancient protruding eaves.

I walked to the center of the patio, toward a weeping willow shrouded in mist. Like phantom beads, the tiny silvery dew-drops on its leaves slid soundlessly into the fountain beneath. A gust of air shook the willow tree, scattering fresh dry leaves all around me. Gripped by an irrational fear, I ran out into the street.

I sat in my jeep determined to wait for Mercedes Peralta. I reached under my seat for a box of tissue paper and felt my camera and tape recorder.

Puzzled, I turned around. I had no recollection of packing anything but my clothes. To my utter astonishment, I discovered a box on the backseat. It contained my tapes and my diaries. Stuck to the box was an unsigned note. I recognized Candelaria's bold handwriting. It read, "A witch's farewell is like dust from the road; it sinks in as one tries to slough it off."

Epilogue

I returned to Los Angeles, and then I went to Mexico to face Florinda. Upon hearing a detailed summary of my experiences, she found it quite extraordinary and inexplicable that my life in doña Mercedes' world began with her own handwritten note, hidden among my clothes, and ended with Candelaria's, hidden among my tapes.

Although Florinda made fun of what she called my compulsive thoroughness, she urged me to see if I could use my numerous tapes to write my dissertation.

Working with the material, I became aware that in spite of the fact that I had had no theoretical plan to organize my objectives, the events in doña Mercedes' house seemed prearranged to introduce me to spiritualists, witches, healers, and the people they deal with and what they do in the context of their daily activities.

Having followed doña Mercedes' activities in healing, and having learned to use her own system of interpretation, I sincerely believed that I had mastered, at least intellectually, the way healers see themselves, each other, and their knowledge. I was certain that my experience and the notes I had collected would suffice to write a dissertation.

However, after transcribing, translating, and analyzing my tapes and notes, I began to doubt my intellectual mastery of healing. My attempt to organize the data to fit a meaningful framework proved to be futile; my notes were ridden with inconsistencies and contradictions, and my knowledge of healing could not fill in the gaps.

Florinda then made a cynical suggestion: either alter the data to fit my theories or forget about the dissertation altogether; I forgot about the dissertation.

Florinda has always urged that I look beneath the surface of things. In the case of my experience with doña Mercedes, she suggested that I look deeper than the possible academic value. She thought my academic bias blinded me to more important aspects. I read and reread the stories doña Mercedes had selected for me and finally understood what Florinda wanted. I realized that if I removed the academic emphasis from my own work, I would be left with a document about human values—human values definitely foreign to us, yet perfectly understandable, if we momentarily placed ourselves outside our usual frame of reference.

With those stories, doña Mercedes proposed to show me that witches, or even ordinary people, are capable of using extraordinary forces that exist in the universe to alter the course of events, or the course of their lives, or the lives of other people. The course of events, she called "the wheel of chance," and the process of affecting it, she called "the witch's shadow."

She claimed that we can alter anything without directly intruding upon the process; and sometimes without even knowing that we are doing so.

For Westerners, this is an unthinkable proposition. If we find ourselves affecting the course of events without directly intruding upon them, we think of coincidence as the only serious explanation; for we believe that direct intervention is the only way of altering anything. For example, men of history affect events with complex social decisions. Or in a more reduced scope, people directly intervene, through their actions, in the lives of others.

In contrast, the stories selected by doña Mercedes make us aware of something that we are not familiar with: They point to the incomprehensible possibility that without directly mediating, we can be more influential than we think in shaping the course of events.

On the whole, Florinda was satisfied with the results of my journey to Venezuela. She said that she had wanted me to get firsthand knowledge of my hidden resources. Her idea was that I had to function effectively in an environment unknown to me, and that I had to learn to adapt quickly to situations outside the boundaries of what I know, accept, and can predict. Florinda maintained that nothing could be more appropriate for bringing out those hidden resources than a confrontation with the social unknown. My life in doña Mercedes' house and my interaction with her patients and friends was that social unknown.

I admitted to Florinda that her admonitions about the woman-warrior philosophy—which were quite incomprehensible to me at the time—actually became the basis for all my acts while I stayed with doña Mercedes.

"There are many ways of behaving when one is in a normal setting," Florinda commented, "but when one is alone, in danger, in darkness, there is only one way: the warrior's way."

Florinda said that I had discovered the value of the

warrior's way and the meaning of all its premises. Under the impact of an unfamiliar life situation, I had found out that not to surrender means freedom, that not to feel self-important breeds an indomitable fierceness, and that to vanquish moral judgments brings an all-soothing humbleness that is not servitude.